KU-252-368

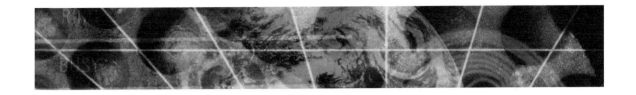

Teaching Guide to Accompany

Strategy
Process, Content, Context

An International Perspective

Second edition

- **Bob de Wit**

  Maastricht School of Management
  The Netherlands

- **Ron Meyer**

  Rotterdam School of Management
  Erasmus University
  The Netherlands

Business Press
Thomson Learning™

Australia • Canada • Denmark • Japan • Mexico • New Zealand • Philippines
Puerto Rico • Singapore • South Africa • Spain • United Kingdom • United States

Teaching Guide to Accompany Strategy: Process, Content, Context

Copyright © 2000 Thomson Learning

Business Press is a division of Thomson Learning. The Thomson logo is a registered trademark used herein under licence.

For more information, contact Business Press, Berkshire House, 168–173 High Holborn, London, WC1V 7AA or visit us on the World Wide Web at: http://www.itbp.com.

All rights resevered by Thomson Learning 2000. The text of this publication, or any part thereof, may not be reproduced or transmitted in any form or by any means, electronic or mechanical, including photocopying, recording, storage in an information retrieval system, or otherwise, without prior permission of the publisher.

While the Publisher has taken all reasonable care in the preparation of this book the publishers make no representation, express or implied, with regard to the accuracy of the information contained in this book and cannot accept any legal responsibility or liability for any errors or omissions from the book or the consequences thereof.

Products and services that are referred to in this book may be either trademarks and/or registered trademarks of their respective owners. The publishers and author/s make no claim to these trademarks.

British Library Cataloguing-in-Publication Data
A catalogue record for this book is available from the British Library

ISBN 1-86152-140-5

First edition published 2000 by Thomson Learning

Typeset by Bob de Wit, Ron Meyer and Saxon Graphics
Printed in the UK by Redwood Books, Trowbridge

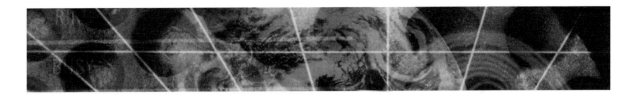

Contents

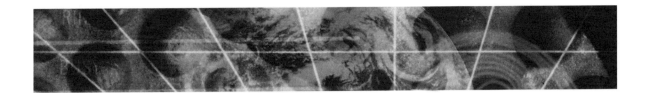

Preface

The stone that is rolling can gather no moss,
for master and servant oft changing is loss.
(Thomas Tusser c.1524-1580; English poet)

As few others, strategy professors know about switching costs - expenses that are incurred when changing over to a new product or service. Usually their knowledge about switching costs is not only of a theoretical nature, but also based on their personal experience. Many professors have invested time and energy in getting to know their old strategic management textbook and cases inside out and now feel locked in to these materials due to high switching costs. The more radically different the new product, the higher are the switching costs.

Yet, despite this barrier, hundreds of professors around the world have switched to *Strategy - Process, Content, Context: An International Perspective*. We are delighted that for so many colleagues the perceived benefits of the book outweigh the costs they expect to incur. Nevertheless, we believe that every effort on our part that can help to enlarge the benefits or lower switching costs should be undertaken. It has been with this intention that we have put together this teaching guide.

In practice, the most significant switching costs are not even due to the change of the actual text employed. Most professors are well acquainted with the readings and debates highlighted in the second edition of *Strategy - Process, Content, Context: An International Perspective* and can quickly adapt their lecturing to this new material. At most, a change of text necessitates a revision of the professor's teaching transparencies, for which we have included a basic set of transparency master copies that could be of assistance. Rather, most time and effort of a professor are normally invested in getting to know the cases and linking the cases to the theories in the text. Especially the latter point - the cross-fertilization of text and cases - leads to high educational added value, but is extremely time-consuming. Consequently, we have targeted the discussion of the cases in connection with the theories in the text as the most important way of supporting professors.

All of the material included in this teaching guide is also available through the International Thomson Business Press website (www.itbp.com). While this version of the teaching guide is necessarily static, the website version of the teaching guide materials is constantly updated, to include new case developments and feedback from other users. We invite you to visit this website and to contribute your experiences, remarks and suggestions, to the benefit of the hundreds of other users of *Strategy – Process, Content, Context: An International Perspective*.

If, after reading this teaching guide, you are still left with significant switching costs or believe that you can not fully benefit from the potential of this book, please feel free to contact us directly. We would gladly be of assistance in answering any questions or in discussing your ideas. Of course, we also welcome any suggestions, feedback or advice that you could give us that could help to improve the next edition. We can be reached by e-mail (b.dewit@dewit-meyer.com and r.meyer@dewit-meyer.com) and by telephone (31-10-4408522).

Finally, we would like to thank the people directly involved in making this teaching guide possible. We have been greatly assisted by the case writers, who have supplied us with all of their available teaching materials. We are also indebted to Pursey Heugens, Marc Huygens, Jaco Lok,

Andrew Mair and Melbert Visscher for helping us to write a large number of the teaching notes. Furthermore, we would like to express our gratitude to Jurgen Hornman, Melbert Visscher and Henk Vos, who have been our trusted bloodhounds, finding out what happened to each company after the case. Last, but not least, we would like to thank the numerous professors, who over the past years have provided us with their valuable feedback, suggestions and support.

Bob de Wit
Ron Meyer
Rotterdam, September 1999

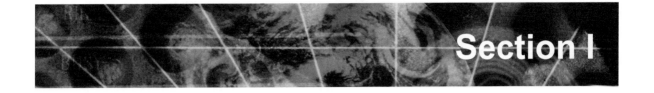

Section I

Teaching Strategy

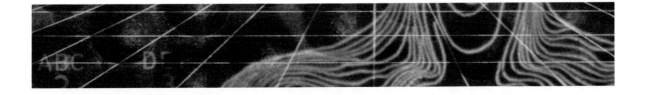

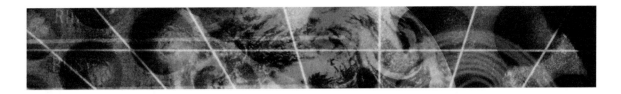

Introduction

The cause of all human evil is not being able
to apply general principles to special cases.
(Epictetus c.60-120; Roman philosopher)

Just as there is not one best way of making strategy, there is not one best way of teaching it either. Throughout the past number of years we have visited many colleagues and observed many different, yet effective, teaching styles, class formats and course structures. Every person has their own preferences, each business school has its own peculiarities and each national context has its own particular needs. It would be impossible to detail how *Strategy - Process, Content, Context: An International Perspective* could be employed to fit with all of these individual circumstances. Each strategy course needs to be individually crafted - we can't give a few simple recipes for designing and running a course.

Luckily, it has been our experience that most professors using or contemplating our book don't want us to tell them how to run their courses. In general they are knowledgeable and experienced, and have intentionally turned away from the simple "how to" textbooks. These professors dislike "instructing" their students on how to follow simplified step-by-step strategy-making procedures. The last thing such professors need is a step-by-step manual instructing them on how to teach a strategy course.

What is required is not a manual, but a guide that helps professors to explore the teaching opportunities offered by the book and aids them in extracting as much value as possible from the book's use. In other words, *Strategy - Process, Content, Context: An International Perspective* is a resource that can be employed in a variety of different ways and professors would like to become quickly acquainted with all of the possibilities available to them. This insight will allow professors to blend the book into their own specific teaching approach.

In light of this need, it is the intention of this teaching guide to outline a number of the ways in which the book could be applied to teaching strategic management. Attention will be paid to the following aspects of course design:

- *Teaching objectives.* What should students learn and what should be the role of the course and the professor in the learning process? In other words, what is the *course mission*?

- *Teaching approaches.* What type of general approach should the professor take to meet the teaching objectives? In other words, what is the *course strategy*?

- *Teaching formats.* How should the professor mix theory and cases and how should class time be spent? In other words, what are the *course tactics*?

- *Teaching set-ups.* How should the course be organized, in what order should the course cover the topics and how much time should be spent on each chapter? In other words, what is the *course structure*?

To illustrate the above choices and just to get an idea of a possible course design, we have included some recent course outlines. After these points, teaching notes will be given that link each case to the appropriate readings. Finally, the master transparencies will be presented that can be employed if lectures are given based on the book.

Teaching Objectives

Perfection of means and confusion of goals characterize our age.
(Albert Einstein 1879-1955; German-American physicist)

What do we actually want students in a strategic management or business policy course to learn? It seems an obvious question to start with, especially to strategy professors. Yet, in practice, the large majority of strategic management textbooks on the market do not make their teaching objectives explicit. These books implicitly assume that the type of teaching objectives and teaching methods needed for a strategic management course do not differ radically from any other subject - basically, strategy can be taught in the same way as accounting or baking cookies. Their approach is based on the following teaching objectives:

1. *Knowledge*. To get the student to clearly understand and memorize all of the 'ingredients';

2. *Skills*. To develop the student's ability to follow the detailed 'recipes';

3. *Attitude*. To instill a disciplined frame of mind, whereby the student automatically attempts to approach all issues by following fixed procedures.

This is an important way of teaching - it is how all of us were taught to read and write, do arithmetic and drive a car. We refer to this type of teaching as *instructional*, because students are *told* what to know and do. The instructor is the authority who has all of the necessary knowledge and skills, and it is the instructor's role to *transfer* these to the students. Thus the educational emphasis is on communicating know how and ensuring that students are able to repeat what they have heard. Students are not encouraged to question the knowledge they receive - on the contrary, it is the intention of instructional teaching to get students to absorb an accepted body of knowledge and to follow established recipes. The student should *accept, absorb and apply*.

However, while instructing students on a subject and programming their behavior might be useful in such areas as mathematics, cooking and karate, we believe it is not a very good way of teaching strategy. In our opinion, a strategic management professor should have a different set of teaching objectives:

1. *Knowledge*. To encourage the understanding of the many, often conflicting, schools of thought and to facilitate the gaining of insight into the assumptions, possibilities and limitations of each set of theories;

2. *Skills*. To develop the student's ability to define strategic issues, to critically reflect on existing theories, to creatively combine or develop theories where necessary and to flexibly employ theories where useful;

3. *Attitude*. To instill a critical, analytical, flexible and creative mindset, which challenges organizational, industry and national paradigms and problem-solving recipes.

In other words, strategy professors should want to achieve the opposite of instructors - not to instill recipes, but rather to encourage students to dissect and challenge recipes. Strategic thinking is in its very essence questioning, challenging, unconventional and innovative. These aspects of strategic thinking can not be transferred through instruction. A critical, analytical, flexible and creative state of mind must be developed by practicing these very qualities. Hence, a learning situation must encourage students to be critical, must challenge them to be analytical, must force them to be mentally flexible and must demand creativity and unconventional thinking. In short, students can not be instructed, but must learn the art of strategy by thinking and acting themselves - they must *discuss, deliberate and do*. The role of the professor is to create the circumstances for this learning. We therefore refer to this type of teaching as *facilitative*.

This teaching philosophy has lead to a radical departure from traditional textbooks that focus on knowledge transfer and application skills, and that have often been written from the perspective of just one paradigm. This book incorporates a number of features intended to help professors to create a course that can meet the ambitious teaching objectives mentioned above:

- *Broad coverage of strategic management field.* Contrary to conventional textbooks, this book covers all three dimensions of strategic management (process, content and context) and deals with a wide range of issues on each dimension. The underlying philosophy is that strategic thinking requires students to have an overview over all relevant aspects of strategy. A capstone strategic management book should help the professor to present the breadth of the field and challenge students to develop a holistic and integrative perspective.

- *Broad coverage of different schools of thought.* While most other textbooks have been written from one perspective or present only a few opposing ideas, this book makes the fundamental differences in opinion within the field of strategic management its focal point. The underlying philosophy is that strategic thinking requires the ability to recognize perspectives and recipes, and the mental flexibility to shift between paradigms. A strategic management book should help the professor to challenge students to use and combine different perspectives when approaching and tackling strategic issues.

- *Academic depth.* This book goes beyond just understanding and applying relatively simple tools and basic concepts. Strategy is more than 'five steps to strategic success'. Students are challenged to understand more complex phenomena and to critically reflect upon them. This intellectual stimulus is reinforced by not shielding students from the uncertainties, inconsistencies and disputes within the field of strategic management. The underlying philosophy is that strategic thinking requires an analytical and critical mind, which can see the limitations of simple recipes. A strategic management book must not pretend that strategizing can be learned by following recipes, but should help the professor to challenge students to question existing ideas and develop a tolerance for theoretical complexity, ambiguity and uncertainty.

- *International perspective.* This book has been explicitly developed for professors who want or need to take an international perspective. This is not only reflected in the geographic diversity of the cases and in chapter 10, which deals with the international context. It is also the broad spectrum of approaches presented and the international perspective sections at the end of each chapter that allow professors to discuss which approach might be more suitable to which country or culture. The underlying philosophy is that strategic thinking requires a culturally adaptive mind. A strategic management book must help the professor to challenge students to understand that 'the best' approach to strategy may depend on the country one is in.

- *Strong link between theory and cases.* In many other books little effort is made to tie cases and theory together, or at best the theory is directly 'applied' to the case. In this book, however, text chapters and cases are closely linked and each case is approached from a variety of perspectives - the theoretical debate is continued as a practical debate on how the case's issues can best be approached. In this way, the case discussions yield two major benefits. First, the theoretical debates become more concrete once they are conducted on the basis of an actual business situation. The usefulness and limitations of each theoretical perspective become much more apparent if students can discuss them in the setting of a practical case. Second, students acquire the ability to employ theoretical concepts in practice, without resorting to 'blind' application. Students learn that approaching practical strategic issues does not call for a 'fill in the blanks' mindset – 'applying' theory is in itself a delicate art. In other words, the underlying philosophy is that strategic thinking requires a mind that can skillfully move from general principle (theory) to specific situation (practice) and back. A strategic management book must help the professor to challenge students to develop this 'vacillation' ability.

These characteristics of the book are the embodiment of our teaching philosophy and teaching objectives. Users of the book do not need to agree, nor do they need to follow our approach. However, it is important to acknowledge that the rest of this teaching guide has been based on the characteristics described above.

Teaching Approaches

The thinker without a paradox is like a lover without feeling; a paltry mediocrity.
(Soren Kierkegaard 1813-1855; Danish philosopher)

Even within the facilitative teaching philosophy, there remains a wide range of teaching approaches that professors can adopt. In our view, the most important choice professors must make is on how to deal with theory diversity. *Strategy - Process, Content, Context: An International Perspective* presents a broad coverage of different schools of thought and professors must decide on how the debate between these different perspectives should be conducted. In principle, there are four ways of structuring a discussion using readings representing rivaling schools of thought:

- *Collection.* The first, and least appealing, teaching approach is to treat the readings as a collection of unconnected readings. In this approach each article is discussed in isolation and the book is viewed as a handy reader bringing together a number of strategy classics. There is no real debate and the different underlying paradigms are not made explicit. This approach is taken if a strategic management course is intended to be no more than an aggregation of individual insights (*non-paradigmatic approach*).

- *Competition.* An alternative teaching approach is to let the various schools of thought compete with one another, to see which perspective has the most descriptive and/or prescriptive value. In this approach, each article is seen a combatant and the book is viewed as an arena from which the most fit school of thought will emerge. In other words, the debate focuses on selecting the best perspective, which may also lead to the discrediting of the other contenders. This approach is taken if a strategic management course is intended to result in one clear-cut, yet dogmatic, theoretical perspective (*mono-paradigmatic approach*).

- *Coexistence.* A more appealing teaching approach is to compare the various schools of thought and to explore how each can contribute to a better understanding of strategy. In this approach the readings are treated as complementary and the book is viewed as a set of lenses, each offering a different, yet beneficial, insight. The various schools of thought coexist and the debate focuses on determining the value and limitations of each perspective. This approach is taken if it is the intention of a strategic management course to acknowledge and respect the richness of theoretical perspectives (*multi-paradigmatic approach*).

- *Connection.* Finally, professors can also opt for a teaching approach whereby they attempt to combine the various schools of thought into a more integrated view of strategy. In this approach the readings are seen as building blocks and the book is viewed as a research laboratory, where the various perspectives are mixed and matched to construct a more balanced and complete understanding of strategy. The debate focuses on gaining insight into the conflicting and complementary relations between perspectives. The discussions can lead to cross-fertilization of perspectives and a higher level synthesis. This approach is taken if it is the intention of a strategic management course to challenge students to leverage the set of theoretical perspectives by employing them simultaneously, instead of sequentially (*inter-paradigmatic approach*).

While the book can be used in combination with all four approaches, we believe that the highest added value is obtained in the cases of 'coexistence' and 'connection'. Especially connection has our didactical preference. Understanding and appreciating different points of view, as in the case of a multi-paradigmatic approach, is an important step in the development of strategic thinking. The ability to switch lenses is essential for the creativity, flexibility and critical analyses needed of a strategist. However, the sequential use of lenses can lead to a fragmented and unbalanced view of strategic issues. The more lenses, the more complex and contradictory the analyses - not uncommonly leading to paralysis by analysis. The student will come to understand the paradoxes described in the book, but will not be capable of resolving them.

Being able to combine and balance the various perspectives depending on the strategic issue and circumstances encountered, as in the case of an inter-paradigmatic approach, is ultimately an essential capability for engaging in the art of strategy. Strategists must be able to make the move from thesis and antithesis to synthesis; otherwise they will not be able to move from thought to action. We therefore always challenge students to try to resolve the strategy paradoxes by blending the various perspectives into a more holistic view of strategic management.

Teaching Formats

Strategy. Power and knowledge. Science when mere knowing; Art when doing is the object.
(Karl von Clausewitz 1780-1831; German military theorist)

Once professors have chosen their teaching objectives and teaching approach, they must determine how to structure the learning situation. In other words, professors must select a teaching format. In general, there are four types of teaching formats from which professors can choose:

- *Theory only.* A traditional university course is one that revolves around the theory, whereby no use is made of cases. Such a teaching format is usually employed if, to paraphrase Von Clausewitz, science and not art is the objective. It is also used if case teaching is too difficult - for example, if one professor must teach a group of more than 100 students.

- *Theory first, then case.* Many professors prefer to supplement a discussion of the theory with a case analysis. Commonly they will spend a class session or the beginning of a class session with a presentation and/or class discussion based on the theory. After this initial exploration, the professor will turn to the case as an exercise for gaining a deeper understanding. This teaching format is usually employed if professors prefer to have a well-structured, theory-driven case discussion. The key questions are 'How can the theories be applied' and 'What are their limitations?'

- *Case first, then theory.* The opposite teaching format is to start with a practical strategic management issue, in the form of a case or otherwise. The class discussion will then focus on understanding the strategic issue and seeking a course of action. Only after the students have finished the case and have developed a 'feel' for the issue, does the professor place it in a broader theoretical context. In other words, the theoretical discussion is grounded in the class's practical case analysis. This teaching format is usually employed if professors prefer an exploratory, theory-seeking case discussion. The key questions are 'What can be learnt from this specific situation' and 'Can these lessons be generalized and transferred to other situations?'

- *Theory and case simultaneously.* Finally, some professors try to combine the theory-driven and case-driven teaching formats by intertwining the two. They will often start with a short theoretical introduction to the topic and then launch into the case. The case discussion will often require a short theoretical intermezzo, for clarification and conclusions, after which the case discussion is resumed. At the end of the case discussion the theoretical insights are consolidated by means of a final overview. This teaching format is usually employed if professors place much emphasis on students' ability to skillfully move from general principle to practical situations and back.

As stated earlier, there is no best way to teach strategy - no teaching format that is best under all circumstances. The most appropriate format will depend on such variables as the number of students, their level and abilities, the skills of the professor and the time available. The most important thing is to make a choice that fits with these circumstances and to follow this choice through in a consistent manner.

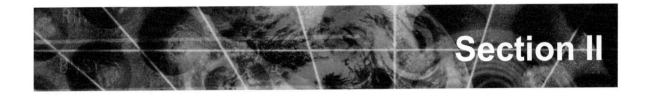

Teaching Set-ups

Introduction
Full-time MBA Course Outline
Part-time Executive Course Outline

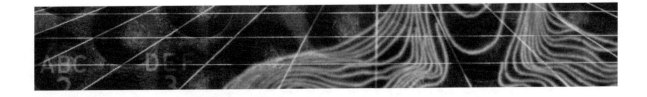

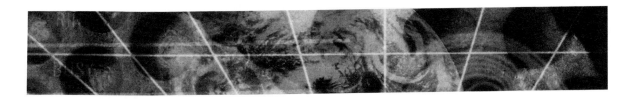

Introduction

There never were, since the creation of the world, two cases exactly parallel.
(Philip Dormer Stanhope 1694-1773; English secretary of state)

When translating the teaching objectives, approach and format into a course set-up, professors must consider a large number of 'design variables'. In other words, strategic management course structures can differ from one another along numerous dimensions. Some design variables can be determined by the professor, while others must be taken as a given. Some of the most important ones are:

- *Course scope.* Professors must decide whether to cover all chapters in the book and whether to skip, or even add, particular topics and readings.

- *Class session sequence.* The order in which topics will be covered must also be determined. Following the chapters in their numerical sequence is a logical choice. However, some professors might prefer to let section III (strategy content) precede section II (strategy process).

- *Class session length.* The length of class sessions can vary from 45 minutes to 4 hours, although the professor does usually not determine this.

- *Class session frequency.* The number of class sessions can vary from 5 to 45 sessions, and is usually also difficult to influence.

- *Class session density.* Class sessions can be clustered into a compact module of 2 to 5 days or can be spread, so that teaching takes place intermittently - 1 to 3 times a week - over a longer period of time.

- *Class session preparation.* Some professors require students to perform activities prior to a class session, for instance to prepare readings, a case and/or an assignment. Other professors integrate these activities into the class sessions.

- *Class session structure.* Each class session can be a mix of activities ranging from listening and discussions to role-playing and assignments. All of these activities can be plenary, in small groups or individual. Each can involve different levels of student-professor interaction.

- *Course cases.* Professors also need to determine which specific cases will be employed. The chapter coverage table in section III can be of assistance for making these choices. Especially if professors want to combine the discussion of two or more issues, this table can help to determine the most suitable case.

- *Course assignments.* Beside class session related work, professors can also assign other duties, such as the writing of an essay, desk research or fieldwork. These assignments can be carried out in groups or individually.

- *Course examination.* It must also be determined how the students' progress will be evaluated. Exams can be written or oral, open or closed book, open answers or multiple choice, individual or group work, and can vary in number, length, weight and level.

With so many variables, it is clear why no blueprint course structure can be given. Professor will need to tailor their teaching set-up to meet their own circumstances. *Strategy - Process, Content, Context:*

An International Perspective is flexible enough to fit with almost any of these. However, to give interested professors a point of reference, we have included our most recent course outlines. We do not think that these particular course outlines will exactly fit the particular needs of any one professor. However, we do hope that they stimulate or confirm your current thinking.

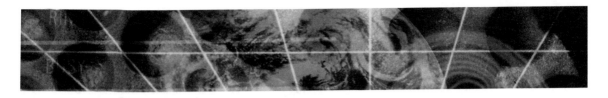

STRATEGIC MANAGEMENT
Full-time MBA Course

Course Description

Strategy. Power and knowledge. Science when mere knowing; Art when doing is the object.

(Karl von Clausewitz 1780-1831; German military theorist)

It is the intention of this course to give an overview of all essential aspects of strategic management. The most fundamental distinction made in the field is between strategy process, strategy content and strategy context. These are the three *dimensions of strategy* that can be recognized in every real-life strategic problem situation. They can be generally defined as follows:

- *Strategy Process*. The manner in which strategies come about is referred to as the strategy process. Stated in terms of a number of questions, strategy process is concerned with the *how*, *who* and *when* of strategy - how is, and should, strategy be made, analyzed, dreamt-up, formulated, implemented, changed and controlled; who is involved; and when do the necessary activities take place?

- *Strategy Content*. The product of a strategy process is referred to as the strategy content. Stated in terms of a question, strategy content is concerned with the *what* of strategy - what is, and should be, the strategy for the company and each of its constituent units?

- *Strategy Context*. The set of circumstances under which both the strategy process and the strategy content are determined is referred to as the strategy context. Stated in terms of a question, strategy context is concerned with the *where* of strategy - where, that is in which firm and which environment, are the strategy process and strategy content embedded.

It must be emphasized that process, content and context are not the 'elements' of strategic management, but its 'dimensions'. Elements can be taken apart and examined in isolation, but this is not the case with the strongly interrelated aspects process, content and context. Strategic phenomena can be examined from a process, content or context *perspective*, as you could look at a box's length, width and height, dependent on where you stand. The exclusive use of any of the three angles gives only a limited view of the object under investigation. To obtain 'depth' of understanding of strategy, it is therefore necessary to merge the process, content and context angles into a *three dimensional view* of strategic management. This course takes such a three dimensional view of strategic management, by paying equal attention to each dimension. In this way, all essential topics in the area of strategic management are covered.

In this course, the remark made by Von Clausewitz in his book *On War* is also acknowledged. As business students are interested in both knowing and doing, this course will not only deal with the 'science' of strategy, but also with the 'art'. In other words, it is the explicit intention of this course to improve students' strategy making competence by emphasizing problem-solving skills and strategic thinking capabilities.

Course Objectives

Some people are so good at learning the tricks of the trade that they never get to learn the trade.

Sam Levenson 1911-1980; American teacher and comedian

One of the occupational hazards of becoming a manager or consultant is superficiality. Unfortunately, getting an MBA is not necessarily an effective deterrent to shallow thinking. Actually, many students enter business programs hoping to quickly pick up the tricks of the trade, without expending too much energy on the laborious task of learning to think strategically. Tools and techniques are more highly valued than developing a strategic problem-solving ability. Some students aspire to become 'spreadsheet wizards', commonly referred to as 'trained monkeys' in the business world.

However, in this course, the emphasis is not on filling in frameworks and applying standard recipes. On the contrary, students will be expected to challenge recipes, question received wisdom, and exhibit unconventional thinking. These are objectives set for this course:

- *Knowledge*. To encourage the understanding of the many, often conflicting, schools of thought and to facilitate the gaining of insight into the assumptions, possibilities and limitations of each set of theories;

- *Skills*. To develop the student's ability to define strategic issues, to critically reflect on existing theories, to creatively combine or develop theories where necessary and to flexibly employ theories where useful;

- *Attitude*. To instill a critical, analytical, flexible and creative mindset, which challenges organizational, industry and national paradigms and problem-solving recipes.

Course Format

Reading makes a learned man, conversation a ready man, writing a precise man.

John Locke 1632-1704; English philosopher

The format of the course is based on a mixture of cases and theory, as it is our belief that understanding both practice and theory, and acquiring the skill to apply one to the other, should be the core of this course. Hence, classes will not be used to review theory which is in the book (this is the student's individual responsibility), but will be employed for case discussion. This discussion should, however, be guided by insights gained in the 'theoretical' readings and should lead to conclusions about the applicability of theoretical concepts in certain practical situations. In general, classes will be structured according to the following schedule:

Topic introduction	9.00 - 9.15
Case introduction	9.15 - 9.20
Case discussion questions 1-2	9.20 - 10.15
Break	10.15 - 10.30
Case discussion questions 3-5	10.30 - 11.30
Conceptual wrap-up	11.30 - 12.00

In order to utilize the limited amount of class time as well as possible, it is expected that students will have read the assigned chapters and have prepared the cases prior to each session (based on the case questions in the appendix). The quality of your preparation and class input will be reflected in your participation grade. Class attendance is not mandatory, but absence from classes will have a negative effect on your participation grade.

Course Schedule

The class schedule, including dates, hours and classrooms is already in your possession. In the table below a further detailing of the contents per class session is given.

Class	Topic	Readings	Case
1	Introduction	Chapter 1	Honda
2	Strategic Thinking	Chapter 2	Virgin
3	Strategy Formation	Chapter 3	Oldelft
4	Strategic Change	Chapter 4	Encyclopaedia Britannica
5	Business Level Strategy	Chapter 5	Southwest Airlines
6	Corporate Level Strategy	Chapter 6	Shell & Billiton
7	Network Level Strategy	Chapter 7	KLM & Alcazar
8	The Industry Context	Chapter 8	Champagne Industry
9	The Organizational Context	Chapter 9	Cartier
10	The International Context	Chapter 10	Cap Gemini
11	Organizational Purpose	Chapter 11	The Body Shop
12	Guest lecture	None	

Course Assignment

The main assignment in this course, beside class participation, will be to write a case or 'solve' a case. The program manager will determine the composition of the groups on the basis of two principles: heterogeneity and non-familiarity.

Work on Existing Case. Student groups interested in working on the solution to an existing case will be given a choice between three cases, which will be presented at the beginning of the course. These groups will be asked to write a strategic plan for the CEO of their case company. In this 'consultancy' role, you must analyze the situation the company is in, suggest alternative strategy directions, and indicate which strategy you find most promising and suggest how the company may go about implementing this strategy. Your strategic plan should meet the following criteria:

- *Length.* The body of the text (excluding executive summary, list of contents and appendices) may be no longer than 30 pages (line spacing 1.5, with regular margins).

- *Description vs. analysis.* The CEO doesn't want you to describe his/her company or the environment, but wants the added value of analysis. You may presume (s)he is knowledgeable about the company and the business surroundings and that (s)he has read the *Strategy – Process, Content, Context* text.

- *Information sources.* It is unnecessary to bring in additional information, since the CEO has supplied you with more than enough. The CEO also has bad experience with consultants who think they are precognizant and claim they know what will happen after the decision date mentioned in the case. Therefore, (s)he would like you to keep your feet on the ground -- no crystal ball gazing allowed!

- *Evaluation criteria*. Your client is a very critical judge of other people's work. Some writing guidelines have been included as appendix to make your task a little easier.

- *Deadline*. The report must be handed in by the last day of class. For every 24 hours (or part thereof) that the paper is late (excluding hours in holidays or weekends) 0.5 points will be subtracted from the paper's grade.

Writing a New Case. Student groups interested in the creation of new cases, which can be used for class discussions in the following years, can choose to write a new case and teacher's guide. These groups will need to work more closely with the course professors, to determine the right company, topic, focus and content. Their assignment will not only be to write an interesting and useful case, but they must also indicate that you can apply the strategy concepts learnt during the course, by writing a teacher's guide, where some possible case solutions should be detailed. The deadline for this assignment is the same as for the other group, but the length, content, information sources and evaluation criteria will be determined depending on the circumstances.

Final Exam

The final exam will consist of a short case with a small number of questions. The questions will require students to be able to apply their knowledge of theoretical concepts to the practical case situation. This exam requires no memorization and is therefore open book. This exam does require deep understanding of the strategy concepts and extensive practice in the application of theory to a business situation. The best preparation for both is class participation.

Course Grading

The assignment accounts for one-third of your final grade. The other two-thirds will be determined by your participation throughout the course and the final exam. In overview:

Assignment	1/3
Final Exam	1/3
Participation	1/3

The class participation grade will be based on the quality, not the quantity, of participation. Absence from class sessions without due reason will result in a lower participation score.

Literature

De Wit, Bob, and Ron Meyer (1998), *Strategy - Process, Content, Context: An International Perspective*, second edition, London: International Thomson Publishing.

Appendix I: On Writing a Strategic Management Paper

On Content

1. *Problem Definition.* A paper must always begin with an indication of why it is being written. Ideally this 'mission definition' should be stated as a problem definition.

2. *Solution Method.* Not only should the writer have a structured method of approaching the problem, but he must also share this solution method with the reader, preferably as early on in the paper as possible.

3. *Analytical Depth.* The most common problem of papers is that they merely scratch the surface of a case, which is usually justified by referring to the page limit. However, the need for brevity may be no excuse for superficiality. The page limit refers to how much one may report, not to how much one may think. One important rule of thumb when striving for depth and brevity is to avoid rehashing the information in the case. You may presume that all the facts in the case are known to the reader, so that you can focus on analysis instead of description.

4. *Use of Theory.* Trying to reinvent the wheel is a cardinal sin for someone striving for an academic education. Theory is the residue of generations of problem solving, is hence usually useful at indicating avenues for attacking a problem and therefore should be used according to need. One must, however, keep the right sequence in mind; for a practitioner theories should not be looking for appropriate problems, but problems looking for appropriate theory.

5. *Structured Reasoning.* Brainstorming is good, as long as it is constrained to one's brain. Wait until the storm is over and things have been straightened out before confiding anything to paper. This should be done in a structured manner, with a clear line of argumentation. Checklists may be used as a structuring tool, but in themselves argue nothing. Checklists need to be explained and woven into the line of reasoning. It is this structured reasoning which is usually more important than the solutions that it bears.

6. *Explicit Assumptions.* Every argument will be partially based on assumptions and estimations. This is no large problem if the writer points them out to the readers, so that readers may determine whether they share them or not.

7. *Motivated Solutions.* Although from an academic point of view reasoning is more important than actual solutions (process more important than the product), business administration is an action-oriented science and therefore necessarily interested in solutions. Hence, it is expected that the paper's line of reasoning is carried through to its logical end, resulting in motivated solutions (including an overview of costs and benefits, and detailed indications of how implementation could be assured) or a well-motivated lack of solution (including alternative lines of action).

8. *Creativity.* Working in a structured manner shouldn't imply that one works through the case mechanically. 'Doing a case' should never become synonymous with 'fill in the blanks' exercises or 'painting by numbers'. Creativity, for instance in terms of original responses to competitive threats, inventive growth strategies or unconventional solutions to implementation problems, is an important element in the strategist's arsenal and therefore actively encouraged.

On Presentation

9. *Clear Structure.* It almost goes without saying that the whole structure of the paper should be clear at a glance. This not only means that the content should be structured (see previous section), but that the structure must be visible to the reader. Obvious helps are clearly named chapters and paragraphs (preferably numbered), use of bold and italic typesetting and use of a structure guide (either a table of contents or a clarifying diagram).

10. *Clear Layout.* Consult a writer's handbook if necessary for rules and hints with regard to margins, page numbers, spacing, listings, tables, bibliographies and footnotes.

11. *Grammar.* It cannot be expected of non-native English speakers that their English rivals that of the Queen, but unfamiliarity with the language may not become an excuse for laxity. Rereading of texts and use of a spelling check program can easily resolve 90% of all errors.

12. *Writing Style.* Although a matter of taste, one may safely assume that a professor grows to dislike unnecessarily woolly, drawn out and boring writing rather quickly, the more so after 20 papers! So, be concrete, to the point and exciting. Dare to be witty, entertaining and different - your reader is human and will probably enjoy it!

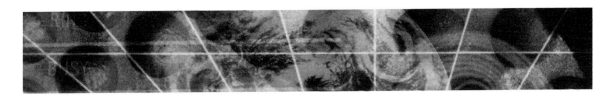

STRATEGIC MANAGEMENT
Part-time Executive MBA Course

Course Description

Strategy. Power and knowledge. Science when mere knowing; Art when doing is the object.

(Karl von Clausewitz 1780-1831; German military theorist)

It is the intention of this course to give an overview of all essential aspects of strategic management. The most fundamental distinction made in the field is between strategy process, strategy content and strategy context. These are the three *dimensions of strategy* that can be recognized in every real-life strategic problem situation. They can be generally defined as follows:

- *Strategy Process.* The manner in which strategies come about is referred to as the strategy process. Stated in terms of a number of questions, strategy process is concerned with the *how*, *who* and *when* of strategy - how is, and should, strategy be made, analyzed, dreamt-up, formulated, implemented, changed and controlled; who is involved; and when do the necessary activities take place?

- *Strategy Content.* The product of a strategy process is referred to as the strategy content. Stated in terms of a question, strategy content is concerned with the *what* of strategy - what is, and should be, the strategy for the company and each of its constituent units?

- *Strategy Context.* The set of circumstances under which both the strategy process and the strategy content are determined is referred to as the strategy context. Stated in terms of a question, strategy context is concerned with the *where* of strategy - where, that is in which firm and which environment, are the strategy process and strategy content embedded.

It must be emphasized that process, content and context are not the 'elements' of strategic management, but its 'dimensions'. Elements can be taken apart and examined in isolation, but this is not the case with the strongly interrelated aspects process, content and context. Strategic phenomena can be examined from a process, content or context *perspective*, as you could look at a box's length, width and height, dependent on where you stand. The exclusive use of any of the three angles gives only a limited view of the object under investigation. To obtain 'depth' of understanding of strategy, it is therefore necessary to merge the process, content and context angles into a *three dimensional view* of strategic management. This course takes such a three dimensional view of strategic management, by paying equal attention to each dimension. In this way, all essential topics in the area of strategic management are covered.

In this course, the remark made by Von Clausewitz in his book *On War* is also acknowledged. As business students are interested in both knowing and doing, this course will not only deal with the 'science' of strategy, but also as with the 'art'. In other words, it is the explicit intention of this course to improve students' strategy making competence by emphasizing problem-solving skills and strategic thinking capabilities.

Course Objectives

Some people are so good at learning the tricks of the trade that they never get to learn the trade.

Sam Levenson 1911-1980; American teacher and comedian

One of the occupational hazards of becoming a manager or consultant is superficiality. Unfortunately, getting an MBA is not necessarily an effective deterrent to shallow thinking. Actually, many students enter business programs hoping to quickly pick up the tricks of the trade, without expending too much energy on the laborious task of learning to think strategically. Tools and techniques are more highly valued than developing a strategic problem-solving ability. Some students aspire to become 'spreadsheet wizards', commonly referred to as 'trained monkeys' in the business world.

However, in this course, the emphasis is not on filling in frameworks and applying standard recipes. On the contrary, students will be expected challenge recipes, question received wisdom, and exhibit unconventional thinking. These are objectives set for this course:

- *Knowledge*. To encourage the understanding of the many, often conflicting, schools of thought and to facilitate the gaining of insight into the assumptions, possibilities and limitations of each set of theories;

- *Skills*. To develop the student's ability to define strategic issues, to critically reflect on existing theories, to creatively combine or develop theories where necessary and to flexibly employ theories where useful;

- *Attitude*. To instill a critical, analytical, flexible and creative mindset, which challenges organizational, industry and national paradigms and problem-solving recipes.

Course Format

Reading makes a learned man, conversation a ready man, writing a precise man.

John Locke 1632-1704; English philosopher

The format of the course is based on a mixture of cases and theory, as it is our belief that understanding both practice and theory, and acquiring the skill to apply one to the other, should be the core of this course. Hence, classes will not be used to review theory which is in the book (this is the student's individual responsibility), but will be employed for case discussion. This discussion should, however, be guided by insights gained in the 'theoretical' readings and should lead to conclusions about the applicability of theoretical concepts in certain practical situations. In general, classes will be structured according to the following schedule:

Topic introduction	9.00 - 9.15
Case introduction	9.15 - 9.20
Case discussion questions 1-2	9.20 - 10.15
Break	10.15 - 10.30
Case discussion questions 3-5	10.30 - 11.30
Conceptual wrap-up	11.30 - 12.00

In order to utilize the limited amount of class time as well as possible, it is expected that students will have read the assigned chapters and have prepared the cases prior to each session (based on the case questions in the appendix). The quality of your preparation and class input will be reflected in your participation grade. Class attendance is not mandatory, but absence from classes will have a negative effect on your participation grade.

Course Schedule

The class schedule, including dates, hours and classrooms is already in your possession. In the table below a further detailing of the contents per class session is given. You are expected to have read all appropriate chapter introductions, as well as the first two readings of each chapter before class.

Class	Topic	Readings	Case
1	Introduction & Strategic Thinking	Chapter 1 & 2	MTV
2	Strategy Formation & Strategic Change	Chapter 3 & 4	Ceteco
3	Business Level Strategy & Industry Context	Chapter 5 & 8	Avon
4	Corporate Level & Organizational Context	Chapter 6 & 9	Philips
5	Network Level Strategy	Chapter 7	Merck
6	International Context	Chapter 10	IKEA
7	Organizational Purpose	Chapter 11	Daimler-Benz
8	Presentation of Assignments	None	

Course Assignment

Your assignment is to relate what you have learnt in the strategic management course to your field research project. More specifically, each group will be asked to prepare a presentation for the last class in which they will *review* the strategy process, content and context of their research company, *analyze* what the strengths and weaknesses of the strategy process and strategy content are, and give *recommendations* with regard to possible improvements. The intention of this assignment is not only to test your knowledge of the strategy concepts, but also to create synergy with your field research project. Your assignment should meet the following criteria:

- *Presentation form.* The outcome of you research must be presented to the entire group and to the professor on the last day of class. This presentation may last no longer than 20 minutes. The supporting transparencies should contain your most important findings and must be multiplied for distribution before your presentation.

- *Presentation content.* Do not spend too much time describing strategy theory, but focus your efforts on adding value by:
  - *Analysis.* Make clear why your company behaves as it does and evaluate whether you think their strategy process and strategy content fit with their strategy context.
  - *Confrontation.* Do theory and practice fit and if not, why not? Are the theories wrong or limited, or is the company making strategic mistakes?
  - *Recommendations.* How can your research company improve its strategy process and strategy content, and how could these changes be implemented?

- *Presentation evaluation.* The presentations will be evaluated by the professor, who will be able to respond directly to the groups' output and will determine the final grades.

Literature

De Wit, Bob, and Ron Meyer (1998), *Strategy - Process, Content, Context: An International Perspective*, second edition, London: International Thomson Publishing.

Teaching Notes

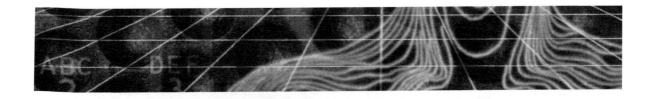

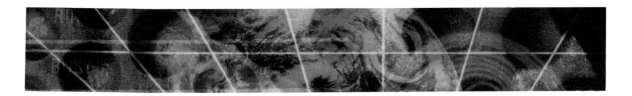

Introduction

Those who have read of everything are thought to understand everything too;
but this is not always so – reading furnishes the mind only with the materials of knowledge;
it is thinking that makes what is read ours.
It is not enough to cram ourselves with a great load of collections;
unless we chew them over again, they will not give us strength and nourishment.
(John Locke 1632-1704; English philosopher)

As Locke correctly observed, true understanding requires more than just reading. Ideas, concepts and perspectives must be 'chewed over' before they can be absorbed in our minds. One of the most common and beneficial ways of achieving this is by means of case discussions. Therefore, 22 long cases and 11 short cases have been included in the book, giving the reader ample opportunity to apply the theoretical concepts to practical situations.

To increase the accessibility of the long cases, three tables have been included on the next pages, clarifying the content and potential usage of the cases. These tables deal with the following topics:

1. *Chapter Coverage.* Table 1 indicates which cases are most suited to which chapters. The extent to which cases and chapters *fit* has been expressed by means of stars. Three stars mean that there is an *excellent* fit between the case and the theoretical issues being discussed in the chapter. Two stars indicate that the fit is *good* and that the theoretical issues can be well illustrated by the case material. One star means that there is only a partial (*reasonable*) fit; the chapter's theory is of secondary importance to understanding the case issues. Table 1 shows that at least two cases have an excellent fit with each chapter.

2. *Industry Sector Coverage.* Table 2 indicates which industries are dealt with in which cases. This table reflects the balanced coverage of service and product companies.

3. *Country Coverage.* Table 3 indicates which countries are dealt with in which cases. Two stars are used to signify that the country is a primary focus of the case. One star means that the country is discussed in the case, but that it is only of secondary importance to the case topic. Table 3 illustrates the broad international coverage of the cases.

As the link between the theoretical chapters and the cases is the most important, the sequence of the cases in the book follows the chapters with which they have the best fit. The teaching notes are presented in the same order.

Each teaching note has been structured in the same way, to make them more readily usable. Each teaching note consists of the following paragraphs:

- *Case synopsis.* This paragraph gives a short summary of the case's key points.

- *Teaching objectives.* This paragraph outlines which major elements of the corresponding chapter's theory can be illustrated using the case.

- *Teaching guideline.* Subsequently, it is explored how they case can be employed, what its strengths are, whether there are any pitfalls and what the professor should keep in mind while teaching.

- *Case questions.* In this paragraph five case questions are suggested that roughly cover the main case issues.

- *Case analysis.* Here a general analysis is given on the basis of the five case questions.

- *What happened after the case.* Each case discussion is wrapped up by a short review of the major events that have happened after publication of the case. This section is regularly updated on our website (www.itbp.com).

TABLE 1
Chapter Coverage

SECTION	I	II			III			IV			V
CHAPTER	1	2	3	4	5	6	7	8	9	10	11
Honda	***	**	**	*	*	*	*	*	*	*	
Swatch	***	**	**	*	*	*	*	*	*	*	*
Virgin	*	***	*	*	*	**	*	**	**	*	
Stantret	*	***	**	*			**	**	**		
Oldelft		*	***	**					*		*
Kao Corporation		*	***	**	*	*	*		**	**	*
Carl Zeiss Jena			*	***					**		*
Encyclopaedia Britannica		**	**	***	*			**	*		
Southwest Airlines	*	*	**	*	***			**	**		
Canon				**	***	**	**	*	**	*	
Shell & Billiton		**	*	**		***		*	**		
Grand Metropolitan			*	*	***				*		*
KLM and Alcazar			**	*	*	*	***	**	**	**	*
The Salim Group			*		*	**	***		*		*
The Champagne Industry			*	**	**		**	***	*	*	**
National Bicycle		*			**		*	***		*	
Teléfonos de México			**	**	*			*	***		*
Cartier		**	**	*	**	**	*		***	**	
Saatchi & Saatchi					*	**		*	*	***	*
Cap Gemini Sogeti (A&B)			**	**	*	**	*	*	**	***	
Burroughs Wellcome							*		*		***
The Body Shop Int'l		*			*	*		**	**	*	***

*** = Excellent fit
** = Good fit
* = Reasonable fit

TABLE 2
Industry Sector Coverage

SECTORS	Consumer Goods	Industrial Goods	Consumer Services	Business Services	Specific Industry
Honda	*	*			Cars, motorcycles, engines
Swatch	*				Watches
Virgin	*		*	*	Diversified
Stantret				*	Cargo airline
Oldelft		*			Optical electronics
Kao Corporation	*				Household products
Carl Zeiss Jena		*			Optical instruments
Encyclopaedia Britannica	*				Encyclopaedias
Southwest Airlines			*		Airlines
Canon	*	*			Cameras, copiers
Shell & Billiton	*	*			Oil products & metals
Grand Metropolitan	*		*		Diversified
KLM and Alcazar			*	*	Airlines
The Salim Group	*	*	*	*	Diversified
The Champagne Industry	*				Champagne
National Bicycle Industry	*				Bicycles
Teléfonos de México			*	*	Telephone services
Cartier	*				Jewelry, fragrances
Saatchi & Saatchi				*	Advertising, consulting
Cap Gemini Sogeti (A&B)				*	IT consulting, software
Burroughs Wellcome	*				Pharmaceuticals
The Body Shop Int.	*		*		Retailing, personal care

28 TEACHING GUIDE

TABLE 3
Country Coverage

COUNTRY	AT	CH	CN	DE	DK	FR	ID	JP	MX	NL	NO	RU	SE	UK	US
Honda								**							
Swatch		**													
Virgin														**	
Stantret												**			
Oldelft										**					
Kao Corporation								**							
Carl Zeiss Jena				**											
Encyclopaedia Britannica															**
Southwest Airlines															**
Canon								**							
Shell & Billiton										**				**	
Grand Metropolitan														**	*
KLM and Alcazar	**	**			**					**	**		**		*
The Salim Group			**				**								
The Champagne Industry						**									
National Bicycle Industry								**							
Teléfonos de México									**						
Cartier						**									
Saatchi & Saatchi														**	
Cap Gemini Sogeti (A&B)						**				*			*	*	*
Burroughs Wellcome															**
The Body Shop Int.														**	

** = Primary focus
* = Secondary focus

AT = Austria
CH = Switzerland
CN = China
DE = Germany
DK = Denmark

FR = France
ID = Indonesia
JP = Japan
MX = Mexico
NL = Netherlands

NO = Norway
RU = Russia
SE = Sweden
UK = United Kingdom
US = United States

TEACHING NOTE 1: HONDA

Case by Andrew Mair

Teaching Note by Andrew Mair and Ron Meyer

Case Introduction

Honda is a popular company to use as a strategy case study in a pedagogic setting. The company first rose to prominence as a strategy example when Boston Consulting Group (1975) published its analysis of the declining British motorcycle industry, in which the competitive threat posed by Honda's advance along the so-called experience curve was highlighted. A well-known essay by Richard Pascale (1984) took issue with one particular aspect of the BCG version of events. This essay is frequently invoked to argue that there may be more than 'one best way' to create strategy, and more specifically that learning from experience, together with luck, may be more important than analytical thinking. Another well-known case study of Honda is by James Brian Quinn (1991, 1996), in his strategy text edited with Henry Mintzberg, in which he describes Honda as an idiosyncratic entrepreneurial firm, much in line with Pascale's portrayal. The summer 1996 issue of *California Management Review* published a lengthy debate on the so-called 'Honda effect' between the BCG camp, for which Honda remains a company best understood as an analytical planner, and the Pascale/Mintzberg camp, which stresses the incrementalist approach.

Besides this strategy process debate, Honda is also at the center of discussion in strategy content issues. Hamel and Prahalad (reading 6.2) lay claim to Honda to argue the importance of technical core competencies, while Stalk, Evans and Shulman (reading 5.2) – also of Boston Consulting Group – propose instead that Honda's success is best explained by broader core capabilities. Honda, in other words, has - unwittingly - become embroiled in some of the major controversies of the strategy field.

This case attempts to explain how Honda can appear to support opposing theoretical perspectives at the same time. The case describes that while many companies, when faced with strategic and other managerial choices, select one option, or trade off one against another, Honda has acquired a strategic capability to reconcile management dichotomies - and hence achieve solutions to management challenges that are denied to other companies.

Teaching Objectives

If used in conjunction with chapter 1, this case can be employed to meet the following teaching objectives:

- *Understanding the concept of strategy tensions.* This case explains how organizations are confronted by tensions between opposite demands that need to be dealt with. In the case these tensions are referred to as managerial dichotomies (link to introduction).

- *Understanding the concept of strategy paradoxes.* In the case it becomes clear that while Honda managers accept the existence of the tensions/dichotomies, they constantly seek to find innovative ways of reconciling them. In other words, they do not see the tensions/dichotomies as false opposites (a puzzle) or as mutually exclusive demands (a dilemma). Nor do they accept that meeting one demand is always at the expense of meeting the other (a trade-off). Honda managers believe that opposites can be bridged (a paradox), but that this transcending of the tension requires creative thinking (link to introduction).

- *Discussion on the reconciliation of opposites.* The case gives many examples of tensions/dichotomies that Honda managers have successfully bridged. Less attention is paid to the cognitive and organizational processes required to achieve successful reconciliation. This allows for a discussion on the use of dialectics and argumentation as creativity enhancing methodologies. This discussion is important as the entire set-up of the book rests on dialectical inquiry and argumentation to stimulate students' critical thinking abilities (link to introduction and 1.4 Mason & Mitroff).

- *Discussion on the nature of strategic thinking.* The case continuously makes clear that Honda's success rests on its ability to break through existing trade-offs and to creatively find new ways for dealing with enduring strategy tensions/dichotomies. This makes the step to the discussion in the following chapter on the nature of strategic thinking quite easy (link to chapter 2).

- *Discussion on cross-cultural management differences.* The case also clearly brings forward the traditional differences between stereotypical Western and Japanese management. The question that can be asked is whether these historical differences still exist and whether they will continue to influence how managers from each nation will develop strategies (link to introduction and 1.5 Hofstede).

Teaching Guideline

The Honda case is not a traditional strategy case study in the Harvard Business School sense. While most case studies attempt to be theory-neutral, so as to provide empirical materials upon which course participants can practice the application of the theoretical strategy perspectives and models they are learning, this case study definitely has a point of view to get across. This case illustrates how managerial dichotomies can be reconciled in a way that the 'best of both worlds' is achieved.

This case has been selected as the opening case because it encapsulates the pedagogical philosophy underlying the book. As at Honda, students are encouraged to understand the tensions posed by opposite pressures placed on organizations. And as at Honda, students must find the most effective way of dealing with these opposites. In chapter 1, four alternative ways of viewing dichotomies are given – as puzzles, dilemmas, trade-offs or paradoxes. The case illustrates that at Honda the dichotomies are viewed as paradoxes – two opposites seem contradictory but can be reconciled through creative thinking. And this is exactly what the book challenges readers to do in all further chapters.

The case is designed to work as follows. After providing a broad background to the company, it presents its fundamental story - that of 'Mr. Kawamoto's Reforms'. This story nicely illustrates two issues. First, the issue of reconciling the individualism-groupism dichotomy at senior management level is examined, which gives valuable insights into managing the strategy process. More subtly, the story also illustrates how easy it can be to misinterpret this reconciliation process as an attempt at a revolutionary swing from one extreme to the other (precisely what occurs in many companies). The bulk of the case then reviews a series of easy-to-understand management dichotomies and presents Honda's 'solutions'. There is no attempt to explain how the solutions were arrived at. The principle behind this pedagogic structure is that of Thomas Kuhn: a young child shown a duck and a goose may not be able to explain the difference between them theoretically, but will certainly recognize the next goose encountered. The Honda goose is shown against a series of different backgrounds in the hope that its silhouette too will be recognizable in front of new, unanticipated backgrounds.

While the dichotomies and constant reconciliation described in the case make the fundamental philosophy of the book clear, they do not pre-empt the debates that follow in the next chapters. This is because the focus in the Honda case is primarily on the *functional* level of strategy - in particular, production operations and product development - and organizational issues. Only at the end does the case raise some strategy dichotomies as discussed in the book, but whereas previously

Honda's reconciliatory management practices were fully described, for strategy they are only hinted at.

A good way to start off the case discussion is to draw attention to Exhibit 8, which incorporates a trade-off line, upon which all types of dichotomies can be mapped. The top right hand corner is the neo-classical economists' unattainable area - which suggests that innovation will have been achieved if it can indeed be reached. The next step is to ask students to create lists of dichotomies through a classroom discussion, carefully managing it to bring out relevant dichotomies and set aside ideas that don't work. It can be very difficult for some course participants to understand this concept if they are not adept at thinking abstractly, so it is worth spending some time on this. One approach could be the following:

- First, create a list from the Honda case (e.g. humane vs. efficient work).

- Second, develop a list of other dichotomies drawn from their own work experience (e.g. what appear to be contradictory pressures on their behavior, such as teamwork combined with individualized reward systems).

- Third, review and get course participants to explain the broad strategy dichotomies.

- Fourth, if a counterpoint might prove useful, reading 5.1 by Michael Porter can be used. Cost and differentiation can be presented as polar points on Exhibit 8 of the Honda case study. Porter is interesting because his points are not at the extremes (firms following the cost strategy must bear differentiation in mind too). He is also interesting because he does not permit a sliding trade-off; any attempt to do so leads to 'stuck in the middle', the bottom left hand corner of Exhibit 8. For Porter, the top right hand corner is unattainable (despite his typical caveats; see Porter, 1996, for his admirable defense of this – we believe fundamentally flawed – approach).

- Fifth, only at this point would we attempt to get course participants to isolate the strategic dichotomies their (former) firm faces - indeed this may best be left until later in the course in the context of the in-depth chapters of the text. The Honda case should nevertheless have made this task less daunting.

Of course, the Honda case can also be used in shorter courses and one-off seminars as a tool to quickly introduce the concept of 'reconciling managerial dichotomies' without participants having read the book. This leaves participants the freedom to focus on the dichotomies that they find most interesting and/or relevant to their practical situation.

Case Questions

1. What are the major strategy tensions/dichotomies that Honda has attempted to reconcile over the past 50 years?

2. Do Honda managers view these tensions/dichotomies as puzzles, dilemmas, trade-offs or paradoxes? Explain.

3. What type of organization and mind-set do you think are needed to reconcile strategy tensions/dichotomies in the way Honda has?

Case Analysis

1. What are the major strategy tensions/dichotomies that Honda has attempted to reconcile over the past 50 years?

The case describes many tensions/dichotomies that Honda has attempted to reconcile, but mostly they have been framed as general management issues or dichotomies at the functional strategy level (e.g.

production and product strategy). Yet, with a little discussion, many of these dichotomies can be reframed as the fundamental strategy tensions discussed in this book:

- *Deliberateness vs. Emergentness.* In the case this tension is identified as the dichotomy of planning vs. learning.

- *Revolution vs. Evolution.* While describing Kawamoto's reforms, it is argued that Honda did not radically switch to a new mode of doing business, nor where the changes gradual and gentle. Honda's approach to change combined revolutionary and evolutionary characteristics.

- *Markets vs. Resources.* In the case this tension is only mentioned in passing as the dichotomy of market positioning vs. developing internal resources.

- *Responsiveness vs. synergy.* At the beginning of the case the dichotomy between individualism and groupism is discussed in depth. At the corporate level this issue is translated into the tension between individual business units responding to the demands of their own businesses, while recognizing the group's potential for achieving synergies through the leveraging of competencies/capabilities.

- *Competition vs. cooperation.* In discussing the relationship with its component suppliers, this dichotomy is brought forward.

- *Globalization vs. localization.* This tension is raised in a slightly different way, as the general dichotomy of Japanese vs. Western management. Looked at differently, the question for Honda is to become a nationless company versus one with a strong Japanese identity.

At this moment the professor might want to complete the full list of 10 tensions, to give students an overview of what is to come, and ask whether students think these additional tensions are also relevant for Honda.

2. Do Honda managers view these tensions/dichotomies as puzzles, dilemmas, trade-offs or paradoxes? Explain.

In the case it becomes clear that while Honda managers accept the existence of the tensions/dichotomies, they constantly seek to find innovative ways of reconciling them. In other words, they do not see the tensions/dichotomies as:

- *A puzzle.* If Honda managers would view the tensions/dichotomies as a puzzle, this would mean that they would strive for the one optimal solution for bringing together the two sides. In other words, seeing a tension/dichotomy as a puzzle means viewing the two sides as false opposites, which logically can be brought together into one best approach.

- *A dilemma.* If Honda managers would view the tensions/dichotomies as a dilemma, this would mean that the two opposites would be mutually exclusive demands. Honda managers would have to choose an 'either-or' solution.

- *A trade-off.* If Honda managers would view the tensions/dichotomies as a trade-off, this would mean that meeting one demand would always be at the expense of meeting the other demand. In other words, Honda managers would accept a static zero-sum game between the two opposites.

Rather, Honda managers believe that the tensions/dichotomies should be viewed as paradoxes, that is, as seeming contradictions. They believe that the two opposites can be bridged, in other words the paradox can be transcended. However, every new reconciliation is not the final resolution of the tension, but merely a better solution than previous ones. This leads to a constant drive to find even better ways of getting the best of both worlds.

A follow-up question to gain more depth would be: *Is it likely that Honda managers and employees think precisely in the way the case suggests, or is this in fact just another Western interpretative imposition?*

This is an open question to which we can give no definitive answer. There is some clear evidence that Honda managers and engineers think more or less explicitly in terms of reconciling dichotomies. The case study presents two examples. Exhibit 11 is Honda's own figure, showing the relation between fuel consumption and the power of the VTEC engine, and Exhibit 12 ('we aren't interested in trade-offs') with its overt dichotomy-resolving language. Mito's book (1990), while less analytical, suggests other examples. Moreover, Honda's 'revealed strategy' can be coherently interpreted in this way. On the other hand, some Western managers from Honda, as well as senior Japanese executives at the company, have seemed somewhat bemused when asked about this way of thinking. Wherever the 'truth' lies, simply posing the above question to course participants - particularly in tandem with a short discussion on explicit and implicit forms of knowledge (link to chapter 2) - can generate useful discussion in class. Of course, it might be that the 'revealed strategy' at Honda described in the case study reflects what is in fact an implicit mode of thinking, possibly tied to Japanese culture, which the case study has misrepresented. Yet, it might still be valid to make this mode of thinking explicit, as the case study does, in order to communicate the underlying conceptual framework to a Western audience (link to reading 1.5 on cultural diversity).

3. *What type of organization and mind-set do you think are needed to reconcile strategy tensions/dichotomies in the way Honda has?*

This question is intended to lead the discussion towards the issues in the following chapters, strategic thinking and strategy formation. The issue of mind-set refers to the discussion that will take place in chapter 2: How much logic and creativity does the strategic thinker need to be able to reconcile tensions? It can already become clear in this discussion that it is necessary for strategists to understand the nature of the strategy tensions, but that analytical reasoning is probably not enough to break through dilemma or trade-off thinking. A certain measure of innovative ability is needed, which suggests that creative thinking probably is an important ingredient of a strategist's art.

The discussion on the organizational characteristics needed to encourage dichotomy reconciliation will anticipate the debates that will take place in chapters 3 and 4, where questions of experimentation and learning are on the agenda.

A follow-up question to gain more depth would be: *Is it really practicable to resolve strategic challenges by first formulating them as dichotomies and then attempting to reconcile them?*

In the answer to this question a distinction needs to be made between using this method as a classroom teaching approach or as an in-company strategy problem-solving approach. This issue is already discussed at more length in the introduction to the teaching guide, of which this teaching note is a part. However, we would like to add the following reflections on the first version of the case (published in Baden-Fuller and Pitt, 1996) in which Martyn Pitt and Peter McNamara report on how the reactions were to the first classroom usage:

> *Overall, students tend to polarise around three positions over the [...] issue. One group, the less experienced, tend to miss the point completely and will need help from the instructor to help them through the issues. A second group argue that it is 'academic tosh', while a third group argue that Andrew Mair is 'really onto something here'. An example of a debate in one executive MBA group illustrates how polarised this debate can become. Individual A, who believed the [dichotomy reconciliation] idea to be valuable, lambasted individual B, who believed the idea to be academic tosh, saying that he believed the relative decline of*

B's firm over many years was largely the result of the inflexible, collective black-or-white but never grey mind-set so well exemplified by B's reaction in class!"

This diversity of reactions indicates that the case study is a potentially challenging one, for two groups of students. Even so, the value of the case in the context of *Strategy: Process, Content, Context* as a whole is that it permits some of the book's key issues to be brought out, debated, and rehearsed through a single, encapsulating, case, towards the beginning of a course. As such, the case can generate enthusiasm and/or be rewarding for some participants - those who were already implicitly converted (the third group above), and those (the first group above) who can thus be more gently shepherded into the daunting intellectual world presented in the book. As ever, the existence of a few skeptics (the second group above) willing to voice their views permits the enthusiasts to deepen their own understanding and sharpen their thinking by defending the case study's analysis of Honda. Meanwhile, the first group can be encouraged to follow the debate in hopes of an intellectual breakthrough. As for the skeptics - sometimes 'hard' managers used to making 'tough' decisions' - they can only be converted to at least accepting such different and 'non-natural' ways of thinking at their own pace. Although this can perhaps be accelerated, if you are working in a traditional academic setting, by a requirement to answer an examination question on the subject.

More on Honda

This case is one of a family of papers that Andrew Mair has written on Honda for different purposes and audiences. A range of support materials is therefore available as background reading for the interested seminar leader, as well as the course participant who is building a longer report on Honda.

Mair, A. (1998) The globalization of Honda's product-led flexible mass production model, in Freyssenet, M., A. Mair, K. Shimizu and G. Volpato (Eds.), *One Best Way? Trajectories and Industrial Models of the World's Automobile Producers*, Oxford University Press, Oxford, pp. 110-138.

> This article describes and analyses the evolution of, and relationship between, Honda's organizational model and corporate strategy since the company was founded in 1948, with a focus on internationalization of the model and strategy. It makes a useful primer on the company's history from a management viewpoint, and would provide good empirical material for addressing issues related to Honda's own strategy dichotomies and their reconciliation as raised briefly at the end of the Honda case study.

Mair, A. (1999) Learning from Honda, *Journal of Management Studies*, January.

> This paper reviews the involvement of Honda in the strategic management debates discussed at the start of this teaching note. The paper is critical of 'case studies' where empirical information appears to have been carefully selected to support a particular strategy viewpoint, which is then supposed to explain a 'success story'.

The two papers above, together with the Honda case study in *Strategy: Process, Content, Context*, fit together well as a package of different but complementary perspectives on the company. Further, more technical, sources include:

Mair, A. (1997) Strategic localization: the myth of the post-national enterprise, in Cox, K.R. (ed.) *Spaces of Globalization: Reasserting the Power of the Local*, Guilford, New York, pp. 64-88.

> This article assesses the relationship between global homogenization and local differentiation at Honda, asking where the boundary lies and how the two are possible simultaneously. The article therefore addresses many of the issues in *Strategy: Process, Content, Context* Chapter 10.

Mair, A. (1994) *Honda's Global Local Corporation*, Macmillan, Houndmills.

> Focuses mainly on organizational structures and processes, largely an empirical study of Honda's arrival in the United States, the establishment of a supplier network and a new employee relations system, as well as Honda's complex relationship with Rover Group in Europe. The final chapter explores Honda's 'global local' multinational organizational form.

Mair, A. (1994) Honda's global flexifactory network, *International Journal of Operations and Production Management*, 14.3, pp.6-23.

> Addresses the dichotomy of how a global company manages the wide-ranging and rapid flexibility increasingly required of production systems to cope with rapid changes in global economic stability, demand patterns, and currency values across the world regions where it produces and sells its products, while at the same time developing deep local roots related to life-time employment and long-term relations with suppliers.

Mair, A. (1998) Internationalization at Honda: transfer and adaptation of management systems, *Employee Relations* 20.3, pp.285-302.

> Looks at the frequent portrayal of Honda in the organization studies literature as an innovative company on the basis of freedom granted to employees to develop new ideas. Shows through an examination of the inter-relationship between global strategy, organizational structure, operations management and the work of individuals, that at least in the case of the operations and organization structures at Honda UK, flexibility for production line employees is combined with restrictive structures and processes.

Finally, for a popular management approach which shares much in common with the Honda case study:

Mito, S (1990) *The Honda Book of Management,* Kogan Page, London.

Feedback and other comments on your experience with the Honda case study should be sent to a.mair@mbs.bbk.ac.uk. All comments received which are used in upgrading the case study or the teaching note will be acknowledged in footnotes to future versions.

References

Boston Consulting Group (1975) Strategy Alternatives for the British Motorcycle Industry, HMSO, London.

Quinn, James Brian (1996) Honda Motor Company 1994, in Mintzberg, H., and Quinn, J. B. (eds.), *The Strategy Process: Concepts, Contexts, Cases,* Prentice Hall International (3rd edition), pp. 849-863.

Pascale, Richard T. (1984) Perspectives on strategy: the real story behind Honda's success, *California Management Review,* 26.3: 47-72.

Porter, Michael E. (1996) What is strategy?, *Harvard Business Review,* November-December, pp. 61-78.

TEACHING NOTE 2: THE SWATCH

Case by Arieh Ullmann

Teaching Note by Bob de Wit and Ron Meyer

Case Synopsis

This case describes the development, launch and success of the Swatch over the period 1978 to 1990. First, a detailed description is given of the structural changes in the worldwide watch industry and the negative consequences encountered by all Swiss watchmakers, including the firm ETA. Then the case concentrates on ETA's turnaround under the leadership of Ernst Thomke and its creation of the Swatch. All aspects of the Swatch enterprise are discussed, including operations and marketing. The case closes at the point in time where Swatch must consolidate its success in the face of growing threats to its position.

Teaching Objectives

If used in conjunction with chapter 1, this case can be employed to meet the following teaching objectives:

- *Introduction of strategy process, content and context topics.* The Swatch case has a very broad scope, touching on almost all of the major strategy topics in the book. This allows for a broad discussion on the major themes of strategic management (link to introduction).

- *Discussion on the impact of the strategy context.* The case describes how the changes that were necessary to turn around ETA were difficult to realize given the strong industry recipe within the Swiss watch making industry (industry context) and the strong political, cognitive and cultural fabric of the firm (organizational context). This can act as an introduction to the issue of contextual determination (link to introduction).

- *Understanding of organized complexity and wicked problems.* ETA is clearly faced with a problem that is not tame and can not be dealt with by employing simple problem solving tools. As such the Swatch case clearly illustrates how companies must operate in environments characterized by organized complexity and that strategy is normally involved in finding solutions to wicked problems (link to introduction and 1.4 Mason and Mitroff).

- *Discussion on the need for logic and creativity.* The case is a classic example of a situation in which excessive rationality lead to a lack of innovation. It is described how creativity is infused into the organization by an outsider and young employees. The question can be raised how to invoke the circumstances needed to induce creativity, how much creativity is needed, and whether creativity must be balanced by logic (link to introduction and chapter 2).

- *Discussion on the nature of strategy formation.* The strategy realized by Swatch can be explained as deliberate, but also as emergent. By analyzing both the planned and incremental aspects of Swatch's strategy formation process, the distinction between these two perspectives can be clarified and the advantages and disadvantages of each can be identified (link to introduction and chapter 3).

- *Understanding the nature of strategy paradoxes.* Indirectly, this case can be used to illustrate that there are no straightforward 'right' solutions to strategy issues, but that strategists must deal with tensions between opposite demands. As such this case can be used to illustrate the approach taken in the rest of the book (link to introduction).

Teaching Guideline

As the chapter coverage table indicates, the Swatch case touches on a wide variety of strategic issues. Due to this richness, the Swatch case can be difficult to teach. If a professor wishes to focus on one issue, it might prove difficult to avoid class discussion going off on a variety of tangents. However, if an integral coverage of all aspects of the case is intended, then the complexity of drawing together a variety of elements within a short period of time might prove quite daunting. Whatever the objective, usage of this case requires strong directing by the professor and disciplined discussion by the students.

The richness of this case is not only a "threat," but also an "opportunity." Its breadth can be exploited in three ways:

- *Introductory case.* The case can be used at the beginning of a course (as we suggest using it directly in conjunction with chapter 1), to give students an overview of issues to come. The central issue of almost each chapter is dealt with in the Swatch case, which makes it possible for the professor to illustrate the topics that will be dealt with throughout the course.

- *Wrap-up case.* The Swatch case can be used as a final wrap up case for the course, because it challenges the student to integrate almost all of the issues discussed during the course.

- *Exam or assignment case.* Again because almost all issues are touched on in this case, an assignment or exam based upon this case will ensure that the most important elements of the course can be covered.

As an introductory case, one of the benefits of the case's breadth is that students must come to grips with the *organized complexity* of ETA's predicament. The entire internal and external contexts are sketched, giving the reader a sense of the complexity and mutual interdependence between issues at ETA. Moreover, while students might think that Thomke took the only sensible route open to the company, it can be made clear that at the time the problem facing ETA was quite a wicked one. We sometimes ask our students to take the 10 characteristics of wicked problems and to see whether ETA in 1980 meets them all. We also try to impress on students how easy it is with hindsight to see the successful path, but how difficult it can be to tackle a wicked problem if its solution is still in the future.

Another advantage of the Swatch case is that it nicely leads into chapters 2 and 3, and the debates between the various perspectives. The launch of the Swatch is an excellent example of a success that can be claimed by the supporters of the rational thinking perspective, as well as by proponents of the generative thinking perspective. Equally, advocates of the planning perspective and the incrementalist perspective can claim Swatch as proof of their position. In other words, this case allows for the debates of chapters 2 and 3 to be foreshadowed. Furthermore, students can be given a practical example of chapter 1's discussion on multiple strategy perspectives. By dwelling on the importance of logic and creativity, as well as deliberateness and emergentness, students will acquire a better understanding of the concept of strategy paradoxes.

As in so many case discussions, a little bit of polarization at the beginning can never hurt to encourage engagement in the debate. Therefore, we usually like to precede the case discussion by a short question: "If you have to choose between the rational thinking perspective and generative thinking perspective (or planning and incrementalism perspectives), which best explains Swatch's success?" A show of hands forces students to take a position, while at the same time giving the professor an indication of whether (s)he might need to play the devil's advocate if one perspective has too few supporters. At the end of class we like to go back to people's initial preferences to see to what extent this is linked to their prior education and their nationality. Usually there is a very significant correlation (link to the 'In International Perspective' sections) and we like to discuss where this preference comes from (linking this to reading 1.5 by Hofstede).

Case Questions

1. Describe the strategy context encountered by Ernst Thomke after becoming managing director of ETA in 1978. In particular, what industry context and organizational context did Thomke encounter?

2. What has been ETA/Swatch's strategy content between 1978 and 1990?

3. What has been ETA/Swatch's strategy process between 1978 and 1990?

4. What do you consider the strengths and weaknesses of ETA/Swatch's strategy process? Did the strategy process fit well with the strategy context and strategy content as identified in questions 1 and 2?

5. Will it be necessary to change the strategy process at Swatch for the future? Why? If yes, how?

Case Analysis

1. Describe the strategy context encountered by Ernst Thomke after becoming managing director of ETA in 1978. In particular, what industry context and organizational context did Thomke encounter?

- *Industry context.* The watch making industry in 1978 was relatively mature, fragmented and moving towards further globalization. Although in general mature, the industry was confronted with significant upheavals due to changes in both production and product technologies (e.g. automation and electronic watches). Despite the high failure rate brought on by these technological changes and increased competition, the industry was still populated by dozens of large and medium sized firms and hundreds of smaller ones. Most of these large and medium-sized firms were highly export-oriented. Few firms were vertically integrated, but rather focused on parts (e.g. movements and cases) or on assembly (*termineurs* and *etablisseurs*). Competition and innovations largely revolved around costs, technical features, luxury and image.

- *Organizational context.* In 1978 ETA was an important producer of movements for the Swiss watch making industry. The company's self-image was that of relatively weak supplier and "victim" of the declining position of the Swiss watch manufacturers. Attitudes within the company were conservative and technology-oriented, and self-confidence was low.

2. What has been ETA/Swatch's strategy content between 1978 and 1990?

ETA/Swatch's strategy content between 1978 and 1990 had the following major characteristics:

- *Vertical integration.* Importantly, ETA decided to redefine its business scope. It no longer wished to remain a movement supplier without any power to influence the direction of the Swiss watch making industry. Instead, the company moved downstream to develop, manufacture, market and distribute its own watches (link to chapter 7).

- *Low price category market.* ETA decided not to try to slowly move down market in an attempt to regain territory lost by the Swiss in the past. Instead the medium price category was left to the Japanese competitors and ETA radically jumped into the low priced market, thus "squeezing the Japanese in the sandwich" (link to chapter 5).

- *New product formula combining quality and low price.* By completely redesigning the concept of a watch and totally "reengineering" the watch production process, ETA was able to improve product quality and lower production costs simultaneously. Importantly, the watch production process could be highly automated, yielding significant economies of scale (link to chapter 5).

- *High fashion positioning*. Instead of positioning the product on the basis of its technical features, as was the tradition within this industry, ETA used innovative designs and the Swatch brand name to differentiate the product as a fashion item, aiming at fashion conscious people from 18 to 30. This strategy required continual updating of watch models.

- *Distribution through fashion retailers*. While Timex and Casio were sold by drugstores and mass retailers, Swatch was distributed through department stores, chic boutiques and jewelry shops.

- *High-powered promotion*. To create brand awareness and excitement, the company used unconventional methods of promotion, combined with heavy advertising.

- *Growth through line extension*. As the Swatch proved successful, the company expanded the Swatch product line to include similar products such as the Pop-Swatch, Maxi-Swatch, Recco-reflector, and Swatch-Chrono (link to chapter 6).

- *Growth through diversification*. Initially Swatch attempted to grow by exploiting the Swatch name, tagging it to a line of clothing and accessories. However, this experiment did not meet profit targets and threatened to damage the Swatch name (link to chapter 6).

3. What has been ETA/Swatch's strategy process between 1978 and 1990?

Although the case does not explicitly discuss the ins and outs of strategic decision-making within ETA, the following strategy process can be reconstructed:

- *Rigid cognitive maps inhibit recipe change*. As described in the answer to question 1, the ETA organization was a very conservative and engineering-oriented company when Thomke arrived in 1978. ETA's organizational paradigm was strongly resistant to change. Managers' cognitive maps were strongly rooted in the pre-electronic period when Swiss watch artisans dominated the industry - external developments were perceived as threats instead of opportunities. The company's culture was also strongly formed by the dominance of craftsmen - it was believed that high quality (and high cost) individually tailored movement production and relation-based business-to-business selling were the keys to commercial success. Furthermore, the organization was strongly departmentalized and bureaucratic, stifling creativity and risk-taking.

- *Autocratic top manager attempts to unfreeze recipe*. As Thomke entered ETA in 1978, he had no clear idea of the strategy that the company should follow, although he did seem to have a general conception of the direction in which the company should start looking for solutions. His first step was to shake up the status quo within ETA, often referred to as "unfreezing the strategic recipe." Because he was an outsider and was challenging the existing political structures and widely held beliefs, it does not seem surprising that the unfreezing was carried out heavy-handedly (earning him the nickname "Ayatollah"). A number of these first activities had to do with the reorganization of the production facilities and a reduction in the number of products.

- *Symbolic action to broaden support for change*. The next step in unfreezing the strategic recipe was to initiate a symbolic project ("Delirium") to create a basis for strategic change. This project had many benefits. It provided the company with a technological challenge, which required the company's craftsmen to experiment and move slightly beyond their traditional ways - it was difficult, but not too difficult. The success of the project legitimized new points of view, illustrated the benefits of experimentation and change, improved morale and increased Thomke's credibility both internally and externally. In particular, the Delirium success gave ETA more authority within the Ebauches SA concern to set out its own strategy.

- *Reorganization to encourage organizational creativity, learning and long-term thinking*. Once Thomke started to gain momentum he explicitly set out to change the organizational structure and culture. His intention was to develop an organization that could do more than just implement - one that could also create, learn and think. To this end he scrapped management layers, cut red tape, stressed cross-departmental communication and fostered an atmosphere in which employees dared to express themselves, experiment and take risks.

- *Focusing the organization on a challenging objective.* As the organization became more geared towards change, Thomke's own thinking had also progressed. His next step was to outline his broad strategic vision for the company ("a watch for the low price segment"). Furthermore, he defined a number of parameters that would have to be met ("price SFr 50, sales target of 10 million within three years, manufacturing costs below Japanese competitors, high quality"). This challenging objective (link to "creative tension" in 4.4 Senge and to "mission, vision and strategic intent" in 11.5 Campbell & Yeung) helped to focus organizational efforts, stimulate creativity and increase individuals' drive and commitment.

- *Empowering change agents and allowing a concept to emerge.* Once the general objectives were set, Thomke let "a couple of kids" (Mock and Muller, both under 30), who presumably were less contaminated by ETA's culture and less wedded to the industry's current recipes, go off to see if they could design a watch to meet the stated specifications. Their new idea was systematically evaluated and improved by inter-disciplinary teams.

- *Improving strategic development capabilities.* To ensure that the evolving watch concept could be further developed and actually marketed, Thomke set out to build organizational capabilities in the field of marketing and distribution. Important players were brought in to assist or work for the company, such as Sprecher (marketing consultant), Imgrueth (president Swatch USA), and Irniger (vice president marketing and sales). Their inputs helped to further develop the concept and the market introduction plan.

- *Formalized market introduction plan.* Finally, a formal plan was developed for the production, marketing and distribution of the Swatch. This plan was based on extensive research, trial runs and test marketing, and called for market introductions to take place in sequence instead of simultaneously, which had the benefit of allowing for learning to take place after each introduction and to be transferred to subsequent introductions.

After 1985 the case does not give sufficient information to judge the strategy process. It does seem reasonable to assume, however, going by the creativity and daring of many of Swatch's activities, that Thomke encouraged a strategy process similar to the process in the early 1980s.

To what extent is this strategy process an example of planning or incrementalism? It seems clear that it has characteristics of both. Looking back at the realized strategy it can be seen that it started rather emergently and became increasingly deliberate over time. In other words, the mix between incrementalist and planning characteristics changed, reflecting changes within the organization. Importantly, however, Swatch seems to have been able to partially bridge the planning and incrementalist perspectives, combining the strengths of both.

The same seems to be true for logic and creativity. The balance was more towards creativity at the beginning, with logic playing a more predominant role later on. However, the most significant characteristic of Swatch's approach is the combination of logic and creativity in a way that the opposites did not collide but rather strengthened each other.

When looking at the strategy process from the angle of strategic change, again the blending of revolutionary and evolutionary elements is apparent. ETA needed to be pushed hard to break through existing cognitive structures and routines, yet not so hard that reorganization exhaustion set in. Enough room and positive energy was created to encourage learning and experimentation, and to structurally build organizational capabilities.

4. What do you consider the strengths and weaknesses of ETA/Swatch's strategy process? Did the strategy process fit well with the strategy context and strategy content as identified in questions 1 and 2?

Strengths of ETA's strategy process. The main strength of this strategy process is that an attempt has been made to combine the positive aspects of incrementalism and planning into a hybrid approach. The most important strategy-making abilities enhanced by this approach are the following:

- *Ability to be creative and recipe challenging.* It is understood that for strategizing it is important to challenge the current way of doing things. A culture has been developed that allows for open, cross-functional discussions to take place, balancing logic and creativity.

- *Ability to experiment and learn.* ETA/Swatch's approach does not assume that new strategic plans can be entirely worked out before coming into action. In other words, plans are not formulated full-blown and only then implemented. On the contrary, ideas are allowed to germinate and are eventually tested, to let strategic plans slowly emerge.

- *Ability to be flexible.* Test marketing, phased introductions and an open mind all contribute to ETA/Swatch's ability to adapt its strategy along the way, if circumstances in its relatively unpredictable environment necessitate a mid-course change.

- *Ability to engage in bold, coordinated action.* Despite elements of incrementalism in the strategy process, the strategic changes realized are often themselves far from incremental. The firm is able to engage in bold and coordinated action due to a broadly shared strategic intent and due to the well-developed plans that are eventually worked out.

Fundamental to all of these abilities is the role of the CEO, Thomke. He is not the typical 'grand master' strategist who makes strategy on his own, but rather he has helped to develop the organization's strategy-making abilities and involves his managers throughout the strategy process.

All of these aspects fit well with ETA/Swatch's strategy context and content. The company is in a relatively dynamic industry, with fast changing fashions, consumer demands and competitor actions, requiring a high level of flexibility and willingness to change. Creativity is a key ingredient of success, yet it is difficult to foresee what types of products will be successful. Under these circumstances ETA/Swatch's approach seems quite suitable.

Weaknesses of ETA's strategy process. With a success story like this, it is often difficult to identify the weaknesses, particularly because some of these weaknesses might only show up over a period of time. Some points that could be brought forward are:

- *Time-consuming and inefficient.* From taking over as CEO until the launching of the Swatch lies a period of five years. While such a turnaround is in itself astonishing, many companies do not have this amount of time to go through a process of cultural change and idea generation. In general, as planners put forward, incrementalism has as a downside that it is time-consuming and inefficient. Trial and error experimentation and an emergent strategy approach are far slower and more costly than the planned formulation and implementation of strategy.

- *Dependence on Thomke.* Without a doubt Thomke played the key role during the transformation of ETA. However, the question is whether the organization's strategy-making abilities are such that they could do without Thomke were he to leave, or would they require a new leader with the same type of qualities.

- *Caught up in a new recipe.* One has to wonder whether Swatch's success will not create a new organizational paradigm that will be resistant to any form of challenge. The more success the company has initially, the more engrained might become cognitive maps, political interests and organizational systems (can also be linked to organizational inheritance and inertia in chapter 9).

5.   Will it be necessary to change the strategy process at Swatch for the future? Why? If yes, how?

Answers given here will depend very heavily on the responses given to question 4. The most obvious line of reasoning would be to discuss what must be done to solve or alleviate the weaknesses mentioned above:

▪   *Lessening dependence on Thomke.* Ideas that could be discussed should focus on two elements. Firstly, increasing organizational strategy-making capabilities (e.g. more room for bottom-up initiatives, management development and establishment of strategy-oriented culture). Secondly, on the development of new leaders for the future (e.g. recruiting high potentials, industry-outsiders and foreigners; human resource policy rewarding initiative and risk-taking).

▪   *Avoiding strategic drift.* Getting too caught up in the current recipe could be avoided in a number of ways. Mason and Mitroff (reading 1.4) offer two key suggestions for keeping an open mind when it comes to finding new solutions to wicked problems. First, to make the strategy process participative, bringing in a wide variety of views and avoiding premature mental closure. Second, to make the strategy process sufficiently adversarial, that is, create enough discussion and debate to draw out the major assumptions and to challenge participants to seek for innovative solutions. A dialectical inquiry approach could serve to systematize doubt, they would argue.

Other Teaching Issues

As stated earlier, this case can be used to illustrate the issues in a large number of other chapters as well. The most important other teaching issues are:

▪   *The nature of strategic thinking.* Was the Swatch the result of rational analysis, or was the entire project the result of a particular state of mind? This case lets students ponder the question of what strategic thinking actually is (link to chapter 2).

▪   *The nature of strategy formation.* Was the Swatch the result of deliberate strategy formulation and implementation, or must the process be largely understood as emergent, as the strategy of Swatch unfolded over time (link to chapter 3).

▪   *The nature of strategic change.* Should the transformation of ETA into Swatch be understood as a continuous process of experimentation, learning and gradual adaptation, or was the process much more discontinuous, encompassing revolutionary breakthroughs and radical shifts in the organization (link to chapter 4).

▪   *Business level strategy.* Swatch can be discussed as a good example of an outside-in approach to business level strategy. Thomke's initial Swatch strategy did not build on the distinctive resource base of ETA, but was focused on filling a defendable market position that Thomke had identified externally (link to chapter 5).

▪   *Corporate level strategy.* Students can be asked whether they know of any diversification activities undertaken by Swatch after 1990. Major moves (see below) have included the Swatch Access and the Smart car (see short case in chapter 2). Both can not be explained as portfolio-oriented investments, but as ways of leveraging Swatch's core competencies (link to chapter 6).

▪   *Network level strategy.* Swatch has helped to consolidate the Swiss watch industry, turning the network structure into a more vertically integrated hierarchy. What are the advantages of this vertical integration and which benefits of the network structure have been lost (link to chapter 7)?

▪   *Maturity of the watch industry.* Swatch is confronted with numerous look-a-likes, a threat of brand erosion and market saturation - classic signs of maturity. Will the watch market mature, turning the competitive game into one of positioning, or can new breakthroughs be created? And if the industry can be reinvented, is Swatch best poised to do so, or should they fear the Japanese competitors with larger R&D budgets and industry outsiders such as information technology firms (link to chapter 8).

- *Strong organizational leadership.* Thomke is a strong leader, but is this good or bad? Has his powerful role been necessary to shape and direct the organization, or has he made the organization unnecessarily dependent on only one person, incapable of engaging in self organization (link to chapter 9)?

- *Global strategy vs. local responsiveness.* At the moment Swatch has a rather global approach to sales markets and produces almost everything in Switzerland. The question is whether a less global approach to sales markets would be useful and whether Swatch should move any production out of the Swiss diamond (link to chapter 10).

- *The role of vision, mission and strategic intent.* Thomke develops a picture of a desired future state that invigorates and directs the firm. This allows for a discussion on the importance of a vision, mission and strategic intent, and the differences between these concepts (link to chapter 11).

What Happened After the Case?

Much has happened to Swatch after the end of the case in 1990. This section presents some of the major moves. More information can be found through our website, www.itbp.com.

- *Smart Car Project.* While there is little doubt that watches have remained its core business, the company has also looked elsewhere to achieve commercial growth. In one of its major moves, Swatch collaborated with car manufacturer Mercedes-Benz to develop the Smart (**S**watch/**M**ercedes/**art**). This project is described in the short case on page 81 of the Strategy book. Since its start in 1995 the Smart project has resulted in the launching of a new automobile brand, but commercial success has been elusive so far. At the beginning of 1999 rumors were circulating that Daimler-Chrysler boss Jurgen Schrempp was thinking about closing the MCC subsidiary producing the Smart, but this has so far been officially denied. However, Swatch's 49% stake in the deal was bought out by Mercedes-Benz in 1998. Nicolas G. Hayek, Chairman of the Board and President of the Swatch Group: "The Swatch Group has fulfilled its role as loyal, competent and efficient partner for the concept, development and production as well as for the marketing, distribution and launch of the Smart car. After the successful Smart introduction, the Swatch Group considers its task concluded and thanks Messrs. Schrempp, Hubbert and their collaborators for an exciting and positive cooperation."

- *Further diversification efforts.* Following its withdrawal from Smart, Swatch launched the idea of a wristwatch that doubles as a telephone. But Swatch Talk has had a limited release and a subdued reaction, because it needed a separate holder for fresh batteries.

- *Growth in luxury watches.* The Swatch group has made a move toward the luxury watch segment, with the acquisition in 1999 of Favre & Perret, and Groupe Horloger Breguet. These purchases are the latest in a spate of takeovers in the luxury-goods industry, where companies are seeking to cut costs by offering several brands under one roof. This move towards becoming a luxury-goods company isn't as strange as it might seem at first. Although Swatch changed the face of wristwatches in the 1980s, as time has moved on Swatch has lost much of its reputation for breaking new ground. With worldwide sales last year increasing a healthy 7% to some CHF 3328.000.000, perhaps the company need not worry much. But little has come of some of its more recent innovations, and observers are wondering how the Swatch brand will be updated for the millenium.

- *Internet time.* It's not all bad news; Swatch's idea for a new time standard intended to take the difficulty out of dealing with multiple time zones on the Internet was well received. Swatch Beat divides a day into 1000 "beats" and has no time zones, and has been greeted enthusiastically by the Internet community. The average number of visits to Swatch's Website has risen from 13 million to 51 million per month. According to a swatch press release; "Key universities i.e. the MIT in Boston at its junior summit meeting, are using Internet Time already since November 1998."

EXHIBIT 1
The Swatch Group companies

Finished watches

Luxury, prestige and top range
- Blancpain
- Omega
- Rado
- Longines
- Breguet
- Favre & Perret

Middle range
- Tissot
- CK watches
- Certina
- Mido
- Hamilton
- Pierre Balimin

Basic Range
- Swatch
- Flik Flak
- Lanco

Private Label
- Endura

Retailing
- Columna
- Swatch Stores

Watches, movements and components
- ETA
- Frédéric Piquet
- Habillage
- SMH Assembly
- Comadur
- Nivarox-FAR
- Omega Electronics

Electronic systems
- EM Microelectronic-marin
- Micro Crystal
- Oscilloquartz
- Renata
- Lasag
- SMH Automobile

General services
- Research and development
  - Asulab
  - CDNP
  - ICB

- Swiss Timing
- SMH Real Estate

- *Financial results*. In geographical terms in 1998 the Swatch Group achieved an 8% increase in sales in Europe in local currency and almost 7% in Swiss Francs. In Asia group sales grew by around 2% in local currency although this was a decrease of around 5% in Swiss Francs due to exchange rates. On the American continent the Group achieved growth of 8% in local currency, 7% in Swiss Francs.

References

Marketing Week, Can Swatch keep up with changing times?, July 15 1999.
South China Morning Post, Swatch adds luxury watch group to expanding empire, September 15 1999.
Swatch Group website, www.swatchgroup.com

TEACHING NOTE 3: BRANSON'S VIRGIN

Case by Manfred Kets de Vries and Robert Dick

Teaching Note by Bob de Wit, Ron Meyer and Jaco Lok

Case Synopsis

The "hippy entrepreneur" Richard Branson is widely admired for his tremendous success in building the Virgin Empire, which has now extended its global reach far beyond its roots in the music industry. Over and over again Branson has proved able to gain the respect of both friends and foes by creatively implementing innovative and often daring business strategies in a wide range of industries. Never one to shy away from new challenges, Branson is always on the lookout for new, unconventional opportunities through which he can expand his empire and strengthen the Virgin brand name. The Virgin name is now known the world over and supports such diverse businesses as an airline, a music entertainment chain, beverages like cola and vodka as well as new financial services.

However, Branson's flamboyance and intuitive style have certainly not always been a guarantee for success. The risk-taking side of his personality has certainly been a liability to Virgin at times and some fear that his entrepreneurial drive for continuous expansion may overextend the Virgin group. Analysts fear that Virgin's latest ventures may negatively affect the brand name and may endanger the synergy between Virgin's various parts. Virgin may also be too dependent on Branson himself - without him the empire might quickly collapse. In this case study students are asked to think about such issues as the tension between rational strategic thinking and generative strategic thinking, the characteristics and importance of strategic leadership, and questions of leadership dependence and succession.

Teaching Objectives

If used in conjunction with chapter 2, this case can be used to meet the following teaching objectives:

- *Understanding possible implications of adopting either a generative or rationalist approach to strategic management.* This case allows for a discussion on the possible advantages and disadvantages of both the generative and the rationalist thinking perspective which are discussed in Chapter 2. When should managers use analysis and when intuition, or can both be combined? The Virgin case clearly shows that strategists who are able to break through orthodox beliefs can be very successful indeed. However, the case does not only emphasize the advantages of the generative thinking perspective - risks and failures are also discussed, and the need in some cases for more traditional strategic thinking is acknowledged. The Virgin case thus offers a good example of the way strategists are forced to deal with the tension between logic and creativity in practice.

- *Relating the generative and rationalist thinking perspectives to management style and organizational structure.* The Virgin Empire is not only characterized by its flamboyant leader, but also by the unorthodox management approach and organizational structure that Richard Branson has designed for it. The Virgin case can be used to teach students that a choice for a specific position in the logic-creativity debate must have implications for the management style and organizational structure one needs to adopt to successfully foster the preferred strategic thinking perspective. The Virgin case offers an example of a business model that seems to encourage the kind of generative strategic thinking that seems to have propelled Virgin's success.

- *Assessing the importance of the characteristics of a strategist and the importance of strategic leadership.* In the case of the Virgin Group it is quite obvious how important Richard Branson's strategic leadership has been to the success of the company. His unorthodox approach and personality allow for a discussion on the possible causal relationship between certain personal characteristics and the likelihood of success.

- *Developing an opinion about the "transferability" of a successful domestic strategy approach to an international context.* Virgin is quickly becoming more and more international, clearly preferring partnerships to internationalizing on its own. It can be discussed whether Branson's unique approach to strategy is likely to be successful in an international setting. Is it true that creativity, mental productivity, and the powers of strategic insight know no national boundaries as Kenichi Ohmae believes?

Teaching Guideline

The Virgin case is fun to use as Richard Branson is a personality that students either thoroughly like or dislike, and this gets students actively involved in the case discussion. Moreover, the Virgin case paints the picture of an entrepreneur who has been highly successful in many successive endeavors, while he is far off from the suit-and-tie, MBA-educated, corporate type that most students want to become. At a very personal level, the Branson role model challenges the stereotype manager/strategist that many students have as an implicit model for themselves. The character 'Branson' forces students to think about who they want to be. We sometimes even make this point explicit by asking students what appeals to them in Branson's style and whether they see him as a role model. A follow-up question is which other 'strategists' they know whom they look towards as a role model, and what appeals to them in the approach taken by their 'hero'. Such an initial discussion can help to get students thinking about how they would like to develop and what they would like to learn, which is a good opening early on in a course.

As Branson is now widely associated with success, rather than failure, and as he seems to have adopted a far more generative than rational thinking perspective, there is a risk that this case can easily serve as a quick and biased confirmation of the superiority of the generative thinking perspective. It is therefore important to ensure that both the advantages and disadvantages of the different perspectives are discussed to create a more balanced view. One of the questions to ask students in this context is whether they think that Branson's newest venture into commercial railway transportation (Virgin Rail) is one step too far (see What Happened after the Case?).

Suggested Questions

1. Describe the nature of Branson's strategic thinking and assess to what extent it fits more closely with the generative or rationalist thinking perspective. How has Branson utilized both intuition and rational analysis to achieve Virgin's success? To what extent is Branson's approach to strategic thinking linked to his personality?

2. Describe the main characteristics of Branson's approach to strategy and management. What do you consider the major strengths and weaknesses of Branson's approach?

3. As Virgin moves further and further away from its original activities in the music industry, are analysts right to worry about possible detrimental effects on Virgin's brand name and on the synergy of various parts of the company? Is Richard Branson himself really the only remaining factor that binds Virgin's parts together?

4. In your opinion, is Branson's business strategy approach transferable to many other countries? Do you think Branson's unorthodox style may get in the way of some of Virgin's international ventures or could his style actually enhance Virgin's international success?

5. What do you think the future holds for Branson's Virgin? Do you think Virgin will need to adopt one dominant thinking perspective in order meet Branson's goal of making 'Virgin' a household name around the world? Or will Virgin find a sustainable way of effectively combining the rationalist and generative thinking perspectives and continue to be successful on an international scale?

Case Analysis

1. Describe the nature of Branson's strategic thinking and assess to what extent it fits more closely with the generative or rationalist thinking perspective. How has Branson utilized both intuition and rational analysis to achieve Virgin's success? To what extent is Branson's approach to strategic thinking linked to his personality?

The generative thinking perspective. In the second reading of chapter 2, "The Mind of the Strategist" (reading 2.2), Kenichi Ohmae argues that the mind of the strategist is not dominated by linear, logical thinking. On the contrary, a strategist's thought processes are "basically creative and intuitive rather than rational." In Ohmae's view, "great strategies ... originate in insights that are beyond the reach of conscious analysis." Logic alone is insufficient for arriving at innovative strategies. What gives strategies extraordinary competitive impact is not logic, but it is "the creative element ... and the drive and will of mind that conceived them." In their article "Strategic Management in an Enacted World" (reading 2.5), Smircich and Stubbart agree with Ohmae: the strategist's task is imaginative and creative, not analytical and objectively rational. According to these supporters of the generative approach to strategy, innovative strategizing is an art as opposed to some advanced form of analytical reasoning.

Richard Branson's mind certainly does not seem to be dominated by linear, logical thinking. The authors of the case describe him as an opportunistic, intuitive entrepreneur, who often finds it difficult to say in what strategic direction he is taking his company. Creativity, surprise and unorthodox thinking have consistently characterized Branson's approach to business strategy. Branson has thus defied traditional business logic over and over again.

The nature of Branson's strategic thinking is best exemplified by his decision to back Simon Drapers' intuitive judgment rather than Nik Powell's business judgment as a response to Virgin's crisis in the early 80s. Instead of cutting costs and pruning out unprofitable bands, Branson chose to invest in new bands and to carry on financing artists whom Draper believed would eventually be profitable. Branson's instinct proved right, since Virgin quickly became very successful with some of the most profitable bands of the 80s. When traditional business practice then dictated that Virgin's success should be consolidated and expansion restricted to complementary activities, Branson decided to establish a new airline instead. Traditional rational thinkers predicted certain failure, because Virgin had no experience, and because the business was very capital intensive, highly seasonal, and very political. But where others had previously failed, Branson succeeded through his creativity and tenacity. With new business ideas such as Virgin's Megastores, Virgin's Direct Financial Services and Virgin Cola, Branson has consistently proved able to break through orthodox beliefs, using his creativity, drive and strength of mind. Richard Branson's mind therefore seems to match Kenichi Ohmae's ideal strategic mind quite precisely.

The rationalist thinking perspective. Some traditional rationalist thinkers may point out that Richard Branson's success involves a great deal of luck, and that some of his failures point to the need for a more rational, analytical approach. Of course one cannot expect to remain successful in so many different ventures forever on just the basis of intuitive gut feeling alone. However, this case shows that Virgin's success can certainly not just be contributed to intuitive luck. Branson has never been blind to rational analysis in his thinking. He may actually have benefited greatly from applying an effective combination of rational as well as generative thought.

Always aware of the bottom-line, Branson not only talks about the need to continuously generate creative new ideas, but also of the need to minimize risk. Soon after the founding of Virgin, Branson offered Nik Powell a 40% stake in his company to counterbalance his creative and expansive drive. More methodical and cautious than Branson, Powell became the ideal, more 'rational' counterbalance in the company, ensuring that proper controls and systems were set up and that the company was managed prudently. Hiring the executives Don Cruickshank and Trevor Abbott in 1984 undoubtedly served a very similar purpose. These executives reorganized the labyrinthine Virgin Empire and created the structure, systems and discipline that were required for the planned floatation of the Virgin Group. By complementing his own creative skills with rational thinkers, and by always protecting the downside, Richard Branson therefore seems to have succeeded in finding a workable reconciliation of the logic-creativity paradox.

The fact that Richard Branson has certainly not ignored the benefits of rational analysis does not mean however that his strategic thinking perspective can also be called 'rational' in the traditional sense. In the balance between logic and creativity, he is clearly strongly inclined towards emphasizing creativity over logic.

Branson's personality. It seems clear from the case that Branson's strong preference for a generative approach towards strategic thinking is not solely a matter of choice, but is tightly linked to his personality. In all aspects of his life, Branson follows his intuition and seeks unorthodox approaches to everyday problems. Starting with his rebelliousness as a schoolboy, up until his attempted balloon trips around the world, Branson's personality has driven him to go against the grain and to imaginatively experiment with new projects. Branson savors thinking 'out of the box', while feeling restless within the confines of 'the way things should logically be done'. A question for further discussion is whether Branson, given this personality, could learn to be more rational. In other words, can an approach to strategic thinking be learned, or is each person's approach largely predetermined by his or her personality structure?

2. *Describe the main characteristics of Branson's approach to strategy and management. What do you consider the major strengths and weaknesses of Branson's approach?*

Main characteristics of Branson's approach to strategy and management:

- *Entrepreneurial.* Whenever Branson becomes interested in a new opportunity, his philosophy is to immerse himself in a new venture until he understands the ins and outs of the business. He then hands it over to a good managing director and financial controller, who are given a stake in it and are then expected to make the company take off. The expansion through the creation of additional legal entities not only protects the Virgin Group, but also gives people a sense of involvement and loyalty, particularly if he trusts them with full authority and offers minority share holdings to the managers of subsidiaries. In this way Branson has been able to build the Virgin empire mainly through organic growth rather than acquisitions, creating entrepreneurs within his empire rather than letting them venture out on their own. Claiming that "small is beautiful", Branson oversees more than 500 quasi-independent small companies interlocked in a collaborative network sharing one strong brand name. Branson prides himself in Virgin's ability to take quick action, allowing it to rapidly take advantage of every new opportunity it comes across.

- *Creative.* Richard Branson's approach is characterized by tremendous ingenuity, always creatively converting temporary setbacks into new opportunities. Branson is not necessarily a pioneer in the sense that he himself invents new products or even new strategies, but prefers what he calls "creative adaptation". He is more than happy to convert somebody else's ideas into successes and encourages his employees to be aware of the "not-invented-here" syndrome that could cause a cognitive blindness that would hamper further innovation. Constantly encouraging his people to "capture every fleeting idea", Branson's creativity lies in the fact that he can pick up good ideas and quickly find ways to turn them into a success, where others usually fail. His personal involvement in the assessment of every new idea, does not usually stem from personal interest in the product itself. He claims for example to have little interest in or knowledge of music, even though his approach to the music industry turned Virgin into a force to be reckoned with.

- *Expansive.* Perhaps a normal characteristic of a true entrepreneur or perhaps a conscious way to avoid becoming a traditional conglomerate, Richard Branson is always looking to expand his empire into new ventures. All profits are immediately reinvested into Virgin - not to become as large as possible, but to become best in the ventures Virgin has chosen to get into, and to continuously invest in new opportunities.

- *People first.* Branson's intention to shape his business around his people is also an important characteristic of Branson's generally generative approach to strategy and management. According to Branson's management philosophy staff should come first, then customers and then shareholders. Virgin people are generally not fired but moved around until they find their niche. Branson encourages his staff to dream above all other things and wants people to work for fun and excitement rather than simply as a means of earning a living.

In his article "Conceptual Mapping" (reading 2.4), McCaskey explains that people are generally very reluctant to change their mental maps, once these maps are able to provide a sensible, simplified picture of the world around them. Once people's cognitive maps have formed, and they have a grip on reality, they become resistant to signals that challenge their conceptions. According to McCaskey people even fight to retain their maps, effectively making themselves captives of their own experience. At an organizational level this cognitive rigidity can lead to organizational blindness to possible threats or opportunities that don't fit into the collective reality map of the organization. This is why Smircich and Stubbart see it as the task of the strategist to manage "the subjective process of reality-building," without creating new cognitive rigidities that may burden the organization in the future. Based on these arguments, it could be said that the strengths of Branson's approach are:

- *Avoiding cognitive rigidity.* Perhaps the most important strength of Branson's approach to strategy and management, is his ability to avoid the collective cognitive rigidity that seems to hamper the strategic creativity of so many large companies. By encouraging his employees to capture every fleeting idea, and by keeping most of Virgin's ventures small and entrepreneurial in nature, Branson seems to have managed to institutionalize some of his personal creative talent. Possible cognitive rigidities developed within some of Virgin's subsidiaries are unlikely to affect the creative culture of the whole organization, because of the semi-independence of these ventures. Branson himself seems very able to escape some of the traditional cognitive biases and rigidities by not involving himself in one particular venture for too long (except for the airline). Once he knows the ins and outs of a new business opportunity, he hands it to capable managers and thereby frees up his mind to assess new opportunities and possible threats more openly. His lack of emotional attachment to most of Virgin's actual products and services may also be a reason why Branson seems able to keep an open mind towards required adaptations and new opportunities. The sale of his record business, the jewel in the Virgin crown, is possibly the most striking example of Branson's ability to destroy in order to create without being tied down by the cognitive and emotional rigidities that would drive most strategists to preserve the status quo.

- *Organizational and strategic flexibility.* A second, perhaps more obvious, important strength of Branson's approach to strategy and management is Virgin's tremendous flexibility. Because of its entrepreneurial structure and spirit, Virgin is able to quickly react to new opportunities and threats and to take required actions almost immediately.

- *Quality and loyalty of Virgin's staff.* The third strength of Branson's approach to strategy and management is the quality of the people Richard Branson has been able to attract to Virgin through his approach. Over the years Branson's 'staff first' approach to Human Resource Management has earned Virgin the trust and loyalty of its staff and has seen them willing to adapt to new circumstances continuously, without requiring above average pay. This atmosphere of trust and loyalty has in turn facilitated open discussions and the continual questioning of the status quo.

- *Strengthening the Virgin brand name.* Last but not least, Branson's creative, 'counter-cultural' approach to strategy and management has undoubtedly strengthened the image of Virgin as a fun, innovative, daring, and successful company. This is an image that is crucial for the strength of the Virgin brand name, from which so many of the Virgin ventures benefit every day.

In the article "The Concept of Corporate Strategy" (reading 2.1), Kenneth Andrews argues that it is the unity, coherence, and internal consistency of a company's strategic decisions that position the company in its environment and give the firm its identity, its power to mobilize its strengths, and its likelihood of success in the marketplace. According to Andrews strategies should be based on an objective analysis of their risks and implications, and should be made explicit to allow for logical consistency testing. If a strategy remains unstated and if it is only implicit in the intuition of a strong leader, Andrews thinks that the organization is likely to be weak and that the demands the strategy makes upon the organization are likely to remain unmet. In chapter 2 it is pointed out that intuitive judgments are usually made on the basis of cognitive heuristics that are inherently biased, as they focus attention only on a few variables and interpret them in a particular way, even when this is not appropriate. This is why many academics urge practitioners to bolster intuitive judgments with more explicit rational analysis. Especially in the case of strategic decisions, time and energy should be made available for rational analysis to avoid falling prey to common cognitive biases. On this basis it could be argued that Branson's approach has the following weaknesses:

- *Too little analysis, too much risk.* Despite the fact that Richard Branson surrounds himself with some 'rationalists' to counterbalance his intuitive nature, many of his strategic decisions seem to be mostly based on intuition. Despite Virgin's tremendous successes, many analysts believe that Richard Branson has often taken too much risk without backing his decisions with proper analysis that could justify these risks. Some of his failures could have possibly been avoided if the long-term consequences of his decisions had been more carefully thought through. Branson's decision to launch the new London entertainment guide *Event* in 1981 best illustrates the risks attached to relying on intuition alone. Within a year the magazine had lost 750,000 pounds, because Virgin was poorly prepared and the magazine required more cash than expected, while rival magazines quickly entered the market. These losses came at a very bad time for Branson, as Virgin was going through a reorganization that for the first time required the dismissal of some staff. If he had adopted a more rational approach, carefully analyzing the risks and consequences, Branson may have been able to avoid inflaming discontent in his company by his risky investments.

- *Too opportunistic.* The previous example points to another possible weakness to Richard Branson's approach to strategy and management. As an entrepreneur he is always on the lookout for new opportunities, without seeming too aware of more traditional strategy concerns like 'risk' and 'strategic fit'. Branson's track record proves that if he feels he can make some quick money by filling some 'gaping hole' in a small or large market, or even by evading taxes, he is likely to act on the opportunity. This opportunistic approach may have led to the investment of scarce resources that could have been better spent on strengthening more profitable core activities. Branson's decision to quickly cash in on the bullish stock market in 1986, without realizing that he and his company may not be very suitable for effectively dealing with the consequences, can also be seen as an example of how Branson's opportunistic strategies sometimes backfire due to a lack of 'due diligence' in his approach.

- *Lack of a proper control structure.* The structure of Richard Branson's company is very complex. Outsiders find it very hard to get a complete structured picture of Virgin, also because many of its offshore branches do not publish financial statements. The secrecy and complexity of the Virgin empire not only obstruct rational analysis by outsiders, but may also stand in the way of the efficient control that is required to make full use of Virgin's potential. Within the complex Virgin structure a lot of money may be tied up in unprofitable activities, not because of the long-term profit potential of these activities but because of the lack of a clear financial control structure. The semi-independence of many of Virgin's subsidiaries may induce their executives to engage in the kind of protective political behavior that could be damaging to the Virgin Group as a whole.

- *Overextending the empire.* Branson's expansion drive has swallowed up all of the cash that Virgin has created over the years. The continued reinvestment of profits in new capital-intensive projects can make a company very vulnerable to unexpected recessions in which it may suddenly become strapped for cash. This is why one could claim that by expanding so aggressively Richard Branson risks losing it all because he is overextending his empire.

3. *As Virgin moves further and further away from its original activities in the music industry, are analysts right to worry about possible detrimental effects on Virgin's brand name and on the synergy of various parts of the company? Is Richard Branson himself really the only main factor that binds Virgin's parts together?*

For most of its young existence the core of Virgin's business was popular music. However Exhibits I and II clearly show that from 1983 onwards Virgin started moving further and further away from its roots by expanding its activities in a wide variety of industries ranging from retailing, to the airline, financial services and even the beverage industries. The sale of the Virgin Music Group to Thorn EMI in 1992 saw the departure of many long-serving staff and clearly marked a departure from its traditional strengths.

Because most of Virgin's activities now seem so unrelated, many analysts worry about the lack of synergy between the various parts of the company. Others fear that the wide range of products and services sold under only one brand name will eventually have a negative impact on the strength of the brand. Traditional business logic dictates that Virgin should focus its key activities more clearly and that it should try to bundle its resources and capabilities in complementary ways, so that it can benefit from synergies and economies of scale. Traditional marketing logic dictates that one brand name should normally only be associated with a small number of related products. It is therefore only logical or 'rational' for many analysts to be worried.

However, chapter 2 explains that rational thinking is nothing other than interpreting problems and selecting solutions in accordance with the prevailing paradigm. The major limitation of this kind of logic is that, according to adherents of the generative thinking perspective, it entraps people in the current orthodoxy. Only according to the current traditional strategy and marketing paradigms can Virgin's approach to diversified expansion and branding be seen as 'illogical'. But does this really mean Virgin's approach is unwise? Instead of accepting orthodox thinking on branding, Virgin may have succeeded in turning the traditional system of beliefs upside down by building a brand that *is* able to support many different products and services. Through its general association with words such as fun, innovation, daring, and success, rather than an association with any specific product or service, 'Virgin' might be a totally different branding concept. Branson may also have succeeded in creating an alternative business model that is flexible and entrepreneurial in nature and that does not require the traditional synergies and scale economies that most other strategists find so important (these issues are further explored in chapter 6).

As for Branson being the sole binding factor between the various Virgin entities, the answer is more complex than first meets the eye. Firstly, there is no doubt that Virgin's business model is centered on Richard Branson; it is primarily Branson's vision and leadership that initiated and shaped Virgin's successes (and perhaps some lesser-known failures). Branson's instinctive ability to recognize opportunities and his creativity in overcoming obstacles has been critical to the survival and success of the company. Virgin appears so dependent on Branson that a sudden departure would seem almost impossible to overcome.

However, beneath the surface other factors may be at work that link the various parts of the Virgin group together. For instance, although the Virgin brand name is still strongly tied to Branson's personal image, it has grown to become a widely recognized uniform symbol that strongly binds together Virgin's various activities, both in the minds of its employees and its customers. Also, virtually all but Virgin's airline business are now run by people other than Branson. Their role in building and maintaining the empire and its success cannot be underestimated. Furthermore, Virgin's corporate culture encourages the entrepreneurial spirit to which the company owes much of it success. These factors might well be able to survive Branson's departure.

4. *In your opinion, is Branson's business strategy approach transferable to many other countries? Do you think Branson's unorthodox style may get in the way of some of Virgin's international ventures or could his style actually enhance Virgin's international success?*

Kenichi Ohmae concludes his article (reading 2.2) by stating: "Creativity, mental productivity, and the power of strategic insight know no national boundaries...they are universal." However, the section "Strategic Thinking in International Perspective" warns against the common cognitive bias of supposing that all others are the same as we are. It questions the assumption that strategic thinking is viewed in the same way around the world. Creativity and strategic insight may be universal as possible human qualities, but they may not be valued equally in all countries. A more generatively inclined approach to strategic thinking might not be understood or accepted to the same extent all around the globe.

Therefore, it can be argued that Branson's unorthodox style may be an impediment when working with foreign partners who do not share his enthusiasm for thinking 'out-of-the-box'. Branson's emphasis on ideas and imagination, as well as his rebellious 'against-the-grain' attitude may not be seen as a strength and it might make more rationally oriented foreign partners somewhat uneasy. Therefore, Virgin must either enter foreign markets alone (which Branson seems not to prefer given the high investments and risks involved), or it must find like-minded partners in other countries. It is a matter of debate whether there are sufficient partners available in foreign markets that would feel comfortable with Branson's approach.

5. *What do you think the future holds for Branson's Virgin? Do you think Virgin will need to adopt one dominant thinking perspective in order to meet Branson's goal of making 'Virgin' a household name around the world? Or will Virgin find a sustainable way of effectively combining the rationalist and generative thinking perspectives and continue to be successful on an international scale?*

Virgin's future will strongly be influenced by whether the company chooses to emphasize *exploration* or *exploitation*. Branson will have to choose whether to continue to engage in new entrepreneurial activities, or whether to focus on expanding and optimizing current activities? Virgin could choose to continue on its entrepreneurial path of creative destruction and generation, sacrificing some of its successes to realize new dreams. It could also choose to significantly expand and optimize its current primary ventures instead, because most of these activities clearly show great growth potential.

Should Virgin decide to focus most of its energy and resources on the international expansion of its current primary activities, Virgin may consequently be forced to integrate more rationality into its approach to strategy and management. Once its activities are expanded beyond a critical scale, Branson might find that a more rational and systematic financial and organizational structure may be required to guarantee continued success. For example, managing fifty or a hundred Virgin Megastores requires significantly different, more rationalized control structures than those required to run merely a few of these stores. If Virgin therefore decides to grow its existing businesses rather than to continue venturing into risky, new opportunities, it is likely that it will have to introduce more and more rationalist tools in order to be able to optimize its businesses.

However, Virgin's track record demonstrates that it is very unlikely that under Branson's leadership, Virgin will opt for this rationalist option. It is indeed much more likely that Virgin will continue to explore new opportunities, reinventing itself continuously, as it has done ever since it was founded. This generative strategic choice may certainly come at a price: certain investments could undoubtedly be better spent on expanding and optimizing already successful ventures. However, this choice may also open up new opportunities that offer even greater potential than the ones in which Virgin is currently engaged. Two major problems may have to be overcome before this 'prospector' option can truly be successful on a global scale. First of all, for this option to remain sustainable in the long run, Virgin's dependence on Branson's personal generative talents will have to be reduced by broadening the base of these talents in the organization. Secondly, more rational methods and structures will have to be developed that allow for the continued expansion of certain successful activities, without this hampering the entrepreneurial spirit on which Virgin thrives. Virgin's current success in striking a balance between the generative and rationalist aspects of strategy is no guarantee for future success. The required balance is a dynamic balance that keeps shifting depending on the prevailing circumstances; the struggle with the logic-creativity paradox is thus indeed endless.

Other Teaching Issues

The case also raises a number of questions that are relevant to other chapters in the book. These teaching issues are:

- *The basis of strategic advantage.* Despite the current popularity of the core competence perspective outlined in chapter 6, Virgin's business units do not seem to share any obvious core competencies. At the same time Virgin cannot be considered to be a traditional conglomerate consisting of a portfolio of profit centers either. The Virgin case can therefore be used as an interesting alternative to the theoretical options offered in chapters 5 and 6.

- *Strategic change: the paradox of revolution and evolution.* Branson's drive and ability to revolutionize different industries without necessarily wanting to be a pioneer or industry leader allows for an interesting discussion on the applicability of the different perspectives on strategic change that are discussed in chapter 4 to the Virgin approach.

- *Strategic networks.* Richard Branson's efforts to emulate Japanese *Kereitsu* success by creating a strategic network of semi-independent businesses and partnerships ("small is beautiful"), all sharing one strong brand name, offers an interesting example in a discussion on strategic networks, which are discussed in chapter 7.

- *The industry context: compliance vs. choice.* Despite the fact that such mature industries as both the cola and airline industries generally leave little room for the enactment of a new environment that is particularly suitable to new entrants, Virgin attacked them as if they left plenty of room for innovative strategic choices. In combination with chapter 8, Virgin's innovative successes in industry contexts that are generally assumed to require full compliance, allow for a discussion on ways in which the tension between compliance and choice can be overcome.

- *The importance of strategic leadership and control.* This case can be used to complement chapter 9 by providing the basis for a discussion on the extent to which strategic initiative should be centralized. Is Virgin's future success solely dependent on Branson's strategic abilities? Can Virgin do without him and should Virgin be able to do without him?

What Happened after the Case?

The case ends in 1995, and since then Richard Branson has been as busy as ever. Virgin's website gives the overview of activities as detailed in exhibit 1. Striking additions to the Virgin Empire include Virgin Express (budget airline), Virgin Cola, Virgin Net (internet service), Virgin Cinema, Virgin Direct (financial services), 40 additional Virgin Megastores, and Eurostar (highspeed Channel train service). In November 1997, Virgin came back into the record business with a new label called V2. A month later, in December 1997, Branson announced the launch of Virgin Bride, a company that will plan weddings and honeymoons (by which point, Branson cheerfully notes, "the customers will no longer be virgins").

EXHIBIT 1
Virgin's current main operating areas and subsidiaries (source: www.virgin.com)

Activities	Units
Financial	<ul><li>**Virgin Direct**: Provides unit trusts, ISAs, pensions, life insurance and a deposit account direct to the public. Virgin Direct sells its products via the telephone, postal services and the Internet. It has no retail outlets.</li><li>**Virgin One**: A highly innovative banking facility that allows people to combine all of their finances into a single convenient account. The Virgin One Account is a secured personal bank account with The Royal Bank of Scotland plc. It is provided by Virgin Direct Personal Finance Ltd.</li></ul>
Business	<ul><li>**The Lightship Group**: The world's leading airship operating company providing airships for advertising and promotional purposes for some of the world's most dynamic companies.</li><li>**Virgin Airship & Balloon Co.**: Market leaders in commercial hot air balloon and operation.</li><li>**Caroline**: International wholesaling distribution of music related products, encompassing both export and import.</li><li>**Virgin Sound and Media**: A leading distributor of value for money CDs, cassettes and videos.</li><li>**Kinko's**: A 24-hour, seven-day a week chain of retail outlets supplying office services to individuals and companies.</li><li>**Vanson**: Vanson Developments primary role is to provide property related advice and services to other Virgin Group Companies, although it is also involved with some direct development projects.</li><li>**Virgin Vouchers**: Corporate incentive vouchers that can be exchanged for goods and services within the Virgin world.</li></ul>

Media Services	▪ **Rushes**: One of Europe's top special effects and post production houses, catering mainly to commercials, music video and feature film makers. ▪ **525 Post Production**: Specializes in telecine, editing, computer graphics and digital effects for the feature film, commercial and music video industries. ▪ **West One Television**: Television and video post production company, across two west London sites: Soho and Notting Hill. ▪ **Virgin Arcadia**: Video production company providing 40 hours of in-flight entertainment every quarter for Virgin Atlantic Airways, corporate video for the Virgin Group and other companies, destination guides, music features, training videos and video press kits. ▪ **Rapido TV**: One of the leading independent UK production companies. Rapido has built up a reputation for high quality youth, factual and educational programming.
Lifestyle	▪ **Virgin Clothing**: A wholesale business selling menswear, womenswear, footwear and accessories to top UK department stores and independent retailers. ▪ **Virgin Vie**: Offers Swiss-formulated skin care, sophisticated color cosmetics and fine fragrances among over 500 affordably luxurious toiletries for women and for men. Five stores in the UK. ▪ **Virgin Bride**: A comprehensive bridal emporium catering for all the couple's needs for the big day, from choosing the venue to finding the perfect location. ▪ **Storm Models**: Model agency representing men, women and sports personalities. Top names include Kate Moss, Eva Herzigova, Elle Macpherson, Kylie Bax and Carla Bruni.
Travel & Leisure	▪ **Virgin Atlantic**: Based at both London's Gatwick and Heathrow airports. Operates long-haul services from Heathrow to the USA, Tokyo, Hong Kong, Athens and Johannesburg and from Gatwick to the USA and Athens. ▪ **Virgin Holidays**: UK based tour operator specializing in long haul holidays to America, the Far East, Australia and South Africa, using Virgin Atlantic flights. Newly formed short haul division offering holidays to Europe. ▪ **Virgin Rail**: One of the largest passenger train operators in Britain, operating two franchises, West Coast Trains and Cross Country Trains Ltd., with more than 1,600 services a week calling at over 130 stations. ▪ **Virgin Express**: a pan-European low fares airline operating scheduled services to nine European cities and charter flights to more than 100 destinations. ▪ **Virgin Hotels**: Diverse selection of over 35 hotels and destinations across Britain, Italy, France, the USA, Australia, South Africa and Majorca. ▪ **Necker Island**: At the north-eastern extreme of the British Virgin Islands. Primarily enjoyed as a private holiday island by families and friends, Necker is also used by corporate companies as a top level incentive destination or inspiring retreat. ▪ **Virgin Balloon**: The largest passenger balloon flight company in the UK, with a fleet of balloons in the UK, Holland and Belgium. ▪ **Virgin Limobike**: Runs six passenger carrying motorcycles, saving passengers vast amounts of time over traffic-jam prone cars or taxis. All riding equipment is supplied and the bikes can carry suitcases. ▪ **Roof Garden**: Private members' nightclub, public restaurant and function venue situated in 1.5 acres of themed gardens 100 ft above Kensington High Street.

Entertainment	• **Virgin Megastores**: Over 80 Megastores in the UK and Ireland, including the world's largest entertainment store on London's Oxford Street. Worldwide, there are Megastores in Canada, Japan, France, Holland, Austria, Belgium, Norway, Italy, Spain and the US.
	• **V2 Music**: Comprises V2 Records and V2 Music Publishing and is engaged in all activities related to releasing records.
	• **Virgin Net**: Provides an Internet service to UK consumers. Designed to be as easy to use as possible, it is targeted at complete beginners to the Internet as well as more experienced users.
	• **Virgin Cinemas**: Engaged in the operation and development of multiplex cinemas in the UK and Ireland and holds the Virgin Cinemas and Megaplex trademarks in these territories.
	• **Virgin Cola**: Manufacturer of soft drinks.
	• **Virgin Radio**: Virgin Radio's music format is based on classic tracks from the last three decades and the cream of today's best music. More than four million intelligent and informed rock-lovers tune in each week.
	• **Virgin Publishing**: Virgin's book publishing company produces world-wide best sellers in all areas of popular culture, including music, sport, TV, movies, comedy and anything that's hot.
	• **London Broncos**: The London Broncos RLFC are the only Super League club based in the South. The Broncos are a professional rugby league franchise and the only sporting interest of the Virgin empire.

As Virgin is now a group of over 200 independent companies, it would be too extensive to mention them all and the time period they started. Therefore, the four most important ventures ('core-businesses') of Branson's empire will be examined in more depth, namely: Virgin Atlantic, Virgin Rail, Virgin Direct and Virgin Entertainment. As with many private groups, the true performance and financial state of the Virgin businesses is hard to determine. It seems, however, that there are three significant profit-earners in the empire and that other businesses require major investment over the next few years:

- *Virgin Atlantic*. The biggest financial success is Virgin Atlantic (which has been profitable for the past three years, after three years of losses), with profits exceeding £50 million a year. The airline has a network of premium routes serving business centers around the world and a superb brand, its Upper Class business cabin. After years of uncertainty, the airline now clearly forms the jewel in the new Virgin crown. Yet, competition over the North Atlantic, where Virgin Atlantic makes at least two-thirds of its profits, is about to become more intense. As part of a deal to win regulatory approval in Brussels and Washington for the alliance between British Airways and American Airlines, precious landing slots at London's crowded Heathrow airport are likely to be given to competing carriers. Making Heathrow more accessible will depress business fares between London and America, which are up to 25% higher than fares to America from other European airports.

- *Virgin Our Price*. The music retailing network, under Branson's control after WH Smith sold back its 75% share, made £16 million in its latest year. This retailing network includes the Virgin Megastores.

- *Virgin Rail*. Richard Branson's newest high profile, high-risk endeavor is Virgin Rail. Through the Virgin Rail consortium, Branson plans to make money from Britain's privatized railways, notorious for their losses and lousy service under public ownership. Turning the railway business around has proven to be extremely difficult though. So far, the venture has not done well, facing immediate large investment requirements and mounting future government fees to be paid after

2002. Virgin's railway lines have also done badly in recent surveys by rail regulators, each of its services becoming less punctual. Passenger complaints have in some months even been higher than they were under British Rail - though Virgin argues that this is because it has encouraged people to complain. In reaction to these reverses, some of Virgin's partners have now imposed demanding financial targets on Virgin Rail. Virgin Rail has generated £12 million in profits last year, but according to estimates by *The Economist*, the firm needs to spend over 1 billion pounds on trains and on its cross-country railway in order to attract new passengers.

Not all of the profits of these units are handed back to the corporate center because of the high investment needs of these businesses themselves. But as the rest of the empire is also cash-hungry, these three profitable areas are expected to help finance many other endeavors, especially the new record company, V2, the prospective health-club chain and the cinema network. Yet it is clear that Virgin Rail still requires huge human and capital investments before it can be turned into another Virgin success, making it an uncertain cash cow. This leaves Virgin Atlantic as Branson's main money-spinner. However, the airline business is highly cyclical in nature and competition seems to be mounting. A sudden recession may prove too much to handle.

Virgin's reputation as a successful joint venture partner is also on the line in the rail business, as Virgin's partners seem to be getting more nervous about the future prospects of their partnerships. But perhaps the biggest threat of all is that for the first time Virgin's brand name may be seriously threatened as it now runs the risk of being associated with a highly visible failure - failure which, in his own words, Richard Branson never considered.

In June 1998, Branson sold 49% of Virgin Rail to Stagecoach (for £158 million), after plans to float the rail venture on the stock exchange did not work out. Also, in general there are signs that Branson is selling off parts of 'non-core' businesses (for instance its 50% stake in the design consultancy Rodney Fitch & Co) to finance his 4 'core' businesses (Atlantic, Rail, Entertainment and Direct). A more structured and transparent organization is also envisioned in the near term, preparing for a float of its crown jewel, Virgin Atlantic (valued at about £1 billion). It seems that by getting into the railway business Richard Branson may finally have overextended his empire. Of course Branson's *track record* in enacting success despite highly unfavorable odds should not be easily forgotten. However, turning around Virgin Rail will require different skills than building Virgin Atlantic. This time Branson is aiming to turn around a bad business, rather than create a new one in an overly regulated market. Will Virgin Rail thus become Branson's Waterloo? Some analysts have speculated that Branson might have to sell Virgin Atlantic in order to finance his newest brainchild. He thus has to sell his past again in order to finance his future. The question is: will he? Right now, it certainly looks that way!

References

Marketing, Financial troubles ahead, September 17, 1998
Sheff, David, The interview: Richard Branson, *Forbes*, February 24, 1997.
The Economist, Eight little Virgins, January 11, 1997
The Economist, Business: Behind Branson, February 21, 1998
www.virgin.com

TEACHING NOTE 4: STANTRET

Case by Igor Touline, Abby Hansen, and Derek Abell

Teaching Note by Bob de Wit, Ron Meyer and Jaco Lok

Case Synopsis

Sergei Sleptsov is one of the many young Russian entrepreneurs who managed to successfully capitalize on new business opportunities that arose after the start of the transformation of the former USSR's planned economic system to a market-economy at the end of the 1980s. His knowledge of the great shortcomings and inefficiencies of the former USSR's distribution system allowed him to see an opportunity to compete against the Aeroflot monopoly in transporting cargo throughout the country and abroad. By creatively working around massive obstacles that would have stopped most businesses dead in their tracks, Sleptsov managed to set up a cargo airline that made millions of rubles right from the start: Stantret Airlines.

After his first successful year, however, Sleptsov started to run into problems that may turn out to be too large to overcome, even for a natural, determined entrepreneur. Sleptsov was faced with a parent company whose behavior and control might threaten Stantret's future. He had also just found out that some of his key employees were probably stealing money from the company. To make matters worse, Stantret was suddenly facing new competition in a business environment that had changed significantly since Stantret's conception. In this case, students are asked to assess the long-term viability of Sleptsov's approach to strategy and management in the changing business environment of the former Soviet Union, and to develop sustainable solutions to some of Stantret's problems.

Teaching Objectives

When used in conjunction with chapter 2, this case can be used to meet the following teaching objectives:

- *Understanding the implications of adopting either a generative or rationalist approach.* This case allows for a discussion on the possible advantages and disadvantages of both the generative and the rational thinking perspectives, which are discussed in Chapter 2. Sergei Sleptsov's example shows that intuitive, generative strategic thinking can often unbolt the doors to success, but that this type of strategic thinking is not always sufficient for consolidating the success in the long run (link to all readings).

- *Assessing the role of the environment in shaping strategy.* As in nearly every strategy case, the environment plays an important role in the Stantret case. The Stantret case can be used to question whether threats and opportunities in the environment can be objectively 'recognized', or whether they are 'in the eye of the beholder'. What is seen as a threat by one person, can be interpreted as a tremendous opportunity by another. In the Stantret case, Sleptsov proved capable of turning what were tremendous threats in the eyes of most, into a very profitable opportunity for Stantret. However, the Stantret case can also be used to argue that despite all his entrepreneurial flair and creative thinking, the 'objective' facts about the business environment finally caught up with Sleptsov (link to 2.5 Smircich and Stubbart).

- *Relating the nature of the environment to the generative and rational thinking perspectives.* The Stantret case can be used to discuss to what extent the nature of a certain business environment requires a specific strategic thinking perspective for sustainable success. In a very volatile, uncertain, difficult business environment such as Stantret's for example, which thinking perspective is likely to have better results? This discussion will serve to show that an assessment of the possible advantages and disadvantages of the two strategic thinking perspectives cannot be properly made without considering the nature of the business environment (link to all readings).

- *Relating the characteristics and style of the strategist to long-term success.* In the Stantret case, it is obvious how important Sleptsov's personality, drive and creative problem-solving skills have been to Stantret's initial success. Without Sleptsov there would be no Stantret. At the same time, however, it can be argued that some of these same characteristics have caused the problems that are now threatening Stantret's long-term survival. Students can be invited to develop possible solutions to this 'entrepreneurial paradox' (link to chapter 9).

Teaching Guideline

The Stantret case is an interesting case to teach in a number of ways. One of the points that usually makes quite an impression on students is that business opportunities are not only found in high growth, high tech industries in high growth economies. We sometimes jokingly refer to this as the 'sexy business' bias of many students – they implicitly assume that better opportunities can be found in software development, multimedia and internet services, as opposed to toilet bowl manufacturing, rodent extermination and funeral services (all three of which have some highly profitable large companies). In the same way, some countries are seen as very promising (until recently South East Asia was hot) while other nations were seen as bottomless pits for careless investors. The Stantret case calls into question the belief that some environments are inherently preferable to others. We therefore make it a point to ask students whether they think that opportunities exist or are created (this issue is further looked into in chapter 8).

To get this issue out in the open, we often start the discussion by asking whether anyone would consider buying Stantret's shares from the current parent company. As the answer is usually a resounding 'no', we ask whether anyone would be interested in buying shares in any Russian company at the moment. This is a good way to exchange information in class on the recent developments in the Russian political and economic environment, and to test whether students have a balanced view of the risks involved in doing business in Russia, or are plainly biased against 'non-fashionable' economies. Sometimes, especially if the large majority of the class is wary of doing business in Russia, we even go further in trying to 'map' the assumptions that students have about the Russian business environment. We often notice that if Russia has just been in the news, this greatly sways the sentiment in the class. This type of discussion makes quite clear to students what is meant by the terms 'cognitive biases' and 'cognitive rigidities'.

Another interesting issue brought forward in the case is the type of behavior often exhibited by entrepreneurs. While the linear reasoning process (identifying, diagnosing, conceiving and realizing) at first seems quite 'logical' to students, the case sketches Sleptsov's intuitive reasoning process in a compelling way. We often ask students whether they believe that Sleptsov's method of reasoning is the exception or the rule among entrepreneurs. And if most people reason in generally the same way as Sleptsov, is this bad, and what are the advantages?

Suggested Questions

1. Describe the risk and feasibility of the business opportunity that Sleptsov decided to act on through his "Air Link-Up"-project. What were the major environmental factors that shaped and constrained this business opportunity? Can you explain why most people in Sleptsov's vicinity did not see the Russian air cargo business as promising at all?

2. Is Sleptsov's approach mainly driven by rational or generative strategic thinking? Assess to what extent Sleptsov's approach, motivation, and personality were particularly suited to Strantret's initial situation. What are the main strengths and weaknesses of Sleptsov's approach to strategic thinking?

3. Describe the problems Stantret is currently facing and identify their possible root causes. To what extent can the causes of Stantret's current problems be attributed to circumstances beyond Sleptsov's control, and/or to Sleptsov's shortcomings as a strategist and manager? Which of the current problems do you consider most threatening to the survival of Stantret? How would you have attempted to avoid some of the problems Sleptsov is now facing?

4. What do you think Sleptsov should do in the face of new, strong competition, and suspected fraud by his managers?

Case Analysis

1. Describe the risk and feasibility of the business opportunity that Sleptsov decided to act on through his "Air Link-Up"-project. What were the major environmental factors that shaped and constrained this business opportunity? Can you explain why most people in Sleptsov's vicinity did not see the Russian air cargo business as promising at all?

At the time Sergei Sleptsov decided to establish Stantret Airlines, civil aviation in Russia was in very bad shape. Government monopolies controlled civilian as well as military transport. A situation had developed in which virtually no aircraft, except those of the military, met strict standards for intensive operation. The Ministry of Aviation Industry's had almost exclusive access to cargo planes and the technical services necessary to fly them. Moreover, across-the-board shortages of engines, spare parts, and fuel, made it seemingly impossible for any independent new cargo airline to set up business in the Russian market. Hence, the first reaction of Stantret's marketing manager to Sleptsov's plans was quite understandable: who would provide not one, but several airplanes to some obscure venture, which had just been established? Where would Sleptsov get fuel, when one kept hearing about Aeroflot being unable to fly because of a huge shortage?

Yet shortages of cargo shipment services had doubled between 1980 and 1990 and were predicted to worsen over the next two decades. This meant that there were opportunities in the cargo market, especially as Aeroflot's service record in terms of price, speed and reliability was very poor, and no other competitors had entered the cargo market. Sleptsov saw that price differences in produce between different regions in the country - especially for perishable goods - provided an excellent business opportunity for an airline that was able to guarantee the timely delivery of goods.

Despite this business opportunity, however, most analysts would argue, in terms of 'objective' risk and feasibility, that the environment in which Sleptsov had to operate was extremely threatening. The Russian cargo transport business could be judged as a high-risk environment, due to the low short-term feasibility (lack of planes and fuel) and uncertain long-term viability (lack of economic stability) of new ventures. Most would have agreed that the constraints Sleptsov was facing were simply too large to justify his efforts. The problems he would have to overcome seemed insurmountable indeed. How could anyone possibly be able to guarantee timely delivery in an environment characterized by delays, shortages, inefficiencies and other problems? Most did not even see the opportunity itself. The government agency ARI, that had the planes to take advantage of the obvious need for cargo services, for example, did not see a business opportunity. It had no incentives to go out and look for customers to engage in new business. As a result of this lack of incentives, their planes were sitting idle most of the time.

In reading 2.5, Smircich and Stubbart argue that the concept of an objective environment (characterized in terms of objective "threats", "opportunities" and "risks") should be complemented by a perspective that recognizes that environments are created through the interpretations and actions of people operating in this environment. They argue that facts never speak for themselves and that so called 'threats' are only threats in the eye of the beholder. The example of Stantret seems to support their case. Even when most people would characterize Stantret's environment as threatening, in Sleptsov's mind the 'risks', 'threats', and 'constraints' merely presented a couple of specific problems that needed to be solved. His creative solutions turned these same 'constraints' into competitive advantages and entry barriers. By seeking business partnerships with the government agencies that could provide the planes and fuel (first ARI and later Molniya), and by providing their managers with the material incentives to help Stantret do business, Sleptsov managed to circumvent obstacles that hampered others like Aeroflot. Through his actions he changed obstacles into advantages, making Stantret a profitable winner, at least in the short run.

2. *Is Sleptsov's approach mainly driven by rational or generative strategic thinking? Assess to what extent Sleptsov's approach, motivation, and personality were particularly suited to Strantret's initial situation. What are the main strengths and weaknesses of Sleptsov's approach to strategic thinking?*

To supporters of the generative thinking perspective, the essence of strategic thinking is the ability to break through orthodox beliefs, which requires a certain measure of creativity. According to this definition, Sleptsov's strategic thinking seems to fit squarely into this category. He was able to break through the widespread belief that fast, reliable, and affordable cargo service was impossible in Russia, by developing innovative solutions to seemingly insurmountable roadblocks. Sleptsov clearly did not follow the rules of the rational thinking perspective. Rather than consciously, explicitly and rationally defining a strategy based on objective analysis of the environment and then implementing this strategy (see 2.1 Andrews), Sleptsov adopted a much more of intuitive, imaginative and incrementalist approach. Acting on his intuitive interpretation of the business environment, he used 'dry runs' and improvised solutions, such as barter trade with officials, to work around problems that could never have been foreseen in advance in all their practical details. Very little attention was paid to formal analysis and planning.

Sleptsov's personality fits with this approach and with the difficult Russian business environment. He was inherently motivated by a drive to prove to himself that he was capable of doing anything. He admitted that the most enjoyable thing for him was to accept a challenge that seems like an insurmountable obstacle and to find the quickest and simplest way around it. The more formidable the challenge, the stronger his commitment to resolve it, and the more enjoyable the success.

However, even though Sleptsov's approach was certainly more creative than logical, one could question to what extent Sleptsov's approach was actually 'strategic'. If strategy can be broadly conceived as a pattern in the organization's course of action, it should be asked whether Sleptsov's thinking lead to any consistent pattern in his organization's behavior. In other words, was Sleptsov's thinking more opportunistic and ad hoc than strategic? His entrepreneurial actions led Stantret into ventures as diverse as air cargo transportation and Argentinean feature films. His short-term, quick win focus and his action-oriented management style may have prevented him from thinking about the long-term effects of his decisions. This would explain why he ignored thinking through the implications of the new market entrants when he first heard about them. It could be argued that the ability to look beyond the ad hoc solution of immediate problems and to assess the long-term implications of actions is an essential characteristic of successful strategists. Was Sleptsov really generating a new way of thinking about competitive strategy in the air cargo market or was he merely cashing in on a short-term market inefficiency, without any conception of the long-term feasibility and viability?

Despite such personal strengths as tenacity, creativity, strong bargaining skills, high energy level, and the ability to see opportunity where others see obstacles, Sleptsov's short-term perspective may have stood in the way of true generative thinking, that would have truly revolutionized the industry in the long run. Therefore, it can be argued that Sleptsov's focus on ad hoc creative solutions to mainly short-term problems does not constitute generative *strategic* thinking in the sense of Ohmae's definition in reading 2.2.

3.   *Describe the problems Stantret is currently facing and identify their possible root causes. To what extent can the causes of Stantret's current problems be attributed to circumstances beyond Sleptsov's control, and/or to Sleptsov's shortcomings as a strategist and manager? Which of the current problems do you consider most threatening to the survival of Stantret? How would you have attempted to avoid some of the problems Sleptsov is now facing?*

After its initial success, Stantret is now facing some critical challenges that may finally prove too hard for Sleptsov to overcome. After successfully solving such problems as fuel and plane availability through cooperation with Molniya, Stantret ran into more vexing problems:

- Stantret was forced to bail out its parent company by paying 13 million rubles in debt, interest and damages.
- One of Stantret's own managers spoiled a major deal with a Japanese trading company.
- Sleptsov discovered that the managers who were responsible for his air shipment operations were holding back money from the company.
- Volga-Dneper, a new serious competitor had quickly accumulated enough equity to buy several large planes, and had forged business relationships with the partner critical to Stantret's initial success: the Ministry of Aviation Industry (MAI).

The first problem can be seen as a symptom of the poor relationship between Stantret and its parent company, which had been opportunistic from the beginning. Stantret had received important amounts of 'seed capital' from its parent in the early stages of its development. However, after this initial financial injection, the parent company turned out to cost money, instead of supplying it. Stantret desperately needed to keep its first profits to pay for its rapid expansion, but was forced to hand over large sums of money and see it go to waste by the ineptitude of its parent company's managers. This problem could not easily have been avoided, as Sleptsov needed the initial support of the parent company to set up his business. Of course, now that Sleptsov has successfully managed to build a business that seems sustainable as an independent business, he should try to get out of the binding relationship as quickly as possible.

The second problem probably has many causes, only some of which Sleptsov can be held accountable for. Probable causes are lack of training due to fast growth in a high-pressure environment, a bad hiring decision, not enough coaching throughout the process, but plain 'bad luck' could also be involved. These first two problems should be considered to be relatively minor, because they can be overcome by changing the relationship with the parent company and by changing the human resource management practices of the firm.

However, the third and fourth problems mentioned above are much more critical and can probably not be fixed quickly, if at all. Their root causes may very well lie within the scope of Sleptsov's control and are probably related to weaknesses in his approach to strategy and management. The suggested answer to the previous question already indicated that Sleptsov's ad hoc, 'quick win' focus and his action-oriented management style may have prevented him from thinking though the possible long-term effects of his decisions.

Realizing that his success formula could easily be copied by others, Sleptsov purposely divided his employees into specialized groups, to make sure that he was the only one to know all the details of his deals. *"Because each whole project exists only in my head, I can avoid rivals - for the time being anyway,"* he is quoted as saying. Oddly, Sleptsov did not extend his fear of rivals beyond the borders of his own organization. In his view, there could be no real outside competitors because any rival would need to use Aeroflot planes, which were constantly grounded due to lack of engines or fuel. In reading 2.4, McCaskey argues that people's conceptual maps determine what elements in the turbulence of daily events they focus on and how they interpret what happens. It is clear that Sleptsov's rigid belief that no external competitor could acquire access to sufficient planes and fuel proved to be false. The sudden appearance of a new competitor that *was* able to compete with Stantret could have been foreseen, had Sleptsov's cognitive map not filtered out all incoming information about competitors' moves

Seeing his own employees as potential competitors, Sleptsov built a basic level of distrust into his organization by dividing up the organization into distinct parts and not sharing important information. Without realizing it, Sleptsov may thus have created an environment that was prone to fraud through building distrust into the structure of his company and through his sole focus on materialistic rewards as incentives for both his employees and his suppliers. His need for full control backfired when the company grew too large to be fully controlled and overseen by one man alone.

Both these problems, new competition and fraud within his company, are extremely threatening to the survival of Stantret. Given the nature of the opportunity Sleptsov seized, any new competitor that has the resources and contacts to get planes and fuel could theoretically provide reliable service at a reasonable price and compete head-on with Stantret. Volga Dnepr's resource base is much larger than Stantret's and at the end of the case it is mentioned that they had already forged ties with MAI. Volga Dnepr also had the backing of a strong foreign partner. There is no question that this competitor could seriously threaten Stantret's future. The question is what Stantret is going to do if MAI decides to exclusively supply Volga Dnepr?

Without a basic level of trust between employer and employees, no company can hope to survive in an environment as threatening as Stantret's. The fraud in his company will damage the fragile culture of Sleptsov's young organization and with the new competition it remains to be seen whether Stantret can survive such a shock.

With the benefit of hindsight one could argue that some of these problems could have been avoided. Sleptsov could have adopted a more balanced approach to strategy and management. Instead of focusing solely on ad hoc solutions to pressing problems, he could have taken more time to think through the possible long-term effects of his actions and to design solutions that could provide a more stable basis for growth. Stantret could have attempted to "lock-in" some of its suppliers and customers, thus creating a higher entry barrier for new competitors. It could also have looked for a foreign partner with a strong equity base itself, or it could have tried to ally itself with new competitors when they were still small. Internally, Sleptsov could have tried to create a more open, trusting environment and could have paid closer attention to the needs of his employees, preempting their incentives to commit fraud. Of course, in real life managers do not benefit from this kind of hindsight, making these kinds of 'obvious' solutions much harder to see and implement than it seems.

4. *What do you think Sleptsov should do now in the face of new, strong competition, and suspected fraud by his managers?*

Stantret is now facing a stronger competitor over which it no longer holds any apparent advantages. It does not have the resources to purchase its own fleet of airplanes and its runs the risk of losing AMI's cooperation to the new competitor. Needing a tight group of hard working people that can build on each other in order to survive in such a threatening environment, Stantret is in serious trouble now that its managers seem to be stealing money from the company. Given these threats, Sleptsov could consider the following options:

- *Restructure and reposition.* Sleptsov could attempt to turnaround Stantret and find a more sustainable competitive advantage on which to base the company. Key issues if this route is chosen are:
    - Securing access to planes and fuel (via AMI, Aeroflot, the military or foreigners)
    - Solving fraud problems (via tighter control or the better alignment of interests)
    - Cutting link to parent company (via management buyout or sale to outsider)
    - Creating competitive advantage (e.g. taking payment in goods instead of cash)

- *Partner or merge.* "If you can't beat 'em, join 'em". Stantret could attempt to strengthen its position by linking up with a strong partner. Possibilities could be:
    - Working together with Aeroflot, to help solve their major problem
    - Linking up with Volga Dnepr to operate complementary routes
    - Finding a foreign airline looking for a local Russian partner

- *Quit and start elsewhere.* Given Sleptsov's obvious talent for creative problem solving and engaging in new business opportunities where others merely see threats, Sleptsov might consider moving on. A good entrepreneur knows when to quit and reallocate his efforts to more promising opportunities.

Other Teaching Issues

The case also raises a number of questions that are relevant to other chapters in the book. These teaching issues are:

- *The paradox of deliberateness and emergentness.* Rather than using a deliberate strategic plan to guide his actions, Sleptsov relied on creative solutions to emerging problems. This approach led to great initial successes but may hamper success in the long run. This case therefore provides an excellent example of the natural tension between the need to plan ahead and the incremental nature in which the development of solutions often takes place (link to chapter 3).

- *The paradox of competition and cooperation.* Sleptsov established tight relationships with the actors controlling resources critical to Stantret. This case thus provides an interesting example of an alliance that is able to solve seemingly insurmountable problems through strategic coordination. Also particularly interesting are the disadvantages of collaboration, especially the dependence that can be its consequence. Sleptsov must determine how to strike a balance between competition and cooperation in his relationship with MAI (link to chapter 7).

- *The industry context: compliance vs. choice.* This case allows for a discussion on the extent to which certain environmental constraints require full compliance or present opportunities for strategic choice (link to chapter 8).

- *The importance of strategic leadership and control.* Throughout this case the question looms whether Sleptsov can, and should, lead his organization in a classic top-down manner. This allows for a discussion on the issue of organizational malleability and the virtues of strong entrepreneurial leadership (link to chapter 9).

What Happened After the Case?

After the case, Volga Dnepr Airlines, the new competitor that had quickly accumulated enough equity capital to buy several large cargo planes, grew exponentially. By 1993, Volga Dnepr had already obtained more than 70 national licenses to conduct cargo charters. In 1994, Volga Dnepr signed a co-operation agreement with Japan's leading trading company, Mitsui Corporation, under which Volga-Dnepr's interests in Japan would be represented by Mitsui. In the same year, Volga-Dnepr established a Beijing office and expanded the number of national licenses to 116. The airline also began operations to Italy, Israel, Hong Kong and many other countries and received certification from the US Federal Aviation Administration to begin scheduled cargo operations between the USA and Russia. Volga-Dnepr's President, Alexey Isaikin, was voted "Russia's Businessman of the Year" in a contest run jointly by the Russian Biographical Institute and the Russian edition of the publication "Who is Who".

By 1997, Volga Dnepr's fleet carried 50 thousand metric tons of cargo, resulting in revenues that totaled US$ 101 million. Its heavy cargo Antonov An-124-100 fleet was responsible for 58% of all international shipments in heavyweight/oversized loads. Among the names of Volga Dnepr's main current competitors (Air Foyle/Antonov, Transcharter, Ayaks, and Polyot), 'Stantret' is nowhere to be found. Despite its fast take-off, Stantret's flight therefore proved short-lived.

TEACHING NOTE 5: STRATEGIC PLANNING AT OLDELFT

Case and Teaching Note by Ron Meyer

Case Synopsis

This case describes the evolution of Oldelft's formal strategic planning system, from the 1970s up until 1987. Oldelft is a medium-sized producer of defense, medical and industrial products, all based on optical-electronic technology. The company is headquartered in Delft, Holland, and is highly dependent on foreign markets, in which it is up against much larger competitors. Oldelft's approach to making strategy is strongly planning-oriented and the company has developed an elaborate company-wide system to arrive at these plans. However, there are people within the company who question the effectiveness of this "three ring circus" planning system. The student is asked to consider which changes could be made to improve Oldelft's strategy-making ability.

Teaching Objectives

If used in conjunction with chapter 3, this case can be used to meet the following teaching objectives:

- *Understanding the design of formal planning systems.* This case describes the entire strategic planning system in use within Oldelft, making it possible to identify all essential elements of this formalized approach to making strategy. The case details how the strategy formation steps, that were discussed in general in chapter 2 (recognition, analysis, formulation, implementation – also link to 2.1 Andrews) are carried out within the organization. All of the important aspects of designing a strategic planning system, such as the planning steps, duration, frequency, horizon, techniques, participants, and the links to other organizational systems can be illustrated in this case (link to 3.1 Chakravarthy & Lorange).

- *Identifying common pitfalls of formal planning systems.* As the strategic planning system used by Oldelft is relatively unsophisticated and mechanistic, almost every common pitfall described in the articles of chapter 3 can be illustrated by this case. Oldelft fails to attune its strategic planning system to other organizational systems (link to 3.1 Chakravarthy & Lorange) and gets caught up in bureaucratic procedures (link to 3.3 Allison and 3.4 Marx). The case offers ample room for discussion on how these ills might be cured.

- *Alternatives for formal planning systems.* The more fundamental discussion that should take place, is whether the formal planning system at Oldelft does more harm than good. Is a planning approach, and in particular a formalized planning system, the best way for Oldelft to make strategy, or should the company consider some of the suggestions of the incrementalists (link to 3.2 Quinn and 3.5 Mintzberg)?

Teaching Guideline

Ultimately, the discussion in this case should revolve around the desirability of having a formal strategic planning system at all and it should elicit a fundamental debate about the need to reconcile the need for deliberateness with the need for emergentness. However, generally it is better to build up to this debate, than to start with it. Given the importance of strategic planning systems in many companies, students should first pay some serious attention to understanding how these systems are organized and operated, without their existence directly being called into question. Therefore, the first few questions here deal with the "mechanics" of strategic planning systems and with the identification of the common benefits and pitfalls of such formal systems. In fact, the discussion should explore how Oldelft's strategy process could be improved without directly challenging the underlying planning paradigm. Once the limits of improvement under the assumption of formal planning have been determined, the discussion can turn to alternative approaches. A remark such as "hasn't the discussion so far been focused on perfecting corporate rain-dancing" can be used to arouse a heated debate.

Suggested Questions

1. How has the strategic planning system been organized at Oldelft? Which steps are carried out by whom and in which order? What is the role and position of the strategic planning department? How long does the planning process take, how frequently is it repeated and what is the time horizon of the plans?

2. How has the strategic planning system been linked to other important organizational systems, such as the monitoring, control and learning system, the incentives system and the staffing system?

3. What do you consider the major strengths of Oldelft's strategic planning system that need to be preserved?

4. What do you consider the major weaknesses of Oldelft's strategic planning system? What could be done to improve this system? How would you go about implementing these changes to the planning system? Who would you involve? What would you consider top priorities?

5. Do you think that Oldelft's choice for a formal planning system was wise in the first place? Should Oldelft scrap its formal planning system instead of reforming it? What alternative ways of making strategy are open to Oldelft and what are their potential strengths and weaknesses? Which approach to the strategy process do you think is the most promising?

Case Analysis

1. How has the strategic planning system been organized at Oldelft? Which steps are carried out by whom and in which order? What is the role and position of the strategic planning department? How long does the planning process take, how frequently is it repeated and what is the time horizon of the plans?

Oldelft's strategic planning system has been set up along the lines of Arthur D. Little's standardized approach. This system has the following key characteristics:

- *Four step process.* Oldelft's system is based on four steps (see page 968), as illustrated in exhibit 1 below.

- *Fifty process participants.* Steps 1a and 2a are the main responsibility of the business segment manager. He is supported by the corporate planner and occasionally by an outside consultant. Besides these two, however, there is widespread participation of relevant (stakeholding) personnel, which includes product managers, sales managers, plant managers, project managers, production coordinators and development unit managers. In general, 10 to 15 managers attend each meeting. Steps 1b, 2b and 4 are carried out by the corporate planner. Step 3, the corporate scrums, involves the participation of the Board of Management (4 people), the directors (heads of the most important departments and business units, 5-7 people), the company controller, the corporate planner and an occasional outside consultant. In all, about 50 of the company's 1300 employees were involved in the planning process.

- *Planner is process facilitator.* The corporate planner, Baas, does not plan, but facilitates the entire planning process, leaving the line managers with the responsibility to make and execute strategic plans. The planner does not have a strong hierarchical position, as a member of the commercial affairs department reporting to the head of the commercial staff, which is a layer away from the Board of Management. However, his role as process facilitator has been sanctioned by top management and he does have a forceful personality.

- *Planning process duration of 1 year.* The entire planning process spans approximately 1 year. Steps 1 and 2 are carried out in the six months period from November to April. Step 3 takes place in May and June, while July through October is needed to complete the post-scrum booklets.

- *Planning process repeated every 2 years.* New strategic plans are drawn up biannually, in the uneven years (1987, 1989, 1991, etc.).

- *Planning horizon of 5 years.* In the strategic plans objectives are set for 5 years into the future. However, the plans only really emphasize the first two years, for which concrete budgeting take place.

EXHIBIT 1
Oldelft's strategic planning steps

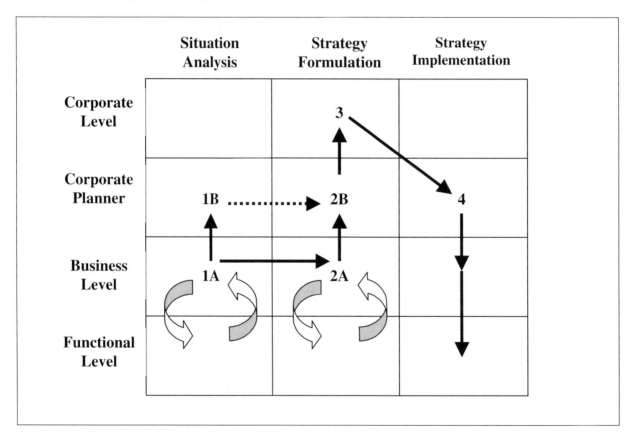

2. *How has the strategic planning system been linked to other important organizational systems, such as the monitoring, control and learning system, the incentives system and the staffing system?*

The answer here is rather straightforward - it hasn't been explicitly linked to any of the other organizational systems. There is no formal monitoring, control and learning system. We may assume that the financial department has a firm hand on the money being spent and will compare this with what has been budgeted, but there are no other progress reviews. Each business unit manager is on his own and there is only an informal review of the old plans during the subsequent planning cycle.

Learning is not an explicit goal of the strategic planning exercise. There is also no explicit link with the incentive system (e.g. promotions and pay raises are not tied to the strategic planning effort) or the staffing system (e.g. staff are not trained to be good strategists nor selected on the basis of their strategic abilities).

3. *What do you consider the major strengths of Oldelft's strategic planning system that need to be preserved?*

In the section 'Defining the Issues' a number of reasons are given for making explicit plans and engaging in formal planning. Most of these can be recognized as strengths of Oldelft's planning system:

- *Direction and cultural turnaround.* Probably the most important contribution of the formal planning system has been the introduction of strategic thinking to this very technology- and production-oriented company. As can be witnessed from the history of the planning system, the company had lost its direction after the founder/entrepreneur had left the company. The company's managers had never developed a capacity for strategic thinking, because the entrepreneur had always been the sole strategist. As the company's fortunes declined, despite excellent products and advanced technologies, something was needed to infuse strategic thinking into their inward-looking, engineering culture. The formal planning system offered a disciplined approach that forced the top 50 managers to regularly think about strategic matters.

- *Broad commitment and internal political support.* The strongly structured ADL methodology is concrete enough to gain the acceptance of the politically dominant engineers, who were prejudiced against the "vague and intuitive" topic of strategy. The involvement of all top managers in the process also ensures their commitment to the process outcomes - very little internal political resistance is met after decisions are made.

- *Coordination of interdependent units and functions.* The relatively broad participation in the planning process encourages the exchange of information between interdependent units and functions and facilitates coordination. In Oldelft this is particularly important, because all business segments share technologies and production facilities.

- *Optimization of decision-making.* The disciplined ADL approach ensures that strategic decision-making is based on rigorous analysis. Furthermore, the relatively broad participation in the planning process and open discussion during the corporate scrums also enlarges the chance of a broader spectrum of relevant information and useful ideas.

- *Programming activities.* Although the strategic plans at Oldelft are not directly linked to operational plans, the strategic planning process does help Oldelft to set priorities, allocate budgets and structure activities.

4. *What do you consider the major weaknesses of Oldelft's strategic planning system? What could be done to improve this system? How would you go about implementing these changes to the planning system? Who would you involve? What would you consider top priorities?*

In general, it is interesting to note here that if the history of Oldelft's strategic planning attempts is reviewed, this very closely resembles the developmental phases described by Marx. In Marx's typology, Oldelft is in phase 3, and needs to progress to phase 4 to have a really effective strategic planning process. From this perspective the major weaknesses and some possible improvements are the following:

- *Plans not made/reviewed frequently enough.* The biannual strategic planning cycle was selected because the company was unable to organize the cycle in a shorter period. The organizational upheaval in the first few cycles, the newness of the exercise and the limited resources of the planning department led to the decision to go through the cycle only once every two years. However, many arguments can be presented why this cycle is too long. Oldelft is situated in a very dynamic environment. Developments in this environment, which actually require a direct strategic response by Oldelft, could linger without an organizational answer for up to two years in the current planning process, which must be unacceptable. One can't afford a leisurely planning approach under turbulent circumstances. A second important reason why a biannual cycle is too long, is the effect this has on commitment to strategic planning in the company. If the strategic planning process is not a part of the fundamental way the company does business, but is perceived as a "circus" one must struggle through each two years, this will not improve commitment. An obvious improvement would be to move to an annual planning process. Another possibility would be to drop the calendar-driven approach altogether and only to engage in strategic planning if the necessity arises - the so-called *issue-driven approach*. An issue-driven approach only works, however, if a strategy review can be carried out in a number of weeks. Oldelft's process, however, takes a year, which is the next problem.

- *Planning process takes too long.* A process-duration of approximately a year is largely due to the bottleneck in the planning department. Most activities, such as the filling of the booklets, the meetings, the reading of reports and the taking of decisions, in themselves could be carried out in a number of months (even weeks). However, after each step the planning department has as a task to process the information it receives before the next step can be taken. They must rewrite the situation analyses and strategic options presented by the business segment managers into a presentable form and must translate the options into comparable financial figures. After the scrums the planning department is also burdened with writing 7 post-scrum booklets. Oldelft itself sees this as a problem, because plans a manager might develop in July must wait a full year before being approved, if the formal strategic planning channel is followed. Hence, the incentive to ignore the strategic planning system and follow informal channels is large. The chance that one responds too slowly to environmental changes is also large. The planning duration could be shortened in a number of ways, there is only one goal - speed. Either write the booklets faster (larger planning department and/or part-time help such as consultants) or let the planners write less (decentralize responsibility for report writing to business segment managers and/or shorten reports). Both approaches would lessen the planning department bottleneck. Further timesavings are, of course, also possible by means of tighter scheduling of meetings and giving more priority to strategic planning over operational matters.

- *Unnecessarily uniform procedures.* As Marx points out, uniform procedures are only necessary to make the planner's life easier. Baas's "hard-nosed approach," requiring managers to fill in pre-printed booklets, to use ADL analytical techniques, and to come to pre-programmed meetings, might have been necessary to get the strategically-inexperienced and unmotivated managers to work. However, in the longer run, putting managers through such paces does not motivate them, does not increase their strategic thinking capability and does not do justice to the different circumstances faced by each business segment. As Marx suggests, "effective strategic business-planning procedures must be flexible and relatively unstructured".

- *Undifferentiated 5 year planning horizon.* In general, five years is a relatively common planning horizon. However, the length of time one wishes to look into the future will depend on a number of factors, such as:

  - Environmental predictability: how dynamic is the company's environment?
  - Organizational capability: how far is the company capable of looking into the future?
  - Horizon of resource commitment: how long will a company be stuck with investments made today?
  - Horizon of strategy implementation: how long is a company forced to look ahead to plan the implementation of its strategy?

The first two points are pressures to limit the planning horizon, while the latter two pressure its' expansion. In the case of Oldelft the high-tech businesses it is in are highly dynamic, thus inherently unpredictable. The company also doesn't seem to have people, time or money to look further ahead than 5 years. On the other hand, some of the fundamental research in which it is investing will not bear fruits within 5 years, thus it requires a longer-term approach. This also applies to the company's involvement in defense (usually NATO) study groups, which are sometimes activated more than 15 years before the final products are sold. Without investment in these study groups the company would lose a considerable amount of turnover in future. Many solutions to these contradictory pressures are conceivable. One important conclusion, however, is that there is no one-best-answer. The chosen planning horizon will be a trade-off of pros and cons. One possibility in the Oldelft case would be to have a different planning horizon for each of the company's SBUs, since each SBU faces different circumstances. Furthermore, the company might consider expanding its present dual planning horizon approach. At the moment the company actually has two planning horizons; one for detailed planning at two years and one for general planning at 5 years. Oldelft might want to add a third horizon at, for instance, 10 years to think about long-term commitments.

- *Excessive quantification and reliance on analytical techniques.* Marx warns of the danger of excessive rationalization. Oldelft clearly suffers from the need to quantify strategy, which is reflected in the central role of the ADL matrix in their planning efforts. All strategic analyses have to be reduced to numbers, so that the ADL matrix can be filled in. It should be noted that the ADL matrix is a useful tool for indicating generic responses to certain business positions (grow, hold or out). However, a position in a certain strategic option zone does not automatically determine the strategy to be followed, but merely indicates what the most obvious thrust of the strategy should be. If used in the above manner, the ADL matrix is a valuable rule-of-thumb tool for decision-making, but also for communication of ideas and intentions (see 6.1 Hedley). Just as the drawback of a hammer is that you can't drive screws with it, so the drawback of the ADL matrix is its limited applicability. For instance, the matrix only indicates the general level of (dis)investment; grow (increase), hold, out (decrease). It does not indicate where or how to invest, in short, its says nothing about the strategy in particular.

    More worrying, is that the suggested quantitative precision and the scientific garb of the whole exercise lulls users into a false sense of significance. Especially those people who dislike the "fuzziness" of strategic management prefer strategy to be something that can be "calculated" and will assign a large measure of importance to the outcome of the ADL matrix exercise (see discussion in chapter 2). At best, however, the ADL matrix can give the strategist a general idea of the most obvious strategic thrust - at worst the numbers being used to fill in the matrix can be manipulated to give any outcome.

- *Lack of control and review system.* Oldelft itself does not identify this as a problem. In an interview the new strategic planner, Van Hoeven, actually says the following: "Everyone gets a post-scrum booklet and they can read...so, we hope they keep, in the back of their heads, the strategic way of doing things". There is good reason to believe, however, that such a laissez faire approach to implementation has its drawbacks. First, as the strategic planning exercise should be a learning process, development can only be achieved by means of feedback. The content of the next plan and the planning procedures used to bring it about will only improve if lessons are drawn from previous strategic planning attempts. If a formal review of the plans is lacking, feedback will only trickle through in an informal, indirect and fragmented way. Secondly, from a motivational point of view a lack of formal review is like asking students to do their homework although there will be no exam. It is a well-known problem that most managers are inclined to let the pressures of daily operational issues prevail above the acknowledged importance of strategic planning. Hence, there must be a countervailing pressure built in to the strategic planning system to assure adequate managerial attention. The knowledge that the product of your planning will be back to haunt you during the next planning cycle can be employed as one of these countervailing pressures. Thirdly, linked to the former point, periodic review of a business segment manager's progress vis-a-vis the goals set in his plan is an excellent control mechanism for top management.

■ *No link to incentives and staffing systems.* If there is no formal review of plans and managers are not judged on their performance vis-a-vis their plans, then it is also difficult to link incentives to the strategic planning system. In Oldelft there is no strict accountability ("we are a team and results can not be attributed to one person") and therefore also no formalized system of "carrots and sticks" for motivating managers. The company does not work with financial incentives and promotions are only indirectly linked to a manager's participation in the strategic planning process and his success at formulating and implementing plans. Although this is partially a cultural matter (the Dutch do not like to reward individuals), there is plenty of room for improvement (e.g. group rewards).

■ *Lack of supportive value system and climate.* Last, but definitely not least, Oldelft's planning system has not been able to capture the loyalty of the company's managers. Managers accept the need for strategic thinking, but view the entire planning "three ring circus" as a burden. Therefore, commitment to wholeheartedly participate in the process is lacking and there is not a strong planning culture. This lack of supportive value system and climate is not only due to all the points mentioned above, but also the result of the following points:

- *Insufficient top management commitment.* Top management only gets involved during the corporate scrums, which doesn't signal the process's importance. Furthermore, the process's half-hearted history (only started because top management was ashamed in front of ADL consultant Nieman, who joined the supervisory board) also does not suggest that the process enjoys top management's support.
- *Appointment of junior manager to position of corporate planner.* While Baas had been a company heavy weight, the appointment of the young and relatively inexperienced Van Hoeven was perceived as a signal that "the storm had passed."
- *Strategic planner situated in commercial affairs department.* After the proposed reorganization, the strategic planner will report to the head of commercial affairs (the politically weakest department in this technology-driven organization). If the strategic planning department had reported directly to the Board of Management, this would have been a clear signal of commitment and importance.
- *Insufficient strategic management training.* While managers were taught to fill in the booklets, true strategic management education was not pursued.

5. *Do you think that Oldelft's choice for a formal planning system was wise in the first place? Should Oldelft scrap its formal planning system instead of reforming it? What alternative ways of making strategy are open to Oldelft and what are their potential strengths and weaknesses? Which approach to the strategy process do you think is the most promising?*

Most of the improvements suggested in question 4 have been focused on reducing the rigidity and mechanistic nature of the strategic planning process. It could be argued, however, that the very existence of a formal planning system has two important detrimental effects (see 3.2 Quinn and 3.5 Mintzberg):

■ *Emphasis on form over substance.* The fact that a formalized planning system exists can give management a false sense of security - they might believe that because they have a system, that they are truly engaged in strategic management. They may unduly focus all their attention on the formal aspects of strategic planning, and forget that any strategy process has many soft and informal aspects. As Quinn points out, the formal planning system is usually just a vehicle for formalizing what has already been analyzed, learned, formulated and decided informally and incrementally. The more hollow the formal system, the more important is the informal process.

Oldelft is actually in such a situation, in which form (the planning system) tends to receive more emphasis than substance (actual strategic thinking).

- *Emphasis on control over creation.* The mechanistic nature of the entire process is in itself a deterrent for entrepreneurial behavior and innovation. Rapid adaptation to changing circumstances and the seizing of opportunities is made very difficult by the slow and bureaucratic procedures of a planning process. Experimentation and the development of a strategy as you go along (emergent strategy) are not encouraged because they can not be formally presented as a plan. And once openly committed to a formalized plan, it is often politically and psychologically difficult to admit failure or to change course, causing companies to become "locked in" to a wrong strategy. In short, an essentially bureaucratic system usually causes bureaucratic behavior:

  - a lack of latitude
  - a lack of flexibility
  - a lack of autonomy
  - a lack of learning ability
  - a lack of self-organizing ability

What should be debated here is whether these two fundamental problems can be overcome by reforming the planning system (as suggested by Marx) or whether the planning system should be replaced by a more informal strategic decision-making system. Such an informal system would probably have many of the following characteristics:

- *Strong leadership role for Board of Management.* The Board, not the corporate planner, runs the strategy process. It is their core business. Their tasks are to:

  - Build a shared vision (see 4.4 Senge)
  - Create awareness and commitment (see 3.2 Quinn)
  - Be teachers and stewards (see 4.4 Senge)

- *Planner as Catalyst.* The corporate planner provokes managers to develop new ideas and assists them in their 'messy' learning processes (see 3.5 Mintzberg).

- *Fast decision-making ability.* The strategy process should be flexible, responsive and quick. Therefore, there should be:

  - Continual bilateral discussions between Board and responsible manager
  - Open communication channels to relevant departments
  - Continually up-to-date business intelligence and possibly an "early-warning system".

- *Entrepreneurial culture.* By dropping as many bureaucratic impediments to entrepreneurial behavior as possible, the company can start to create a culture in which risk-taking, experimentation, dissent, initiative and flexibility are the norm.

Other Teaching Issues

This case can also be used to illustrate some points in connection to other chapters. Besides chapter 3 this case can also be used in conjunction with a number of other chapters:

- *Encouraging strategic thinking.* While the discussion in chapter 2 deals with the nature of strategic thinking, this case can be used to explore the issue of creating organizational circumstances that facilitate and encourage strategic thinking (link to chapter 2).

- *Realizing strategic change.* This case can also be employed to discuss the link between strategic planning and strategic change – how should strategy formation be organized to enhance the organization's ability to learn and change (link to chapter 4).

- *Advantages and disadvantages of portfolio techniques*. Oldelft's use of the ADL matrix has benefits and drawbacks that can be discussed (link to 6.1 Hedley).

- *The impact of the organizational context on the strategy process*. Oldelft suffers from many of the causes of inertia and this strongly influences the way the company's strategy process is, and can be, run (link to chapter 9).

- *The importance of an organizational mission*. The case describes how the company has a technological "mission" ("to reveal the invisible"), but not really a sense of mission (link to 11.5 Campbell & Yeung).

What Happened after the Case?

Van Hoeven left the discussion with the students at the Rotterdam School of Management in a state of surprise - he didn't understand why there was so much criticism of such a fine strategic planning system. He had more or less defined his role as caretaker of the system, making small improvements here and there. He did not have the mandate, intention or the ambition to redesign the way things were run. It should therefore come as no surprise that in the following years few alterations were made to the system.

A few years after the case, Oldelft merged with a fine-mechanical instrument maker, Enraf-Nonius, and changed its name to Delft Instruments. Mr. Kingma (who used to be VP Technical Affairs) replaced chairman of the Executive Board, Mr. Duinker in those years. This move in the medical equipment sector further lessened the company's exposure to the quickly declining defense business. However, the company's financial position remained weak, and this situation was not improved by an American embargo on essential parts. This embargo was imposed after the company was found guilty of supplying night vision equipment containing American parts to Iraq prior to the Gulf war without an American export license.

Due to declining sales and profitability, Delft Instruments was forced to take some dramatic action. In March 1998, Mr. Kingma led Delft Instruments into a merger with Nucletron, a company specialized in radiotherapy equipment for cancer treatment. Simultaneously, the physiotherapy activities of Enraf-Nonius (revenues of Dfl. 75 million) were sold to the US-based Henley Healthcare for Dfl. 15 million, forming Henley/Enraf-Nonius. Delft Instruments would remain responsible for the supply of electrotherapy products to the new Henley/Enraf-Nonius combination. In addition, a seven-year lease and service agreement was concluded between Henley/Enraf-Nonius and Delft Instruments to avoid the relocation of operations.

After this reshuffling, Delft Instruments consisted of seven Business Units (see exhibit 2) and two Production Units (Mechanical Parts Production in Delft, The Netherlands and the Advanced Instruments Manufacturing in Brunssum, The Netherlands).

EXHIBIT 2
Delft Instruments industry activities and business units as of March 1998
(Source: Delft Instruments Press Release March 6, 1998; www.delftinstruments.com)

Industry	Products	Business Unit
Medical	Radiotherapy	Nucletron
	Imaging systems	Oldelft
	Medical equipment	Oldelft Benelux
Defense/aerospace	Observation equipment	Delft Sensor Systems
Industrial/scientific	Tank gauging	Enraf
	Image intensifiers	Delft Electronic Products
	X-ray diffraction	Nonius

In May 1998, after the integration of Nucletron and Delft Instruments was completed, Mr. Kingma resigned (to pursue other interests) in favor of Mr. De Groot, former Board Member of Getronics, a large Dutch information technology company. Mr. De Groot announced a major restructuring and rationalization of the company, as 25% of total activities was still unprofitable. A provision of Dfl. 50.7 million was formed for this purpose and a plan called *Target 2001* was devised.

Key elements of Target 2001

The new focus was on market niches in the medical and industrial sectors, together with a strong emphasis on software, as can be judged from the altered corporate mission statement of Delft Instruments: *'To be a leading global supplier of high quality instruments, systems, software and services in selected niches of the medical and industrial markets, mainly based on our own design and creation'* (Annual Report 1998). The strategy was aimed at providing high-tech, high-quality niche products to professional customers, based on proprietary unique technology and knowledge of high-precision mechanics, electronics, software and radiation (more specifically X-ray, radar, radioactivity, thermal and light technology). The major moves include the following:

- The marketing and sales activities of Oldelft where integrated into those of Nucletron and the manufacturing and assembly of Oldelft products were outsourced. The Electro-Optics activities in Delft (Delft Sensor Systems) were closed, after completing their running defense contracts. The Nonius activities in Delft were scaled down. The direct participating interest in the unsuccessful production joint venture with Bharat Electronics (called BE-Delft) in India was sold.

- In August 1998, Delft Instruments signed a co-operation agreement between Nucletron (its subsidiary), Siemens Medical Systems, Oncology Care Systems Group (Concord, California, USA) and ELEKTA Oncology Systems (Crawley, UK) for the marketing and sales of Nucletron hardware and software. In addition, Nucletron also took over its distributor in India (Nucletron Trading Private Ltd.) to become effective as of January 1999.

- In March 1999, Oldelft and Nucletron announced the moving of the X-ray diagnostics activities to the premises of Nucletron in Veenendaal, The Netherlands. Also, the operation would be conducted under the Nucletron name, with only the Oldelft trademark still being used. What remained of Oldelft were the Ultrasound activities in Delft.

- Measures were also taken to slim down the staff of the company's head office in Delft. Only the successful sales and service activities of Oldelft Benelux would be further expanded at the same rate as before.

- In April 1999, Delft Instruments sold their headquarters in Delft to an investor for Dfl. 7 million. Also in that same month, Delft Instruments announced that it was discussing the sale of their Business Unit Delft Electronic Products to the US-based Burle Industries (expected to become official in June 1999).

All this restructuring activity has resulted in Delft Instruments currently being a holding company of an international group of companies with some 1100 employees and annual sales in the order of Dfl. 400 million. With Target 2001, Delft Instruments is trying to solve the financial problems of the last few years and to achieve an improvement of its balance sheet. *'It is the group's financial mission to secure good balance sheet ratios and returns in order to guarantee continuity, facilitate future expansion and create shareholder value'* (Annual Report 1998). The following financial goals are part of Target 2001:

- A capital base of at least 35% of total assets

- Net profit after taxation of at least 7% of net sales

- A 10-15% yearly increase in net earnings per share as from the year 2000

- Higher annual growth rate than the market

As can be judged from the figures in exhibits 3 and 5 below, these goals are very ambitious (for instance looking at the net margin of less than 3% the last few years). In an interview in the leading Dutch financial newspaper *Het Financieele Dagblad* of June 2 1999, CFO Mr. Dekker stated that these goals were to be met by divesting non-core businesses. He also stated that with the new focus on medical and industrial products, the defense business could now be classified as non-core.

EXHIBIT 3
Financial Summary 1994-1998 in Dfl. Millions (Source: Annual Report 1998)

		1998	1997	1996	1995	1994
Results	Sales	380	473	474	473	453
	Other operating income	27	9	17	-16	0
	Salaries and social security	-138	-159	-158	-162	-151
	Depreciation	-13	-14	-15	-14	-17
	Costs of materials and sub-contracting	-155	-177	-190	-168	-167
	Other operating expenses	-95	-95	-96	-90	-89
	Operating profit	6	37	32	23	29
	Financial income and expense	-12	-17	-15	-14	-16
	Taxation	0	-6	-4	0	-1
	Extraordinary income and expenses	-38	0	0	7	-4
	Net income	-44	14	13	16	8
	Cashflow	-30	28	28	30	24
Assets	Fixed assets	103	99	102	105	106
	Inventories	150	152	150	144	155
	Accounts receivable	221	261	253	214	175
	Liquid resources	3	5	4	5	4
	Total assets	477	517	509	468	440
Liabilities	Group equity	114	153	137	130	113
	Long-term external liabilities	66	82	93	81	94
	Short-term external liabilities	297	282	279	257	233
	Total equity and liabilities	477	517	509	468	440

EXHIBIT 4
Sector figures in Dfl. Millions (Source: Annual report 1998)

		1998	1997
Net sales	Medical	195	311
	Industrial and Scientific	135	134
	Miscellaneous	50	28
Operating results	Medical	11	29
	Industrial and Scientific	5	18
	Miscellaneous	-9	-10
R&D costs	Medical	31	29
	Industrial and Scientific	21	15
	Miscellaneous	4	3

EXHIBIT 5
Five year summary key ratios (Source: Annual report 1998)

		1998	1997	1996	1995	1994
Net sales	Increase in net sales in %	-19.7	-0.3	0.4	4.5	17.3
Results	Net profit as % of sales	-11.5	3.0	2.7	3.4	1.5
	Net profit as % of average equity	-32.7	9.7	9.8	13.5	6.4
Equity	Equity as % of average total assets	23	30	28	29	28
Working capital	Current ratio	1.4	1.5	1.5	1.4	1.5
	Quick ratio	0.8	0.9	0.9	0.9	0.8
	Inventory as % of sales	39	32	32	30	34
	Working capital in Dfl. Millions	99	139	139	111	114
R&D	R&D costs in Dfl. Millions	56	47	48	43	43
	R&D costs as % of sales	14.7	10.0	10.2	9.1	9.5
Employees	# of employees at year-end	1.194	1.413	1.428	1.633	1.711
Per share data	Cash flow	-3.91	3.81	3.76	4.23	3.43
	Net earnings	-5.63	1.90	1.76	2.24	1.00
	Cash dividend declared	0	0.75	0.70	0.50	0
	Stock dividend declared	0	1/50	1/52	0	0

EXHIBIT 6
Net sales in Dfl. Millions by geographic region (Source: Annual report 1998)

	1998	1997
The Netherlands	63	61
Other EU countries	125	158
North and South America	98	105
Rest of world	94	149

References

Delft Instruments Annual Report 1998
www.delftinstruments.com
Het Financieele Dagblad, Delft wil in 2000 zekerheden terug (Delft wants securities back in 2000), June 2, 1999.

TEACHING NOTE 6: KAO CORPORATION

Case by Sumantra Ghoshal and Charlotte Butler

Teaching note by Bob de Wit and Ron Meyer

Case Synopsis

Kao is Japan's market leader in detergents and shampoos, and runner up in disposable diapers and cosmetics. In 1990 the company had sales of Y620.4 billion (approximately US$ 4 billion), largely in Japan and South East Asia. However, in the late 1980s Kao has acquired a number of companies in the US and Europe and has committed itself to further internationalization. Its strategic intent is to belong to the 3 or 4 global detergent/cosmetics/personal care companies that they believe will eventually survive.

Kao is particularly interesting due to its corporate philosophy. The company believes that competitive advantage stems from the superior attainment and usage of information. Therefore information must flow freely throughout the organization and all individuals must be equipped to continually learn from the information obtained. This concept of a "learning organization" is achieved by having a very flat organizational structure, an open, non-hierarchical culture, broad participation in strategy development, extensive information systems and a state of mind that emphasizes that learning is an essential never-ending process. The strategy process can be characterized as continual, largely informal, participatory, flexible and incremental.

The key question raised by the case is how this strategy process and the company's learning ability can be maintained as they further internationalize. The company will grow in size and complexity, while more nationalities will become involved in strategy development. The company must learn how to remain a learning company.

Teaching Objectives

If used in conjunction with chapter 3 this case can be used to meet the following teaching objectives:

- *Understanding the building of a learning organization.* This case describes the manner in which Kao has been able to transform itself into a learning organization. The company's structure, culture, leadership and systems are described, allowing for a discussion on the circumstances that are necessary to create an organization capable of continual learning (link to 3.2 Quinn and 4.4 Senge).

- *Understanding the role of leadership in a learning organization.* Of particular interest in the Kao case is the role of the CEO, Dr. Maruta. He does not play the traditional role of master planner and architect of implementation (Commander Approach or Change Approach). On the contrary, he creates the circumstances under which ideas and strategies can arise and grow within the organization (Crescive Approach). Maruta's leadership style can be taken as a starting point for a discussion on the influence of leadership on learning. More broadly, the impact of various leadership approaches on the strategy formation process can be explored (link to 3.2 Quinn, 4.4 Senge, and 9.3 Bourgeois & Brodwin).

- *Discussion on learning as part of the strategy formation process.* Kao's focus on learning is an integral part of their thinking about how to manage the strategy formation process. Therefore, this case allows for a discussion on the link between learning and strategy formation (link to all readings).

- *Discussion on the advantages and disadvantages of the incrementalist perspective.* Kao's strategy formation approach is strongly inclined towards the incrementalist perspective. Therefore, this case allows for a discussion on the strengths and weaknesses of incrementalist approaches to strategy formation (link to all readings).

Teaching Guideline

It is our experience that it is essential to have at least one good case on a Japanese company somewhere in the course. Few topics are so widely discussed and so poorly understood by most students as the functioning of Japanese corporations. Biases, both overly positive (e.g. undefeatable) and overly negative (e.g. hierarchical and uncreative), are common, as are sweeping generalizations about Japanese companies. The Kao case is excellent at challenging these biases and generalizations. For instance, Japanese culture scores high on Hofstede's measures of power distance (i.e. hierarchical) and masculinity (i.e. aggressive and competitive), yet Kao is a flat, open and egalitarian organization. Japanese companies are said to internationalize through internal growth, yet Kao has staged a number of significant acquisitions (Andrew Jergens and Goldwell). In all, the Kao case can help to sketch a more balanced and heterogeneous picture of Japanese companies.

The Kao case is not a particularly difficult case to teach, although it does combine the issues discussed in chapter 3 (learning), chapter 4 (change), chapter 5 (competing on capabilities) and chapter 10 (internationalization). Primarily, however, the case deals with learning and therefore it is linked to chapter 3. It makes an excellent companion for a case on formal planning systems, such as the one on Oldelft. While the Oldelft case focuses on the formalized and planned processes of analysis, formulation and implementation, the Kao case emphasizes the informal and incremental processes of learning, adaptation and change. Therefore it is often quite useful to use them directly after one another. The case can also be used to combine the discussions in chapters 3 and 4.

We usually start class by asking people whether they knew that Jergens and Goldwell had been acquired by Kao (most don't know this). We then provocatively ask people whether they would consider working for Jergens, Goldwell or other Kao subsidiaries. Many will indicate that they would like to, but usually a few people express uneasiness about a possible lack of freedom at these subsidiaries and limited career opportunities at the senior management levels. It is felt that the company might be a learning organization in Japan, but that foreign subsidiaries are not part of these dynamics and are probably run on a different basis. We don't directly pursue this issue any further, but indicate that this is the key question that our discussion should arrive at by the end of class. How can learning in a closely-knit and culturally homogeneous organization be extended to new company subsidiaries that are culturally and physically distant, and with which few relations exist? In other words, how can one create transnational learning?

The build up of the class discussion is that we start by trying to understand what makes a company a learning organization. Then we link learning to the entire strategy process - what role does organizational learning play in strategy formation. After this has become clear, we move to the question of the internationalization of learning.

Case Questions

1. What is learning and what is a learning organization according to Kao? How is organizational learning different than, for instance, a person learning from reading Peter Senge's article?

2. How has Kao been able to build a learning organization? What is their corporate philosophy and what type of structure, culture, systems and leadership roles has the company developed to become a learning organization?

3. How does Kao go about forming strategy? What are the strategy formation process's main features?

4. What are the advantages and disadvantages of Kao's current strategy formation process?

5. How would Kao need to adapt or change its strategy formation process to accommodate further internationalization? What type of action would you recommend?

Case Analysis

1. *What is learning and what is a learning organization according to Kao? How is organizational learning different than, for instance, a person learning from reading Peter Senge's article in chapter 3?*

At Kao learning is simply defined as gaining a better understanding of the truth. More specifically, it is believed that organizational learning has the following characteristics:

- *Continual.* Learning does not take place at fixed moments, but is viewed as "a frame of mind, a daily matter." In this way, every activity can lead to further learning.

- *Collective.* Learning is not an activity that an employee carries out individually behind a desk, but a process that takes place through open discussions and the investigation of concrete business ideas. In Kao everyone within the organization is expected to participate in this joint learning process, helping not only himself to learn, but also all others, whether above and below him.

- *Intuitive.* Learning is also viewed as largely intuitive - by doing and discussing, managers often unknowingly internalize knowledge (the Zen Buddhists speak of kangyo ichijo, internalized intuition). This places an important emphasis on the development of tacit knowledge over the attainment of formalized/codified knowledge.

Hence, a learning organization is simply an organization in which the process of daily, collective and largely intuitive learning is well developed. A person reading an article differs on all three counts. Reading an article is not continual, but incidental learning; it is not collective, but individual learning; and it is not intuitive, but largely formalized learning. In other words, reading an article is a long way off from organizational learning, although it can be an ingredient of the process.

2. *How has Kao been able to build a learning organization? What is their corporate philosophy and what type of structure, culture, systems and leadership roles has the company developed to become a learning organization?*

Building a learning organization is not a matter of changing the organizational structure or tinkering with the incentive system. In isolation these actions will not result in a learning organization, although they could be elements of a more encompassing effort to build up a company's learning ability. To really become a learning organization, Kao has taken systematic action on a number of fronts.

Corporate philosophy. Most importantly, the company truly believes in the importance of learning. Dr. Maruta, the president of Kao, states that Kao is "an educational institution in which everyone is a potential teacher." All employees, including Maruta himself, are seen as students of the truth, continually seeking new insights and better understanding. It is the company's fundamental assumption that such learning, drawn from scarce information, is the ultimate source of competitive advantage and therefore needs to be carefully nurtured: "The company that develops a monopoly on information, and has the ability to learn from it continuously, is the company that will win, irrespective of its business."

Organizational culture. Linked to this underlying philosophy is an organizational culture that reinforces the importance of information, knowledge and its acquisition through learning. To facilitate the daily, organization-wide, and largely intuitive learning that Kao believes is essential, the company's culture emphasizes a number of principles:

- *Equality*. Kao rejects authoritarianism, believing that collective learning can only take place in an organization where people discuss matters on an equal footing. Interaction and the spread of ideas require that opinions are judged on their own merits, independent of rank and therefore the principle of equality is central to Kao's culture.

- *Openness*. Joint learning also requires the free flow of information and ideas. Therefore Kao's culture emphasizes that every employee should have full access to all information and that all discussions should be held out in the open, where everyone is free to hear what is said and to participate if needed.

- *Mutual assistance*. Organizational learning also requires individuals and departments to take an active interest in each other's problems and development. If each individual or department tries to optimize only its own learning, everyone loses, because there is no cross-fertilization. Therefore mutual assistance is stressed as a key principle.

- *Individual initiative*. Although the organization must learn together, ideas are born and knowledge is spread by initiatives taken by individuals. Therefore, the collective nature of organizational learning requires a strong cultural emphasis on the good of individual initiatives.

- *Proactiveness*. Finally, it is a commonly held view within Kao that learning should not be solely based on previous experience. As Maruta puts it, "past wisdom must not be a constraint, but something to be challenged." "Yesterday's success formula is often today's obsolete dogma." The emphasis is rather on what has been learnt today that can be useful tomorrow (link to the discussion on mental models in chapter 2).

In short, the values and beliefs held by managers within Kao regarding learning are very strong and are a main factor in shaping Kao as a learning organization. However, this culture is further reinforced by other organizational elements.

Organizational structure. To allow for the equality, openness, mutual assistance, individual initiative and proactiveness mentioned above, Kao has designed a very flat organizational structure, without significant boundaries or titles. There is relatively little hierarchy and not a strict separation of tasks - the organization functions fluidly and flexibly, with various parts interacting and assisting each other where necessary, which Kao refers to as "biological self control".

Organizational systems. As horizontally shared information is essential to Kao's organizational learning, the company has placed a strong emphasis on developing information systems so that the most up to date information is available to all members of the organization. Everyone has access to the Logistics Information System (ordering, inventory, production and sales data) and the Market Intelligence System (market research, sales, and marketing data). Further information exchanges and networking opportunities are created through regular R&D conferences and through the open physical lay out of the Kao building.

Leadership roles. Finally, the way that top managers define their roles within the company has a significant impact on Kao's learning ability. As Senge (reading 4.4) argues, leaders can not learn on behalf of their organizations, but must assist their organizations to learn. Senge identifies three critical roles of leadership in a learning organization, each of which is also applicable to Kao:

- *Leader as designer*. Leaders must understand that learning cannot be commanded, but that a "social architecture" must be created that will support organizational learning. In Kao, the company leaders have designed the needed organizational structure and systems, and have fostered the essential organizational culture.

- *Leader as teacher.* Leaders should not be authoritarian experts, but must coach, guide and facilitate everyone in the organization. In Kao this is exactly the case - Dr. Maruta does not push one vision of reality, but aids employees in coming up with their own ideas.

- *Leader as steward.* Most fundamentally, leaders should not be motivated by a desire for power, but by their desire to serve other people and the organization, so that these can function optimally. Here too, it seems that Kao fits the mould. Maruta seems very much a "servant leader," who creates trust and commitment by his unselfish desire to serve others and the organization as a whole.

3. How does Kao go about forming strategy? What are the strategy formation process's main features?

The remark about Kao's joint venture with Colgate-Palmolive on page 991 really gets to the essence of Kao's strategy process: "The way the two firms decided on strategy was totally different. We [Kao] constantly adjust our strategy flexibly. They [Colgate-Palmolive] never start without a concrete and fixed strategy. We could not wait for them." In other words, Colgate-Palmolive's approach to strategy formation was inspired by the planning perspective, while Kao approach was much more in line with the incrementalist perspective.

When examined more closely, Kao's strategy formation process can be seen to have the following characteristics:

- *Creating issue awareness.* Within the open and participatory culture of Kao, it is every person's responsibility to identify the critical issues to which the organization must respond and to bring these issues to the attention of all relevant colleagues (link to chapter 2, page 80). In other words, the definition of threats and opportunities, and the focusing of organizational attention take place continuously, informally, horizontally and intuitively. There are no formalized, periodic procedures using rational analytical techniques to ensure that issue identification takes place, nor is it a task assigned to only a small number of senior managers.

- *Developing ideas and legitimizing new viewpoints.* Once issues or problems have been identified, clusters of affected or interested individuals form around them (referred to as self-organization, see page 160 and 9.2 Stacey). These people may meet formally or informally to exchange information and jointly develop ideas on how to proceed. At this stage there will not yet be any fixed proposals, so that discussions can be truly open, without any individual defending a predetermined point of view.

- *Obtaining contributions, consensus, credibility and commitment.* As the ideas developing in these small groups become increasingly clear, they are shared more widely. The prevailing principle at Kao is referred to as tataki-dai; "present your ideas to others at 80 percent completion" so that others can criticize and contribute to them before they become a proposal. Not only does this enhance the quality of the idea, but also it helps to create zoawase - a common perspective or view. This is also the point at which higher management levels are involved. They too can contribute to the evolving ideas and by their participation lend weight and credibility to the plans. As consensus emerges in this fashion, all of the participants in this strategy formation process also become increasingly committed to making the strategy a success.

- *Implementation, systematic learning and reformulation.* None of Kao's managers believes that the strategy formation process is over once the initial plans have been formulated. A first set of plans is merely a snapshot in the learning process - as an issue grew into an idea, which grew into a proposal, which grew into a plan, so the strategy should continue to grow as the knowledge and wisdom of the organization continue to expand. Hence, no one expects the plans to be fully implemented as formulated. On the contrary, everyone is focused on obtaining feedback information that can lead to learning and can be used to adapt and further develop the strategy.

- *The role of vision*. A common vision about the organization's purpose, identity and strategic intent is both the outcome and the guiding principle in the above process. In other words, Kao's vision is not static or top-down, but is developed in the same incremental manner as described above. However, at the same time, Kao's vision is less variable than its strategies and thus acts as a guiding principle in the incremental strategy formation process. The company's vision helps managers to focus on the right issues and points managers in certain directions where they should seek solutions and new opportunities. In short, the company vision helps to determine the pattern in the stream of organizational actions.

These points underscore that learning and incrementalism are two sides of the same coin. When looking at learning, the focus is on the competence development process - how organizations continually and gradually obtain information and increase their knowledge and abilities. When looking at incrementalism, the focus is on the strategy development process - how organizations continually and gradually create patterns in their streams of decisions and actions. The two are wrapped up in one another, proceeding in unison.

4.   What are the advantages and disadvantages of Kao's current strategy formation process?

The advantages of Kao's current strategy formation process have become quite clear from the discussion above. Their strategy formation process is flexible, adaptive, and open to learning, which is particularly important in unpredictable environments. High participation and a crescive approach by top management (link to 9.3 Bourgeois & Brodwin) lead to more bottom-up information and ideas, the continual improvement of proposals, and broad understanding and commitment throughout the organization.

The case writers are particularly kind toward the company and do not mention any disadvantages encountered by using this approach. However, based on the readings in chapter 3, the following potential disadvantages can be identified:

- *Disadvantages of "finding out"*. Learning and incrementalism are based on the principle of feedback - the results of current activities are used to adapt future activities. Feedback is also referred to as output- or error-driven, because learning is based on past successes and mistakes (we refer to this as 'finding out'). The alternative is feedforward, whereby future activities are based on forecasts and estimates. Feedforward is also referred to as input- or forecast-driven, because estimates are made of what will probably happen (we therefore speak of 'figuring out'). The most common problems of feedback are inefficiency and the danger of irreparable mistakes. Learning by trial and error can often be time- and resource consuming compared to thinking things through in advance. Furthermore, some "errors" can not be repaired. By trying out something in the market a company can damage its name or make investments that can not be recovered. The main problem of feedforward, on the other hand, is that many things can not be forecast or thought out in advance. Kao seems to be trying to combine both feedback and feedforward to get the best possible results. However, the threat of inefficiency and irreparable damage remains.

- *Threat of strategic drift*. This argument is put forward by Johnson in chapter 9. Companies that employ an incremental approach to strategy formation run the risk of making adjustments that are not radical enough. Because Kao has a strong bias toward incremental action (get started and learn as you go along), they might find it more difficult to formulate and execute far-reaching plans, such as take overs, large capital investments or shifts in technologies. The case, however, does not suggest that this is a problem.

- *Threat of slower decision making*. Above it was argued that trial and error learning might be time-consuming. To this it can be added that the participatory decision-making system and need for consensus can also be relatively slow. Especially in circumstances where the speed of decision-making is essential (a crisis or a sudden opportunity), Kao might be at a disadvantage. In general, however, it should be recognized that the length of the decision-making process ("time-to-decision") is usually less important than the length of the total decision and implementation process ("time-to-results"). Slower decision-making might be more than compensated by quicker implementation. Investing time during the decision-making process to produce high quality plans that are widely understood and enjoy broad acceptance often facilitates rapid action, making the total amount of time spent from issue identification, through diagnosis, to conceiving and realizing less than in other firms.

- *Threat of political infighting.* An inherent threat of flat organizations with widespread participation is (as everyone at a university knows) political infighting (link to 3.3 Allison). The wide variety of opinions and the diffusion of power can easily lead to confrontational political processes, without a clear-cut source of authority to resolve disputes. Kao seems to avoid these problems by a strong, homogeneous, cooperation-oriented corporate culture and a shared strategic intent.

- *Difficult to internationalize.* As the company internationalizes, keeping up the shared culture and strategic intent will be increasingly difficult. The organization will be larger, made up of more nationalities and divided by larger physical distances. There will be fewer informal contacts and differences of interests are likely to grow. Openness, trust and commitment will be difficult to maintain under these circumstances. If ideas need to be surfaced and consensus needs to grow between people at scattered locations around the world, the ease of interaction is likely to decrease, while decision-making time is likely to increase. Furthermore, the threat of political infighting is likely to grow as well.

- *Difficult to integrate acquisitions.* The very particular attitude toward learning and the strategy formation process at Kao, makes it very difficult for other organizational cultures to be integrated into the Kao system. At corporations with highly formalized strategic planning systems, companies that are acquired need to adapt themselves to a number of procedures and regulations governing the strategy process. The often-used metaphor is that of a new "part" that must be slotted into the organizational "machinery". At Kao, however, learning and strategy formation have not been formalized into policies and procedures that can be easily transferred to an acquired company. The Kao way of doing things has grown out of a philosophy and is engrained in the beliefs, informal rules and tacit organizational routines prevalent throughout the company. Dr. Maruta's own metaphor is that of an organism. Taking this metaphor one step further, it can be questioned whether a foreign body can be made compatible, or will be rejected if implantation is attempted. In other words, how can managers at the acquired firms be integrated into the Kao way of learning and strategy formation if their culture is radically different? The more exceptional Kao's culture, the more difficult it will be to absorb foreign cultures into the organization.

5. *How would Kao need to adapt or change its strategy formation process to accommodate further internationalization? What type of action would you recommend?*

This is a difficult question, particularly as it goes a step further than the literature provided to students in this chapter (actually, this question can be used to point ahead to issues that will be discussed in chapter 10). Students will probably come up with a broad range of suggestions at this stage, varying from obvious to profound. At a minimum, the lecturer will want to ensure that the following issues are touched on:

- *A Japanese or transnational company?* Kao seems to believe in the transnational corporation (see Bartlett and Ghoshal in chapter 10) judging by its vision that "headquarters' functions would be dispersed to SE Asia, the US and Europe, leaving the Tokyo headquarters the role of supporting regionally based, locally managed operations by giving strategic assistance." Compared to the current situation this would require a significant amount of decentralization and growth of an international management cadre. The question is whether this can be achieved without destroying

Kao's unique learning capability. As mentioned above, Kao's learning organization is currently dependent on mutual trust, openness, understanding and involvement. These are maintained by a common culture, interdependence, parallel interests and frequent informal contacts - attributes that are more typical of a medium-sized firm, based in one location, with a homogeneous culture. Will a bigger company, with more foreigners, spread all over the world not frustrate the company's ability to learn? Shouldn't Kao remain a Japanese company with foreign interests, with the headquarters' in Tokyo remaining as the focus of its learning activities? Should Kao develop a diverse group of global managers from a variety of national backgrounds, or rely on a core group of Japanese expatriate managers that relate each foreign operation to Tokyo headquarters?

- *A formal or informal company?* Kao must also wonder whether its lack of hierarchy (the "paperweight organization"), lack of organizational boundaries ("biological self-control") and lack of formalized procedures all remain possible as the organization grows both in volume and geographically. How can communication be as frequent and as informal as within the Tokyo headquarters? How can control be exerted over subsidiaries far away from the center? Can this be achieved "informally" or are systems and procedure necessary to ensure that the foreign subsidiaries remain a part of the larger learning organization?

- *An acquiring or organically growing company?* As mentioned in the answer to question 4, transferring Kao's learning capability to a company that has been acquired is terribly difficult. Yet, both in Europe and in the United States, Kao has staged major acquisitions as an important part of its foreign market entry strategy. The question is whether the benefits of these takeovers (instant market share, existing brand names, local management and market knowledge) really offset the costs (cultural incompatibility, difficulty to share learning, difficulty to transfer learning capability). Shouldn't Kao take the longer and rougher road of organic growth, if this eventually leads to the leveraging of Kao's learning capability?

Other Teaching Issues

The case also raises a number of issues that are relevant to other chapters in the book. These other teaching issues are:

- *Strategic thinking.* Dr. Maruta is clear that he believes that learning and strategic thinking are not entirely rational and conscious, but require intuition and imagination. This case can therefore be used to link in with the discussion on the nature of strategic thinking (link to chapter 2).

- *Strategic change.* The case describes Kao as a learning organization, much in line with the continuous change perspective. However, the internationalization process started is not an evolutionary change, but promises to be a revolutionary change, especially if it entails the integration of numerous foreign acquisitions. The case therefore allows for a discussion on how revolutionary the internationalization process should be made (link to chapter 4).

- *Competing on capabilities.* Kao believes that there are no structural competitive advantages. Its' emphasis on continual learning stems from the belief that competitive advantage comes from constantly being one step ahead in the development of new capabilities. As a consequence, the company sees its ability to learn new capabilities as its most important resource. In this light the case allows for an interesting discussion on the link between the learning organization and competing on capabilities (link to chapter 5).

- *Multi-business level strategy.* Kao's portfolio of businesses seems rather odd. On the one hand the company seems to be concentrating on a few core technologies (fatty chemicals) and core capabilities (new product development and marketing household goods). The company's move into cosmetics (Sofina) fits nicely with the notion of diversification based on the core competence perspective (Kao as a capabilities predator, link to Stalk, Evans & Shulman). On the other hand the company has a specialty chemicals and floppy disk division, with few if any links to the rest of the portfolio. It can be discussed whether this portfolio makes sense and what type of corporate management style would be needed to deal with this situation (link to chapter 6).

- *Managing cooperative relationships.* The case also describes a number of joint ventures that Kao has engaged in, as well as the tight links the company has with independent (hansha) wholesalers and storeowners. It is interesting to note how some of these relationships are symbiotic (in particular the vertical ones) while others are partly competitive and partly cooperative (especially Kao's horizontal links). Interesting questions can be discussed, such as 'Would you set up a joint venture with Kao, given their ability to learn from you?' (link to chapter 7).

- *Influence of the organizational context.* As discussed above, Dr. Maruta does not fit the traditional "command and control" mould of the strong CEO who makes the strategic plans and orders the hierarchy to carry them out. On the contrary, the company's organizational structure is flat and top management does not exercise a great amount of control over strategy development. Dr. Maruta's style closely resembles the crescive approach (link to 9.3 Bourgeois & Brodwin) and the firm seems to be relatively "chaotic" (link to chapter 9).

- *International competitiveness and global strategy.* Building on the answer to question 5, a central issue that warrants further discussion is the form of Kao's international expansion. As argued above, the physical proximity of Kao's divisions to one another might be a necessary ingredient to make a flat and informal organization work. Centralization in Japan might allow for the necessary common culture and multitude of lateral relationships to evolve, which help to make Kao a learning organization. Bartlett & Ghoshal discuss these issues further. It is also interesting to question whether Japan might be the right home base for continued innovation (link to Porter, chapter 10).

- *A sense of mission.* Kao is a company that not only has a relatively clear mission, but also seems to have a strong sense of mission. In terms of Campbell & Yeung's mission model, Kao has a well-developed strategy component in the mission (link technological excellence to an outstanding comprehension of consumer needs), but also an extensive system of values (equality, the importance of learning and open communication, co-operation). This results in a set of clear-cut behavioral standards (no secrets, biological self control, symbiotic relationships). Only the organizational purpose is not evident from the case (link to Campbell & Yeung, chapter 11).

What Happened after the Case?

In the 1998 *Business Week* Global 1000 Kao ranked no. 472 worldwide (no. 441 in 1997) and no. 46 in Japan based on a market value of $9,258 million. Total net sales grew from ¥771,270 million in 1993 to ¥901,402 million in 1997. The share of the Household Products division in total net sales declined slightly from 83.1% in 1993 to 78.2% in 1997, due to an increase in the net sales of the Chemical Products division, where a strong demand for CD-ROMs led to higher sales for Kao's Information Technology products. Within the Household Products division, the Laundry and Cleansing Products group was responsible for 39% of total sales in 1997, with Personal Care and Cosmetics following closely at 34.7% of total net sales, even though the market for personal care products was hit by tumbling prices and intensified competition.

Kao, which has a few well-known brands in Europe and the United States like Guhl, Jergens and Goldwell, is not a company that receives very much media attention in the West. The reason for this is probably that Kao has attempted no real major acquisitions in the 1990s. However, there is much to report about Kao, as it has been quite active since the case was written. Here is an overview of some of the major developments:

- *Acquisition of Bausch & Lomb's skincare business.* The only noticeable acquisition by Kao has been the purchase by the Andrew Jergens Company (a wholly owned subsidiary of Kao Corporation) of Bausch & Lomb's skincare business for $135 million in cash and the assumption of certain liabilities in May 1998. This purchase added Curel, a line of therapeutic skin lotions, and Soft Sense, a moisturizing lotion, to the existing product line. "Curel and Soft Sense complement our existing business and fit with our strategy of becoming a leading skincare company", said William J. Gentner, president and CEO of Andrew Jergens (*Chemical Market Reporter*, June 8, 1998).

- *Growth in Southeast Asia.* Over the last few years, Kao has successfully increased sales in Asia in product categories such as facial cleaners, sanitary napkins, and laundry detergents. To meet the growing demand in the South East Asian region, Kao has invested aggressively and has expanded its facilities throughout the region. New plant operations were started in China and Japan, and in 1995 Kao Vietnam was established. The largest sales increases in 1997 were achieved in Indonesia, China and Thailand. Sales outside Japan have grown from 20.9% in 1993 to 24.1% in 1997, largely due to growth in the Asian market. Kao is thus still very focused on Japan and the South East Asia region, which has made it vulnerable to the current Asian crisis.

- *New product development.* Ground breaking product development is the basis for Kao's sustained profitable growth. R&D expenditures on a consolidated basis totaled $ 353 million in 1997, which amounted to 4.5% of consolidated net sales. This R&D effort resulted in the development of the Bioré Pore Pack deep cleansing strip in May 1997, which was a huge success from the beginning. Bioré is marketed as a mid-priced family brand in Japan. In the US it is sold in a repackaged form and targeted at a younger audience, historically not Jergens' main customer group (which are mainly women of 35 and above). In Europe, the Bioré brand is sold in a tie up with the Beiersdorf's Nivea brand (Nivea Kao Bioré). The strips were patented, but soon after they were introduced rivals launched similar products (for instance, Unilever's Ponds brand has already launched its own version). Nevertheless, the Bioré innovation has been very good for overall sales (it was the best selling skincare product in the US in the beginning of 1998). Analysts estimated that the US sales (through Jergens) of the Bioré products alone would reach ¥22.5bn (US$169.1m) in 1998. Also, a range of new facial products has been added to the very successful range of strips. It is expected that these new products will be as successful as the strips for quite some time, although Kao management does not want to wait to see how long it will last, and are pursuing further innovations (*Accountancy*, October 1998).

- *Sale of information technology business.* Kao's most recent big move has been to sell off the bulk of its information technology activities in December 1998. This product group, with operations in the US, Canada, Ireland and Germany, generated sales of approximately ¥40 billion in 1997. It was sold to Zomax Optical Media, a US compact disc maker, for about US$60 million (*Financial Times*, December 4, 1998).

Kao's strategy expressed in the 1998 Annual Report was to pursue growth in profitable areas. Shareholders' expectations will be met by strengthening its position through strategies based on the following five concepts:

- *Concentrate resources on core businesses.* These are household products and chemical products. Kao wants to realize profitable growth through development of unique products, taking advantage of their capacity to pursue integrated R&D in such areas as fatty chemicals, surfactants, polymers, and biological science. Their aim is to continually reinforce the company's expertise. The approach will enable Kao to improve their capital efficiency and realize profitable growth. The selling off and rationalization of the information technology business reflects this strategic element.

- *Develop innovative products that will create new markets.* Kao's most important business field is household products, a market that has been described as mature or saturated. Despite this, Kao has found that consumers respond enthusiastically when new products are brought to the market which propose new lifestyles (for instance the Bioré Pore Pack). Kao intends to continue its pursuit of original, breakthrough products that promise to create untapped markets.

- *Increase the power of Kao brands.* Kao's numerous brands are very powerful. Many of their so-called number one brands are in the top 20 of most powerful brands in Japan in 1997. The company's R&D, marketing and sales capabilities sustain these brands. Also, Kao wants to upgrade its number two and three brands, by continuously improving existing products, adding new products to each brand lineup, and carrying out aggressive marketing strategies for key brands. Kao will also target some of these brands, particularly those in the personal care category, at world markets, developing them into global brands. These global brands will be the main pillars in their marketing strategy, designed to position Kao as market leader, starting in Asia, where the markets for Kao's key categories of products are expected to grow in the medium-to-long term. In North America and Europe, Kao will continue to market unique personal care products that have the potential to create new markets.

- *Accelerate growth through a strategic approach and develop new businesses.* Kao's determination to develop new fields of business is strong and will continue to be one of its main business strategies for the 21st century. Such areas as health care and beauty products, and specialty chemicals, appear to have the greatest potential as sources of new business, in view of the particular strengths Kao can bring to bear. Kao will accelerate operations and raise efficiency as it moves into new fields of business. A strategic approach will continue to be explored for such options as acquisitions and alliances (acquisition of Bausch & Lomb's skincare business and the tie-up with Germany's Beiersdorf for marketing and sales of Bioré Pore Pack).

- *Continue efforts to reform operations.* An ongoing company-wide effort to reduce costs, called TCR (Total Creative Revolution), has been pursued along with a drive to increase product quality. As a result of TCR efforts in all production and procurement activities in the 1999 fiscal year, cost reductions amounting to over ¥10.0 billion (US$75.7 million) were achieved. Kao will continue to carry out a campaign to reduce costs and improve efficiency in areas not directly related to production. The effect of these measures will be to raise corporate competitiveness even further.

As stated in the above strategy, Kao is looking vigorously for new markets, both product-wise and geographically. Despite the ambition to become more globally active, Kao has only been marginally successful. The US operations (especially the Andrew Jergens company) have done well and also in Europe a larger market share was realized. But still, the non-Asian operations accounted for only 18% of total sales in 1998 (opposed to the 71% of total sales for Japan and 11% of total sales for the rest of Asia and the Pacific region).

In the document 'Business Results 1999' (www.kao.co.jp), the following projections were made for the fiscal year ending March 2000:

> "Kao Corporation projects growth in operating income and ordinary income as it continues strenuous efforts, including the adoption of the newly introduced EVA management system, to improve profitability, and consequently secure greater earnings. Large growth is projected in net income mainly due to eliminating costs incurred in the withdrawal from the information technology business, and profitability in Japan is expected to increase steadily with ROE projected to be approximately 10%."

The household products will see a sluggish year, and an overall lower level of sales is expected (due to an expected stronger yen and the recession in Asia). Chemical products will see lower sales because of the withdrawal from the information technology business and a stronger yen. Operating income of the chemical products is expected to increase due to the elimination of operating losses in the information technology business. The dividend policy of the company will be based on a payout ratio to non-consolidated net income of 30%.

> "In addition to continuing efforts to maintain steady dividends, Kao will endeavor to conduct management activities that increase real corporate value from a shareholders' viewpoint by utilizing the newly introduced EVA management system. The company intends to apply its internal reserves to fund demands anticipated in the areas of future development of global business, expansion of the company's business areas, investment in rationalization and the strengthening of current businesses."

EXHIBIT 1

Five Year Financial Summary, in billions of yen
(Source: Annual Report Kao Corporation 1998 and Business Results 1999)

	1999	1998	1997	1996	1995	1994
Net sales						
Household	731.2	696.8	705.3	675.9	653.5	642.6
Chemicals	193.3	210.5	196.1	159.7	143.2	131.3
Total	924.5	907.2	901.4	835.6	796.7	773.9
Japan		662.2	684.3	661.9	641.7	627.3
Outside Japan		245.0	217.1	173.7	155.0	146.6
Operating income	91.6	73.1	72.3	66.7	62.1	61.9
Net income	34.7	24.5	27.6	24.5	23.7	22.2
Capital expenditures	69.0	59.0	65.3	79.3	72.2	78.1
Depreciation and amortization	71.2	81.4	73.6	70.6	73.6	71.5
R&D expenditures		37.8	37.9	37.5	40.0	37.0
Advertising expenditures		65.4	61.0	58.6	55.6	56.1
At year-end						
Total assets	751.7	778.8	807.1	756.8	709.3	714.8
Total shareholders' equity	451.7	424.4	379.6	359.8	342.0	324.4
Per share (Yen)						
Net income	55.98	40.10	45.92	40.85	39.49	37.02
Cash dividends	16.00	15.00	14.00	12.50	11.50	10.50

Note: Years ended March 31

EXHIBIT 2

Financial Overview of Previous Year's Results
(Source: Business Results Kao Corporation 1999)

	Billions of ¥		Change %	Millions of US$
	1999	1998		1999
Net sales	924.5	907.2	1.9	7,669.8
Net income	34.7	24.4	41.7	288.0
End of year:				
Total assets	751.7	778.7	-3.5	6,235.8
Total shareholder's equity	451.7	424.4	6.4	3,747.6
Per share:	¥			US$
Income	55.98	40.10	39.6	0.46
Cash dividends	16.00	15.00	6.7	0.13

Note: Year ended on March 31st

TEACHING NOTE 7: CARL ZEISS JENA

Case by Manfred Kets de Vries and Marc Cannizzo

Teaching note by Bob de Wit, Ron Meyer and Melbert Visscher

Case Synopsis

This case describes a turbulent and almost catastrophic episode in the history of Carl Zeiss Jena from the fall of the Berlin Wall at the end of 1989 until the formal launching of Zeiss Jena and Jenoptik as separate legal entities on 1 October 1991. Dr. Jörg Dierolf was the first West German executive to arrive in East German Jena to supervise the challenging and historic restructuring of this world-famous precision optical instrument producer.

Carl Zeiss Jena, which was established in 1846 by Carl Zeiss, has a history that is characterized by turbulence and discontinuity. In the aftermath of the Second World War the company in Jena had to be rebuilt from scratch after American evacuations and Soviet dismantling. Under East German Communist rule the Carl Zeiss Jena 'people's-own enterprise' was placed at the center of an industrial combine (Kombinat) which integrated the optical and mechanical precision instruments sectors of the economy and became the flagship enterprise of the German Democratic Republic.

In the sixteen months after the fall of the Berlin Wall the situation at Carl Zeiss Jena changed from autocracy to near-anarchy. The company had to be converted from a highly bureaucratic, highly overrated and highly centralized company into an able competitor in the Western market economy. Initial reorganizations were hampered by cultural and political legacies from the Communist era. Moreover, social unrest and demotivation were sparked by the thousands of layoffs that were necessary. After eighteen months of negotiations an agreement was reached between the government privatization agency, Treuhand, the former West-German Carl Zeiss Oberkochen and the State of Thüringen to restructure the Jena company with the help of Western management. This eventually led to the separation of the company into two legal entities on 1 October 1991, Zeiss Jena and Jenoptik.

Teaching Objectives

If used in conjunction with chapter 4 this case can be used to meet the following teaching objectives:

- *Understanding environmental discontinuities as an impetus for strategic change.* This case describes the dramatic collapse of the East German command economy and the impact it had on Carl Zeiss Jena. This allows for a broad discussion on the effect of external discontinuities on organizations and the difficulties companies have responding to such sudden shifts (link to introduction, 4.3 Tushman, Newman & Romanelli, and 4.5 Strebel).

- *Understanding the sources of organizational inertia.* Carl Zeiss Jena suffers from a wide range of structural sources of inertia. Not only is the firm bureaucratic and lacking basic marketing and management skills, but the company is also constrained by social and political considerations. The case can therefore be used to understand the variety of barriers to change and to illustrate how deeply engrained they often can be (link to 4.3 Tushman, Newman & Romanelli, 4.5 Strebel, and 9.5 Rumelt).

- *Understanding the pace, magnitude, levels and spheres of strategic change.* The case gives a detailed account of the most important changes throughout the company. This allows for an analysis of the pace and magnitude of the changes, and for an understanding of the various levels and spheres of change (link to introduction).

- *Discussion on the advantages and disadvantages of evolution and revolution.* The case describes how Carl Zeiss Jena goes through a relatively revolutionary change process and how its successor Jenoptik must now decide how revolutionary it wants/needs to be to proceed (link to all readings).

- *Discussion on the possibility of creating continually learning organizations.* It is clear that Carl Zeiss Jena's predicament was at least partially due to its own lack of learning ability. Proponents of the continuous change perspective would therefore advocate building up the company's ability to continually learn and renew itself. The question is whether this is truly possible (link to all readings).

Teaching Guideline

Some students might at first believe that a case focusing on such a once in a lifetime event as the reunification of Germany is not particularly representative for the type of strategic change situations that they will be facing. However, we like to point out to them that while this particular 'discontinuous' change might be unique, discontinuous changes occur in many different forms on many different occasions. For instance, the political discontinuity confronting Carl Zeiss Jena is encountered by many companies in countries with rapidly shifting political landscapes. But even in 'politically stable' nations, governments can often radically change the rules of the game, for example by deregulation and privatization. Furthermore, companies may encounter economic discontinuities (e.g. the South East Asian economic crisis), technological discontinuities (e.g. the Internet), competitive discontinuities (e.g. a sudden new market entrant), etc. One way to make this point is to start off the discussion with the question whether students believe that this case is unique and whether they can think of recent examples of companies also confronted with sudden environmental shifts.

When starting on the case it is often useful to reiterate the general structure before 1989 (Zeiss Oberkochen and Zeiss Jena as two separate companies) and as of October 1991 (Carl Zeiss Oberkochen with a subsidiary in Jena and Jenoptik as 'rump' organization). While a part of the analysis will follow the entire change process involving both companies, the final questions to which Dr. Dierolf seeks an answer focus on his company, Jenoptik.

Case Questions

1. Describe the change path of Carl Zeiss Jena from 1989 to 1991. Judging by the magnitude and pace, how would you characterize the strategic change process at the company?

2. What do you consider the major barriers to change faced by Carl Zeiss Jena's management during the period from 1989 to 1991?

3. What do you consider to be the main strengths and weaknesses of the strategic change process up to October 1991? What would you have done differently?

4. How revolutionary would be your approach to further strategic change if you were in Dr. Dierolf's shoes in October 1991? What would be the advantages and disadvantages of your approach?

5. What would you need to do to transform Jenoptik into a learning organization? Explain.

Case Analysis

1. *Describe the change path of Carl Zeiss Jena from 1989 to 1991. Judging by the magnitude and pace, how would you characterize the strategic change process at the company?*

At the end of 1989 Carl Zeiss Jena was faced with a strong change force that required the company to respond. As the change force could not be rolled back and the available time was limited, the only possible change path according to Strebel was restructuring. This relatively revolutionary approach corresponds with the magnitude of the external changes encountered (broad scope and high amplitude). Comprehensive action on all eight fronts described by Mintzberg and Westley (table 4.2) was deemed necessary to save the company from bankruptcy. However, although quite revolutionary, the strategic change process at Carl Zeiss Jena did allow for ample consideration of the interests of the employees and much of the company was 'salvaged from the wreckage' in such a way that its fundamental character was left in tact. The ultimate revolutionary change under such circumstances – scrap and rebuild – was purposefully not chosen.

The organization was given a sharp shock at the end of 1989, but the shock waves reverberated throughout the company until well into 1991. The initial response of the East German managers was one of trying to gradually cope with the radically changed environment. Gattnar spent most of his time managing political and social tensions, which prevented him from involving himself with the operations of the company. Initial reorganization plans had hardly been implemented due to the chaotic situation in and around the company. According to Gattnar "we were always rushing from one crisis to another".

After the restructuring agreement had been reached following 18 months of negotiations, the decisions started to succeed each other more rapidly. Among the Western executives brought in was Dr. Jörg Dierolf, who had quite a reputation as a turnaround specialist. The change force was tackled by laying off excess workers, dividing the assets into two legally separate entities (Jenoptik, which was to remain independent, and Zeiss Jena, which was to be acquired by Carl Zeiss Oberkochen) and implementing the delayed product divisional structure. According to Strebel the scope of discontinuous change is usually highly focused on organizational structures and systems to facilitate control of the transition and limit the possibility of disintegration. This focus on structure and systems means that the reorganizations mainly affected the two middle levels of the state of the organization as depicted in table 4.2 by Mintzberg and Waters. During the division of the assets of Zeiss Jena local managers complained that "meetings are occupied with the present problems, rather than future strategic activities". This indicates that there was a lack of attention for the direction of the company, especially for Jenoptik. Zeiss Jena was to be focused on its core business, but Jenoptik still had many problems to overcome.

If this is placed in the restructuring path depicted by Strebel it becomes clear that the streamlining measures executed by the Western executives were directed at tackling the change force and decreasing its impact. Resistance factors such as rigid structures were addressed, but attention had yet to be given to the company's direction in order to adjust employees to their new environment. This means the restructuring process had reached its half way point in 1991.

2. *What do you consider the major barriers to change faced by Carl Zeiss Jena's management during the period from 1989 to 1991?*

Of course, many (sub) categories of barriers can be identified here. However, the following can be identified as major barriers to change in this particular case (link to 4.5 Strebel and 4.3 Tushman et al):

▪ *Rigid structures and systems.* As a 'people's-own enterprise' (VEB) Carl Zeiss Jena's structure had been purely based on the set up of the production facilities since the priority was on manufacturing. The introduction of a product division structure proved to be a very difficult step, worsened by the fact that every production facility had a separate union. Moreover, the organization chart seemed to be designed to avoid responsibility. Furthermore, administrative systems proved to be inaccurate and systems for product costing were non-existent.

- *Closed mindsets reflecting business beliefs and strategies that are oblivious to the forces of change.* Many local managers who worked closely with Western executives were astounded to find out how overrated their impression of the competitive value of Carl Zeiss Jena proved to be in the market economy. At the end of 1989 it had been expected that if there were one company that had to be able to compete in a market economy, it would be the GDR's flagship Kombinat. However, the attitude at Carl Zeiss Jena was entirely production oriented, with little emphasis on factors such as cost, speed and market suitability.

- *Entrenched cultures and organizational history.* Carl Zeiss Jena inherited two strong cultural legacies. On the one hand, there was a strong Zeiss culture that had produced the overrated view employees had of the company. On the other hand, communist propaganda had created a false sense of economic security in East Germany. As these two elements of tradition had been intertwined over the last 45 years, it would prove difficult to filter out the elements that could hamper change, in order to retain the healthy loyalty that employees felt for the company.

- *Social and political arena.* With the end of Communist rule came the call for the removal of managers who had collaborated with the old regime. Gattnar stated that to simply remove all the managers would be impossible due to the fact that most of the knowledge about the company was in the heads of these managers. Removal would mean undermining the existence of the company. Furthermore, the thousands of layoffs that were necessary caused tremendous social unrest that almost stifled operations in many instances. This matter had to be dealt with very delicately in order to find an economically and socially acceptable solution for all parties. The State of Thüringen was involved in order to facilitate the reaching of such a solution.

- *Individual resistance to change.* When frame-breaking change is implemented slowly the individual resistance to change grows due to increased uncertainty. This led to an increased demotivation, especially since many employees had high expectations about the reunification. The fact that their company proved to be overrated brought people very close to the naked truth. The adaptation to the market economy involved a significant individual transformation as well. It was not uncommon for people to want to go back to the old days of stability.

3. *What do you consider to be the main strengths and weaknesses of the strategic change process up to October 1991? What would you have done differently?*

Students can think of many different answers here, but the following list covers the main strengths and weaknesses that can be identified:

Main strengths:

- Attempt to minimize (social effects of) layoffs
- Deployment of Western managerial help and consultants
- Tripartite involvement (Treuhand, state of Thüringen and Zeiss Oberkochen)
- Legal separation of Zeiss Jena to focus on core business
- Freedom of division heads to select their own subordinates

Main weaknesses:

- Lack of accurate, up-to-date information for employees
- No evident vision of future activities by leaders

- Long decision making time to reach reorganization agreement
- Delays in implementing product divisional structure
- Predominantly short-term orientation

In general, what students see as strengths and weaknesses will depend on whether they prefer revolution or evolution. Some students might have preferred a more revolutionary approach, by dismantling the company and selling off bits to more commercially viable companies (maybe including management buy-outs). Others might have their doubts whether it all had to go this fast and might wonder whether a longer period of transition would have given the former-East German managers more time to learn the necessary skills to save more of their company (and more jobs).

These different points of view will lead to many possible answers as to what could have been done differently. Some issues that might be discussed include:

- *Shared vision vs. short-term orientation.* A point of major strategic importance is the question whether the Western executives should have started to build a shared vision within the company. Some might argue that this was necessary since employees complained about the focus on short-term activities. Others might argue that short-term orientation is inherent to the turnaround process.

- *Provision of information and worker participation.* Uncertainty had increased and rumors were sparked by the lack of employee information. Employees were also largely left out of the turnaround process, although it was intended to be to their benefit. Some might argue that it would have been better to play a more open hand, by informing and involving employees in the decision-making process. However, others might argue that this would have made the process even more political and volatile.

- *Speed of decision-making and implementation.* It can be discussed whether the decision making process concerning the reorganization could have been speeded up or slowed down. Some might argue that state-initiated 'emergency surgery' would have been better – short term pain for long term gain. A quicker reorganization might have cost less, and might have led to a more rapid recovery. Others might argue that given more time and government backing, managers at Carl Zeiss Jena could have obtained the necessary skills to turnaround the entire company without dismemberment.

4. *How revolutionary would be your approach to further strategic change if you were in Dr. Dierolf's shoes in October 1991? What would be the advantages and disadvantages of your approach?*

Basically two generic options can be discussed here: Bold restructuring and gradual revitalization:

- *Bold restructuring.* This means continued revolutionary change. As Jenoptik still faces many problems with a high priority, the company should push forward and further transform itself. On the 'direction' side of the equation, Jenoptik should quit unpromising product lines, and focus its energy and scarce resources on a few areas where a profitable future seems likely. On the 'state' side of the organization, this would entail further cuts in personnel, further restructuring of activities, a total reorientation of the culture from 'broad line' to 'niche player', and a reengineering of the entire value chain within the company. Furthermore, investors have to be found and joint ventures and cooperation agreements have to be formed. This top-down redesign approach would have the major advantage that energy and resources would only flow to activities with a future and that profitability could be quickly established. Moreover, the company's market position and reputation could quickly be salvaged, before too much damage had been done. The downside is that the forces of change might overwhelm the company and lead to insurmountable management problems – the company might be biting off more than it can chew. The managers' and employees' ability to change might be over taxed, leading to stress, chaos, and more (hidden) resistance to change. Also, it might be difficult at this stage to determine the best strategy and structure for the future. Room might be needed for experimentation and incremental strategy development.

- *Gradual revitalization.* Dr. Jörg Dierolf can also opt for a more evolutionary approach. Almost two years of turbulent change have had a tremendous impact on Jenoptik's employees. It must not be forgotten that the employees' personal lives have also been strongly affected by the fall of the Berlin Wall. Instead of continuing the revolutionary change and risking fatigue and resistance to change, Dierolf could choose for a path of medium paced continuous adaptation. He could try to stem the bleeding by reorganizing or divesting the worst cases, but allow for other product divisions to reform themselves. After all, growth requires a plough, not a sword – axing products is easy, but getting the product divisions to proactively put forward new strategies requires more skills. Dierolf must create an environment in which managers learn and develop their abilities, and this might require some measure of stability. However, the time needs to be available to allow for this gradual approach. As Paul Strebel puts it: "Revitalization can only be implemented if the firm can protect itself from the negative effects of the change force long enough to accomplish the necessary cultural turning point." Continuous change is thus more long-term oriented than revolutionary change. Jenoptik seems to be ready for a more long-term approach now that the legal separation has become a fact and the most radical changes are in the past.

5. *What would you need to do to transform Jenoptik into a learning organization? Explain.*

Students can come up with a number of possible courses of action. First it might be useful for students to sum up the main characteristics of the situation in October 1991, before reflecting on possible courses of action.

Situation in October 1991. Carl Zeiss Jena had been a highly centrally controlled company during the 45 years of Communist rule. The Biermann era had been a one-man show, based on hierarchy and 'carrot and stick' control. This had left a lasting impression on the employees that they were little more than cogs in the machine. Gattnar experienced the inertia of the socialist management culture when he made his first attempts to decentralize. The traditional approach of centralized control by Zeiss' management thus stood in sheer contrast with the views of the proponents of the learning perspective.

While Gattnar and his colleagues tried to adapt the organization to a market economy, the high levels of resistance in the organization and the constantly emerging crises forced management to adopt a short-term, problem-solving approach. When Gattnar's position had become precarious, the first Western executives arrived in Jena, but they too adopted a problem-solving approach. As soon as they arrived, Dierolf and Späth were also focussed on short-term survival, with little time to spare for developing organizational learning abilities. Dierolf and Späth learnt for the organization and then implemented their decisions top-down.

Courses of action. When looking at possible courses of action to be taken it becomes clear that building a learning organization requires systematic effort on a number of fronts so that learning is supported throughout the company. Three issues can be discussed in this respect:

- *Type of leadership.* One of the keys to continuous learning is motivation that must be facilitated by the leaders in organizations. The West German executives who were brought in were turnaround specialists, primarily focused on the short-term. If turnaround is seen in the light of the discontinuous change perspective, the short-term focus of these executives can be explained. After all, frame-breaking change must not take too long in order to avoid resistance to change.

The question then arises whether the managers who are good at turning around the company, should also be in charge of further developing the company and teaching it to learn.

- *Organizational systems*. From the description of the October 1991 situation it becomes clear that the focus of Jenoptik was clearly on 'short-term events', not on 'long-term processes'. This is not surprising since the dust had not settled yet after the fall of the Berlin Wall. But learning is a long-term process and requires a long-term approach. To create a learning organization, Jenoptik will need to institute the organizational structures and systems that encourage people to participate, share information and ideas, and remain open to new ideas. Important elements include the strategy formation system (are employees encouraged to participate in strategy development?) and the human resource management system (how are employees selected, encouraged and rewarded?).

- *Attitude of employees*. In learning organizations elements such as structure, systems and leadership reinforce a culture characterized by openness, curiosity, initiative and tolerance. However, the employees need to accept the system and be able to operate in such an environment. Creating the right conditions for a learning culture thus involves a great deal of anticipation with regard to the employees' perception of the organization and their attitude towards learning. Changing people's attitude is not a question of days or weeks. Especially in countries and organizations where people have long been discouraged from questioning, doubting, experimenting, daring, debating and taking action, it is extremely difficult to break through established attitudes. On a positive note, Michael Hiller did notice that the people at Jena were good problem-solvers in a day-to-day tactical sense and most employees had already understood that change was necessary. However, in his opinion they would need coaching to develop longer-term, strategic thinking, which lay outside their previous experience. It must also be doubted whether all employees would be able to adopt a more open learning mentality. Therefore, the question is with which segment of the employees the creation of a learning organization would be possible.

Other Teaching Issues

A number of issues raised in this case are also relevant to other chapters of the book. These other teaching issues are:

- *Strategy formation*. In November 1989 Klaus-Dieter Gattnar, deputy general manager and future successor to Biermann, and his colleagues had started talking about contingency plans to be able to anticipate the adaptation to the market economy. Advocates of the planning perspective stress the advantages of planning - direction, formalization and long-term thinking. Incrementalists would point out that the planner's faith in deliberateness is misplaced and counterproductive. The sheer complexity and magnitude of the changes Carl Zeiss Jena faced, raises the question to what extent planning (if at all) is possible under such conditions (link to all readings in chapter 3).

- *Organizational leadership vs. organizational dynamics*. It became clear in the Zeiss case that traditions and culture played a significant role in the reorganization process. Opinions differ as to what extent organizational inheritance predetermines an organization's future path or as to what extent managers can show initiative to intervene in organizational processes (link to introduction chapter 9). Three readings in chapter 9 will help clarify the sources of inertia that hinder leaders to shape their organizations at will (link to 9.2 Stacey, 9.4 Johnson and 9.5 Rumelt).

- *Organizational purpose*. Carl Zeiss Oberkochen and Carl Zeiss Jena were clearly based on two different conceptions of organizational purpose. This case allows for a discussion on what the responsibilities of the corporation should be, and how this can be at odds with the corporation's need to be profitable (link to chapter 11).

What Happened after the Case?

After October 1991 the legal separation of Carl Zeiss Jena had become a fact. Therefore the companies' developments since 1991 time have to be viewed separately.

Carl Zeiss Jena GmbH.

1995   Carl Zeiss Oberkochen acquires the shares held by Jenoptik GmbH (then company of the state of Thüringen) in Carl Zeiss Jena GmbH.

1996   The enterprise Carl Zeiss celebrates its 150th birthday.

The headquarters of the Carl Zeiss Group and the company Carl Zeiss, which controls and coordinates global activities, is Oberkochen. The majority of the company's business groups are managed from here: Consumer Optics, Medical Systems, Opto-Electronic Systems, Semiconductor Technology and Industrial Metrology. Jena is the second core location of the Carl Zeiss Group and is responsible for Microscopy and Opto-Electronic Systems.

Jenoptik GmbH.

The most important developments since October 1991 of Jenoptik GmbH are depicted here in chronological order:

1994   January 1. Jenoptik GmbH is transformed into a holding company. Jenoptik Technology GmbH is founded and takes over the operative business in the fields of automation   and medical engineering, micro fabrication and special purpose technology.

   October 1. Meissner + Wurst is taken over by Jenoptik GmbH.

1995   July 1. From Jenoptik Technology GmbH three new companies emerge: Jenoptik Automatisierungstechnik GmbH, Jenoptik Laser/Optik/Systeme and Jenoptik Infab.

1996   January 1. Jenoptik is organized as a joint stock corporation.

   April 18. Majority interest is acquired in the telecom company Krone AG of Berlin.

   October 1. A new shareholder structure is introduced for Jenoptik AG (Aktiengesellschaft). Institutional investors and private investors own 50% plus one share, while the former 100% owner, the State of Thüringen, owns the rest of the stock.

1997   December 12. Jenoptik AG takes over ESW-Extel Systems Wedel.

1998   June 16. Jenoptik AG shares are listed for the first time on the Frankfurt stock exchange.

Jenoptik has grown dramatically since 1991 and a successful technology group has emerged with global operations. Earnings for the fiscal year 1997 amounted to DM 2,609 million, which meant that earnings more than doubled for the year. Dr. Lothar Späth is still with Jenoptik, currently as chairman. Jenoptik AG now has the following three business divisions with the division's major companies depicted in brackets:

- Clean Systems Technologies (Meissner + Wurst, Jenoptik Infab, and Zander)
- Telecommunication Technologies (Krone, Meissener Nachrichtentechnik, and ElkoPlus)
- Photonics Technologies (Jenoptik Laser/Optik/Systeme, Extel Systems Wedel (ESW), Jenoptik Automatisierungstechnik).

TEACHING NOTE 8: ENCYCLOPAEDIA BRITANNICA

Case by Jeffrey Rayport and Thomas Gerace

Teaching note by Bob de Wit, Ron Meyer and Melbert Visscher

Case Synopsis

This case describes how drastic technological developments have significantly altered Encyclopaedia Britannica's business environment and how the company has reacted to these changes. Since its foundation in 1768, the Encyclopaedia Britannica has grown to become the flagship of general reference books. For more than two centuries, the expensive print versions of the oldest English language encyclopaedia enjoyed an enviable position among reference works. Since 1964 the Encyclopaedia Britannica has also expanded its reach around the world by publishing the encyclopaedia in several languages. In 1990 the company seemed to be running better than ever.

However, in the following years Encyclopaedia Britannica was forced to make a significant transition from its historical past. The digital age had boosted electronic publishing, which had led to erosion of the sales of printed reference works. Searchable CD-ROMs, which included sound, video and graphics besides the text, started to replace printed reference works. Although Encyclopaedia Britannica had already entered the digital arena in the 1980s and had launched Compton's Multimedia Encyclopaedia in 1989 and a CD-ROM version (without multimedia) of the Encyclopaedia Britannica in 1994, the company did not seem to be able to cope with the radically altered business landscape. Competition, from among others Microsoft's Encarta, was fierce and Britannica management believed that CD-ROM was just an 'interim technology'. With the tremendous growth of the Internet around the corner, the ailing Encyclopaedia Britannica faced an uncertain future.

Teaching Objectives

If used in conjunction with chapter 4, this case can be used to meet the following teaching objectives:

- *Understanding that a company's past often has major implications for the company's ability to change its strategy.* This case makes a clear distinction between the 'paper age' and the 'digital age' strategy of Encyclopaedia Britannica. The difficulties encountered by the company in this transition make clear how difficult it is to break away from the organization's heritage. Shaking off its old habits and beliefs, and changing its structure, systems, skills, and strategy is visibly difficult for Encyclopaedia Britannica – and the organization's past always influences it's future to some degree (link to 4.1 Hammer, 4.3 Tushman, Newman & Romanelli and 4.5 Strebel).

- *Understanding environmental discontinuities as an impetus for strategic change.* In this case Encyclopaedia Britannica is faced with major technological changes which undermine the company's competitiveness. This allows for a broad discussion on the effects of external discontinuities on organizations and the difficulties these companies have in responding to such sudden shifts (link to introduction, 4.3 Tushman, Newman & Romanelli, and 4.5 Strebel).

- *Discussion on the possibility of forecasting and anticipating the magnitude, pace, levels and spheres of strategic change.* The occurrence of discontinuous change often leads to questions concerning the predictability of such events. Even if the occurrence of certain events can be expected, it is still very difficult to estimate the impact of these events on the company's operations (link to introduction).

- *Discussion on the revolutionary or evolutionary nature of strategic change processes.* Advocates of the continuous change perspective would stress the gradual and long-term nature of continuous change. Proponents of the discontinuous change perspective would deny the fact that organizations develop gradually. The advantages and disadvantages of each perspective can be compared and used to propose possible courses of action for Encyclopaedia Britannica (link to all readings).

Teaching Guideline

For students this case is an excellent example of the impact that the 'digital age' can have on companies' strategy and operations. As a provider of information through 'paper' general reference works, Encyclopaedia Britannica has been especially sensitive to the drastic changes in the field of information technology. To get an impression of how representative this case is, we often start class discussion by asking students how many other industries will be transformed by digitalization in general, and the internet in particular. We subsequently ask students to think of other technological discontinuities they know of that have shocked industry incumbents (e.g. mini-mill technology in the steel industry, biotechnology in the pharmaceutical industry). Then we ask them to identify examples of non-technological discontinuities, such as:

- political discontinuities (e.g. the impact of political changes in Russia and South Africa on the diamond industry, and deregulation on the telecommunication industry);
- economic discontinuities (e.g. the impact of the Asia crisis on the banking industry, and shifts in the dollar exchange rate on the airplane industry);
- social discontinuities (e.g. the impact of health scares on the food industry, and of fashion trends on the clothing industry).

The intention of this short exercise is to make clear that external discontinuities are not exceptional events, but that they happen quite often, and therefore warrant our attention.

In tackling this case, it has been our experience that it is very useful to analyze Encyclopaedia Britannica's strategy in the 'paper age' first, before turning to the point of discontinuous change. This gives students a better appreciation of the magnitude and scope of the strategic change involved in dealing with the technological discontinuity. After analysis of the discontinuous change we challenge students to advise Encyclopaedia Britannica on what next step to take. It is usually hardly necessary to hint that the dramatic growth of the Internet requires Encyclopaedia Britannica's utmost attention. This provides for an excellent link with the section "What Happened after the Case?".

Case Questions

1. Describe Encyclopaedia Britannica's strategy in the 'paper age'. Why do you think that the company was so successful until the end of the 1980s?

2. How did the introduction of CD-ROM and on-line services affect the encyclopaedia industry and what impact did this have on Encyclopaedia Britannica's traditional competitive advantage?

3. How did Encyclopaedia Britannica react to the rapid shifts in its environment? Why did the company behave as it did?

4. Are you in favor of a more revolutionary or a more evolutionary approach to further change at Encyclopaedia Britannica?

5. What strategy would you advise Encyclopaedia Britannica's management to follow? How can the company reform and reposition itself to survive in the 'digital age'?

Case Analysis

1. Describe Encyclopaedia Britannica's strategy in the 'paper age'. Why do you think that the company was so successful until the end of the 1980s?

Encyclopaedia Britannica's approach to the market can be summarized by highlighting four key elements that are described in the case:

- *Direct sales method.* At the beginning of the twentieth century, Britannica came into American hands. An inexpensive Britannica version was sold via mail order, while a home sales force was established to sell the encyclopaedias door-to-door, following a trend in the United States. It was the direct sales method that expanded the market in the years leading up to the Second World War. In the 1980s, Britannica continued the direct sales method by leasing space in bookstores and placing an employee in the store to promote sales. Mailing lists were often bought from those bookstores in order to send direct mailings to the bookstore's customers.

- *Product format.* The novelty of the first Britannica edition was the mixing of long essays on important subjects with short entries for technical terms and other subjects. After the third edition Britannica started to use original contributions of respected British and French scholars instead of using independent sources. These product characteristics made Britannica renowned for its high quality encyclopaedia and subsequently made the name Encyclopaedia Britannica equivalent with knowledge. This would prove to be an important asset of Britannica in the 1990s.

- *Product range.* In the 1960s, Encyclopaedia Britannica acquired Compton's Pictured Encyclopaedia and the G&C Merriam Company, which owned Webster's Dictionary. Compton's Encyclopaedia was positioned in the market as a less expensive alternative to Britannica, attracting many student users. Compton's had a tradition of using text and graphics on the same page. These acquisitions appear to have been complementary to Britannica's operations.

- *International scope.* Although Encyclopaedia Britannica was also used outside English speaking markets, sales were limited due to the language barrier. After 1964, however, the Encyclopaedia Britannica was published in many foreign languages, including Portuguese, French, Spanish, Italian, Chinese, Hungarian and Russian. The content of the foreign language encyclopaedias was usually adapted to country specific interests. Britannica used the arrangement of co-production to expand internationally. In the 1990s, Britannica experienced a downside to its international expansion - the company was confronted with problems regarding international protection of its intellectual property.

Hence, it can be concluded that Encyclopaedia Britannica had built up a considerable competitive advantage based on the following factors:

- *Distribution.* Encyclopaedia Britannica had an excellent door-to-door sales force, skilled at selling a non-essential, high priced item as an investment.

- *Brand name.* Encyclopaedia Britannica had a very strong brand name, associated with high quality, accuracy, and completeness.

- *Economies of scale.* Encyclopaedia Britannica had been able to offset the extremely high fixed cost of continuously updating its products by achieving a high market share and by reusing its texts in translated versions in other countries.

2. How did the introduction of CD-ROM and on-line services affect the encyclopaedia industry and what impact did this have on Encyclopaedia Britannica's traditional competitive advantage?

The direct effect of the 'digital revolution' was that Encyclopaedia Britannica's environment changed in the following way:

- *New, unconventional competitors.* Britannica suddenly faced new competitors striving to fill the same customer need for 'reference works'. These new competitors were from the field of software development and on-line services.

- *Rapid drop in demand.* Widespread electronic availability of information cut deeply into people's need to consult or buy a printed encyclopaedia. For an investment comparable to the price of an encyclopaedia, consumers could purchase a personal computer and CD-ROMs. This caused a sharp decline in sales.

The result was a plunge in revenues and significant losses during the period 1990-1992. As for Encyclopaedia Britannica's competitive advantage, this evaporated quite rapidly during this period. Actually, most of the factors that had been competitive advantages in the past, had become disadvantages in the 'digital world':

- *Expensive distribution network.* Britannica's door-to-door sales network was well suited to high-priced, high-margin printed encyclopaedias, but entirely unsuitable for cheaper CD-ROM products. However, Britannica was stuck with its distribution network, while it also had no experience in marketing via the retail channel.

- *Expensive production system.* Britannica's high quality standards and comprehensiveness had led its encyclopaedias to be very expensive. The new CD-ROMs made use of cheaper archive material and aimed at significantly higher sales volumes to earn back the fixed costs.

- *Established brand name.* Britannica had a 200-year tradition and benefited from the authority that this long pedigree brought with it. This made managers at Britannica somewhat wary about experimentation and pioneering initiatives.

3. *How did Encyclopaedia Britannica react to the rapid shifts in its environment? Why did the company behave as it did?*

Encyclopaedia Britannica started building its electronic presence at the beginning of the 1980s through a combination of licensing agreements and acquisitions. Through acquisitions Britannica increased its commitment to electronic publishing and improved its organizational skill base. In March 1989, Encyclopaedia Britannica and ESC announced Compton's Multimedia Encyclopaedia (CMME). The addition of color, sound and animation proved a radical change from the print version. The CD's search capabilities and its organization proved to be its greatest innovations. The product proved very successful and Compton's New Media division was counting on an explosive growth of the CD-ROM encyclopaedia market.

Judging from these efforts, the Encyclopaedia Britannica organization seemed to be following the changes in the field of electronic publishing very well until the beginning of the 1990s. Especially the Compton's New Media division seemed to be geared towards the rapidly growing market for electronic encyclopaedias and other educational applications. However, the first years of 1990s were profitless for Britannica. Sales plummeted and Britannica suddenly faced competitors from totally different backgrounds, like Microsoft that launched Encarta. Britannica responded with the following measures:

- *Adaptation at the periphery.* Britannica's management initially judged that CD-ROM was only an 'interim technology,' and therefore they had an argument not to swiftly reform Britannica's core business. Instead, Britannica's management decided to use the Compton division for product innovation purposes. Unfortunately, by not quickly shifting to the CD-ROM technology, Britannica slipped into a negative spiral. The slow adaptation led to sharp declines in revenues and profitability, which eventually meant that by the mid-1990s Britannica had no capital to invest in new product development any more.

- *Sale of Compton's New Media.* In 1993, Encyclopaedia Britannica sold its successful and innovative subsidiary Compton's New Media. While selling Compton's New Media brought in some desperately needed cash after three profitless years, it also indicated that Britannica had little idea of the competencies it would need to survive in the 'digital world'. Selling this company decreased Britannica's chances of learning from Compton's New Media with regard to the electronic publishing business.

- *Too little, too late.* When in 1994 Encyclopaedia Britannica did finally market a CD-ROM product, it did not include multimedia, while competitors' products did. Furthermore, Britannica's products were a lot more expensive than the competition.

In short, Encyclopaedia Britannica followed a slow and gradual adaptation path, while the environmental change was severely discontinuous. Furthermore, Britannica's change trajectory seems to be reactive and opportunistic, as opposed to proactive and visionary, as the sale of Compton's New Media suggests. Some hypotheses to explain this behavior could be the following:

- *The failure of success.* Britannica had a long, proud and successful history. The company had been the market leader for as long as most people at the company could remember, and there was a shared understanding (paradigm) within the firm explaining the causes of this success. Britannica's management implicitly believed that they understood the 'rules of the game,' and were superior players. Hence, the company's past success became the seed of its eventual downfall. Tushman, Newman & Romanelli argue that "a proud history often restricts vigilant problem solving and may be a source of resistance to change. When faced with environmental threat, organizations with strong momentum may not register the threat or may respond by heightened conformity to the status quo and/or increased commitment to 'what we do best'."

- *The competence trap.* Britannica might not have only become caught up in its past successes (and related cognitive maps), but also in its past competencies. As Britannica had developed an excellence in producing and distributing high quality printed encyclopaedias, this had become engrained in the organization's routines, procedures, systems, structure and culture. Moreover, for decades the organization had hired, retained and promoted people who had exhibited exceptional talents in these areas. The competencies need to produce and market electronic encyclopaedias did not neatly fit with the current organizational profile and therefore were very difficult to introduce.

- *Internal politics.* Another important factor may have been the significant internal political ramifications that every strategic change carries with it. A major change, like a switch to CD-ROM technology, would greatly improve the interests and career opportunities of the Compton people within the Britannica hierarchy. It can be assumed that many employees whose skills would be less valued in the 'digital world' were probably heavily in favor of a cautious and gradual exploration of the CD-ROM technology.

- *Risk aversion.* Even when top management does not filter out external signals that the environmental changes are revolutionary, this does not mean that decision makers are willing to make high risk revolutionary changes within the organization. They may prefer to wait 'until the dust has settled,' arguing that it is often better to be an early follower than a risk-taking pioneer. This is clearly the position of Encyclopaedia Britannica's management, who wanted to see which technology would finally prevail. Britannica's management also preferred to spread its risks by placing a low profile 'side bet' on CD-ROM technology via its Compton's division. Remaining flexible and slowly increasing commitment as the developments in the environment become more clear can be a wise policy – but it can also leave you hopelessly behind if you are the only one not taking the risk.

4. *Are you in favor of a more revolutionary or a more evolutionary approach to further change at Encyclopaedia Britannica?*

A Britannica press release of April 1995 stated: "Technology and the Information Age have radically transformed our landscape and will require our company to make a significant transition from our historical past. To continue to grow and develop our business, we must reinvest. Our goal is to preserve Encyclopaedia Britannica as an institution and to continue to develop new products and explore alternative sales channels." When environments change as sharply as they did for Britannica, frame-breaking change can not be avoided. Discontinuous environmental change usually requires major shifts throughout the entire organization. However, the longer a company waits to make these major changes, the more radical, comprehensive and dramatic the changes will be. It is clear that the slow pace of adaptation by Britannica's management has created a crisis and has made the available time span for change very limited. Thus revolutionary changes seem almost inevitable. Yet, two routes are still available, depending on the perspective chosen:

- *Revolutionary change.* This argument is the easiest to make under the crisis circumstances of 1995. Heavy losses have been incurred, competition is racing ahead and the company is up for sale. In this situation proponents of the discontinuous change perspective would argue that it is obvious that only radical reengineering can turn around the company. For Britannica it is 'reform' or 'receivership'. The new CEO, Esposito, might be the needed new leader, able to think outside of established orthodoxy, and powerful enough to brush away any resistance to whole-scale restructuring.

- *Evolutionary change.* While the current crisis has limited the margins for gradual change, proponents of the continuous change perspective would still warn against the revolutionaries' promise of the 'big bang solution'. They would fully agree that Britannica needs to change, but would emphasise that change will not be a one time effort, but a continuous process for the coming years, as the digital world is still in high state of flux. Therefore, they would argue that Britannica should avoid the 'pressure cooker approach' to all at once change, in favor of a continuous learning mode. Emphasis should be placed on gearing the organization up for a long-term exploration of the digital world, instead of opting for the quick fix.

5. *What strategy would you advise Encyclopaedia Britannica's management to follow? How can the company reform and reposition itself to survive in the 'digital age'?*

Of course, students can come up with a variety of answers to this question. At a minimum they will have to deal with the following issues:

- *New media.* If printed encyclopaedias are definitely headed in the direction of the 'typewriter,' Britannica must decide what types of new media to focus on. Will CD-ROMs remain an important technology or will they be totally displaced by on-line services? If so, what types of on-line services could Britannica provide?

- *Competitive advantage.* If Britannica does refocus itself on on-line services, the question is how it can earn money doing so. The obvious solution of asking for a subscription fee may be unacceptable to a new generation that are used to getting information for free. Britannica's problem is similar to so many information providers on the internet – how do you attract people to your website and how do you generate income from the ensuing traffic?

■ *Printed encyclopaedia.* With the sales of the printed encyclopaedia falling at such an alarming rate, students will need to decide what to do with the traditional product line. Should it be retained, changed or discarded?

■ *Sales force.* What should Britannica do with its large door-to-door sales force? Can this distribution channel be reformed to gain a competitive advantage, or should the sales force be disbanded?

■ *Ownership.* Britannica has been put up for sale, and the firm's management must ask itself who they would prefer as a parent company. Would Britannica do better with a hands-off investor as owner, or would it be preferable to link up with a media company searching for content?

Other Teaching Issues

A number of issues raised in this case are also relevant to other chapters of the book. These other teaching issues are:

■ *Strategic thinking.* With the benefit of hindsight it is clear where Britannica went wrong. In the case it became apparent that Britannica's managers had very strong cognitive maps that filtered out signals that the environment was undergoing a fundamental change. Could this miscalculation have been avoided by more thorough analysis, performed in a more disciplined and explicit manner, as proponents of the rational thinking perspective would argue? Or was Britannica's major problem that their culture was too uniform, and there were too few imaginative people able to think out of the box (link to chapter 2)?

■ *Strategy formation.* Should managers proactively chart a viable course of action or flexibly adapt to unfolding circumstances? Advocates of the planning perspective would probably stress the usefulness of scenario development and contingency planning under the circumstances faced by Britannica. Incrementalists, on the other hand, would argue that Britannica can not make long term plans, but should more proactively experiment with new ideas (link to chapter 3).

■ *Business level strategy.* The sudden environmental shifts have had quite an impact on Encyclopaedia Britannica and the company must now reconsider its competitive strategy. From an outside-in perspective Britannica should closely follow the developments in the market and fully adapt itself to them. From an inside-out perspective, however, Britannica should more thoroughly consider what its remaining strengths are and find an environment in which these strengths can be applied (link to chapter 5).

■ *Changing rules of the game.* The encyclopaedia business is a great example of how a once distinct industry can lose its separate identity and can be swallowed by an emerging industry, all due to technological innovations. The producers of encyclopaedias have found out that they are 'content providers' in the new, broad information technology industry. This case is therefore an interesting example of what Hamel and Prahalad (8.4) refer to as the 'space without boundaries'. It is also arguably an industry characterized by increasing returns (8.5 Arthur). This case also allows for a discussion on the extent to which firms have the opportunity to shape their own environments (link to chapter 8).

■ *Organizational inertia.* Britannica is also a good example of an inert organization. Almost every possible factor that can contribute to organizational inertia is present at Britannica. The interesting question to be debated is whether this inertia should be overcome through strong top-down leadership, or whether a certain measure of creative chaos would be preferable, to get changes going (link to chapter 9).

What Happened after the Case?

The turmoil in the encyclopaedia industry caused by the availability of the CD-ROM technology intensified in the 1990s due to the growth of the internet. The rise of the internet has severely affected revenues according to analysts. Britannica has reacted by moving itself beyond encyclopaedias. Britannica has reassessed its core business and with the launch of Encyclopaedia Britannica Internet Guide (EBIG) it seems to have transformed itself from information provider to an internet directory / navigation director. EBIG had spun out of the related links that Britannica included in Britannica Online. EBIG features eBLAST (Encyclopaedia Britannica Links and Search Tool), which is a World Wide Web navigation service. According to Britannica's website EBIG "boils down the overwhelming amount of information available on the internet into a manageable set of only the highest quality web resources... it's the encyclopaedia for the 21st century." The rejuvenated Encyclopaedia Britannica is a multi-product electronic publisher that has diversified its distribution channels to include retail, education and direct marketing.

Other encyclopaedias are also expanding to the internet directory market. Encarta, which has a 60% market share in the CD-ROM encyclopaedia market, is offering its own version of an internet directory with Encarta '98. Britannica is also facing Excite and Yahoo as competitors, who have been in the business longer than Britannica. The EB 98 Multimedia CD-ROM however has topped the charts of best-selling CD-ROMs. The 1999 version has further improved the user's experience in three main areas: ease of access, productivity and multimedia.

1996   Purchase of Encyclopaedia Britannica by Jacob Safra.
        Britannica disbanded its home sales force and moved the CD-ROM and the print version into retail stores.

1997   Launch of the Encyclopaedia Britannica Internet Guide (EBIG).
        Britannica lowered its prices for Britannica Online (the site had around 11,000 subscribers in 1997) from $ 150 a year to $ 85 a year.

1998   1 October. Partnership with the New York Times on the Web. Britannica's Ready Reference Encyclopaedia has been added to The New York Times on the Web's archives product.
        4 October. Partnership with the Washington Post Newsweek Interactive (WPNI) to further develop eBLAST and create a new, yet to be named, co-branded version that will be launched early in 1999.

Encyclopaedia Britannica products featured in Britannica Online (Dec 1998):

Britannica Digital Products	*Britannica Print Products*	*Merriam-Webster Products*
Britannica Online	Britannica Ready Reference	Elementary Dictionary
Britannica CD 99 Multimedia Ed.	EB Reference Suite	Intermediate Dictionary
Britannica CD 99 Standard edition	Britannica Book of the Year	School Dictionary
Britannica CD Ultimate Ref. Suite	Great Books of the Western World	Collegiate Dictionary 10th ed.
Discovering Dinosaurs CD-ROM	1998 Great Ideas Today	School Thesaurus
Britannica Profiles Black History	Britannica Atlas	Collegiate Thesaurus
	The Annals of America	Geographical Dictionary 3rd ed.
	Encyclopaedia Universalis	New International Dictionary
	1999 Medical and Health Annual	Biographical Dictionary
	1999 Yearbook of Science and the Future	
	Britannica First Edition Replica Set	

TEACHING NOTE 9: SOUTHWEST AIRLINES

Case by Don Parks and Ivan Noer

Teaching note by Bob de Wit, Ron Meyer and Melbert Visscher

Case Synopsis

The start of Southwest Airlines' operations goes back to 1971 when the company started flying three Boeing 737 jets in Texas. Due to regulations concerning flights from Dallas Love Field airport, Southwest Airlines was forced into a role as a commuter airline. Southwest could only fly to cities in Texas and Texas' four neighboring states from Love Field. As a niche carrier, Southwest Airlines provided low-fare, high frequency, short-haul and no-frills flights. While the airline industry in the United States had just experienced its worst performance in the deregulated era of the late 1970s, Southwest Airlines was expanding its operations and its steady growth continued during the following 25 years.

In terms of originating passengers, Southwest had become the seventh-largest major airline in the United States in 1991. Its fleet had grown to 124 Boeing 737 jets which flew more than 20 million passengers annually to 32 cities in 14 states. Even the severe airline industry recession of the early 1990s did not seriously affect Southwest. In fact, Southwest was one of only two major U.S. carriers that showed a profit in 1990. Southwest had stuck to its 1970s strategy of low-fare, high frequency, short-haul and no-frills service using a point-to-point system rather than the hub-and-spoke system many others airlines used. Southwest had the lowest cost structure in the industry and proved to have very high ratings in overall customer satisfaction. Southwest's workers showed high productivity and extreme loyalty. In 1991 Southwest's total operating revenues amounted to $ 1,313 million, showing growth in traffic and load factors that were higher than the industry average. The case ends with the question of how Southwest can further build on its competitive advantage and expand beyond its regional base.

Teaching Objectives

If used in conjunction with chapter 5 this case can be used to meet the following teaching objectives:

- *Analyzing and understanding the importance of industry structure.* The airline industry has a complex structure, yet it is understandable without detailed technical knowledge of the industry. This case therefore is useful for exploring the elements making up an industry's structure, i.e. the five forces (link to introduction and 5.1 Porter).

- *Understanding the distinction between industries, markets and businesses.* Southwest is a niche player within the airline industry, and only operates in a few geographic markets within the U.S. This makes it possible to clarify the concepts of industry, market and business (link to introduction).

- *Understanding of competitive scope, competitive advantage and positioning.* Southwest has positioned itself within the airline industry by selecting a limited competitive scope and by developing a unique competitive advantage. The case can therefore be used to explain the concepts of scope, advantage and positioning (link to 5.1 Porter).

- *Understanding the role of resources in achieving competitive advantage.* In the case Southwest's unique resource configuration is explained, with an emphasis on the company's intangible resources. This allows for a discussion on the importance of intangible resources and how they contribute to competitive advantage (link to introduction and 5.4 Barney).

■ *Discussion on the distinction between outside-in and inside-out perspectives.* The success of Southwest can be claimed by both the advocates of the outside-in and inside-out perspectives. This allows for a discussion on the major differences between these two views (link to all).

■ *Assessing the factors leading to sustainability.* The main issue in the case is whether Southwest can continue to expand and remain profitable based on the current competitive advantage. The discussion will therefore eventually focus on the issue of sustainability and the factors that contribute to long term competitive advantage (link to all).

Teaching Guideline

As an introduction to this case it might be useful to ask students what they expect from an airline they fly with and which services they find important or unimportant. Another step can be to ask students which services they would want to give up in order to pay lower fare prices. Encourage students to think about which factors, according to them, determine an airline's quality and discuss the possibility of combining low-fares with high quality.

Many students know Southwest Airlines and its successful history. A few might even have come across Herb Kelleher in one of Southwest's Boeing 737 airplanes dressed as the Easter Bunny. Interesting results emerge when students are asked to sum up what they know about Southwest and in what way this airline differs from the other major American airlines. Many students are surprised to hear that Southwest has achieved the highest ratings in customer satisfaction in the airline industry in the United States since 1992.

In conjunction with chapter 5 this case allows for a very interesting discussion on the sources of competitive advantage. Approaching the case from the two extreme perspectives, the inside-out and the outside-in perspective will give students the opportunity to evaluate both viewpoints and form an opinion. Students should be made aware of the complex sets of activities that shape a sustainable competitive advantage. Summing up the sources of competitive advantage usually makes students very aware of the fact that these are closely interrelated and that the one often can not exist without the other. It should be pointed out to students that difficulty in untangling the separate sources of competitive advantage often indicates a high degree of sustainability.

The professor can proceed by discussing the future sustainability of Southwest's competitive advantage and possible strategic options. Students should be encouraged to think about the possibility of Southwest proactively changing its environment or of Southwest having to comply more to industry rules when expanding. This provides for a link with chapter 8. This case can also be used in conjunction with chapter 3 and chapter 9 touching on the deliberateness and emergentness of strategy formation and the role of leadership in the organization respectively.

Case Questions

1. Analyze the structure of the airline industry in the United States. How attractive do you think this industry is? How important do you think a high market share is for airlines?

2. Analyze the resource base of Southwest. What would you consider to be Southwest's key distinctive resources?

3. What is Southwest's current competitive advantage?

4. How sustainable do you think Southwest's competitive advantage is?

5. What do you think should be Southwest's strategy for the coming years?

Case Analysis

1. Analyze the structure of the airline industry in the United States. How attractive do you think this industry is? How important do you think a high market share is for airlines?

A structural analysis of the airline industry can be made using Porter's 5 forces framework. Such an analysis can span an entire class session, but here the analysis has been limited to a number of main points.

- *Rivalry among existing competitors.* At the time of the case, in 1991, the airline industry in the United States was in the midst of cut throat competition, resulting in a low price level and industry wide losses (Southwest was one of the few companies not in the red). Reasons for this high rivalry include:
  - *Low growth.* The economic downturn and Gulf War were cited as causes.
  - *Overcapacity.* The major airlines to surface after the deregulation in the late 1970s had all switched to a hub-and-spoke structure, and had expanded their networks to keep customers within their systems.
  - *High fixed/variable costs.* The cost of flying an empty seat is almost the same as flying an occupied paying one. Airlines therefore encounter high pressure to enhance load factors (the average number of seats occupied per plane). As any income above variable costs is preferable to flying an empty chair, there is a strong downward pressure on prices.
  - *Low product differences.* Airline services were generally not highly differentiated.
  - *Low brand identity.* Although airlines were trying hard, brand loyalty remained weak.
  - *Some switching costs.* Airlines tried to lock in customers through Frequent Flier Programs and through the use of computer reservation systems.
  - *Low informational complexity.* Customers could easily compare prices, despite efforts by the airlines to make things less transparent through differential pricing.
  - *High corporate stakes and exit barriers.* All airlines were single business firms.
  - *Balanced competitors.* A number of competitors of comparable size dominated the playing field.

- *New entrants.* Entry barriers into the heartland of the airline industry (big hub and spoke networks) are high, although there are many niches with much lower entry barriers. Especially on point-to-point services and in the charter business entry barriers are much lower, the reasons being:
  - *Capital requirements.* Setting up a hub and spoke system requires significant investments, although nowadays airplanes can be leased, crews can be hired on short contracts, and activities such as ground handling, maintenance and ticketing can be outsourced. On point-to-point routes, capital requirements are much lower.
  - *Economies of scale.* Hub and spoke systems have been developed to achieve economies of scale, to ensure a higher load factor for each plane in the system. Entrants do not benefit from these scale economies.
  - *Low proprietary product differences.* There are no legal or technical imitation barriers.
  - *Medium switching costs.* New entrants might find it difficult to seduce customers away from their Frequent Flyer Programs.
  - *Medium brand loyalty.* New entrants might find it difficult to convince customers of their safety and service, without a track record.
  - *High access to distribution.* Most travel agents are independent.
  - *Expected retaliation.* New entrants can count on a strong response from the incumbents.
  - *Access to necessary inputs.* Getting the best slots at the best airports can be a problem.

- *Bargaining power of suppliers.* One of the major factors that increased the operating costs of airlines at the beginning of the 1990s was the rise of jet fuel prices. Exhibit 6 of the case shows that fuel and oil are the second largest source of operating expenses per available seat-mile. The other important suppliers to the airlines are the manufacturers of aircraft. Their relatively strong bargaining power can be analyzed as follows:
    - *Concentration.* In the area of large airplanes (above 150 passengers), only three major players dominated the market, Airbus, Boeing and McDonnell Douglas. In the smaller planes there were many more competitors.
    - *Cost relative to total purchases high.* Aircraft are a major investment.
    - *Medium differentiation of inputs.* Different manufacturers have different qualities, but only to a limited degree.
    - *Medium switching costs.* Airlines often prefer aircraft from one manufacturer to minimize maintenance costs.
    - *No substitution or integration.* There is no substitute input and no threat of forward or backward integration.
    - *Importance of volume to supplier.* The aircraft manufacturers yearn for volume, to achieve economies of scale.

- *Bargaining power of buyers.* Buyers have a fair amount of power, although a distinction must be made between business and economy passengers:
    - *Low buyer volume/concentration.* Some business buyers purchase tickets in significant volumes, but generally buyers are fragmented and buy in low volumes.
    - *Low switching costs.* Only frequent flyer programs lessen this power.
    - *Moderate transparency.* Most buyers will engage a travel agent to navigate through the price offerings.
    - *Price sensitivity.* Economy passengers will be much more price sensitive than business passengers. Business passengers will be much more concerned with transfer times, on-time performance and business travelers' facilities.

- *Threat of substitutes.* Only in Europe are the airlines being challenged by high-speed trains.

Competition in some markets and on some routes can differ considerably in intensity. Competition on busy routes is fierce, but the load factor is usually high. On routes with less competition and hardly any alternatives, airlines might be able to achieve higher margins. All in all, however, this structural analysis does not suggest that the airline industry is particularly attractive. Some niches might be more profitable, but the industry as a whole does not seem to hold out great promise.

As for the importance of market share, Buzzell and Gale would probably argue that in the airline industry being the market leader is particularly important. Their arguments would be:

- *Market leaders profit most from economies of scale.* In the airline industry, with its system wide load factors, economies of scale are significant.

- *Market leaders profit most from risk aversion among customers.* In the airline industry, many business people will prefer a well-known brand.

- *Market leaders profit more from bargaining power towards buyers and suppliers.* In the airline industry, buying planes and running frequent flyer programs becomes easier if you are the biggest.

- *Market leaders have more power to block new entrants.* In the airline industry, market leaders can hinder smaller rivals in getting slots and can attack them through targeted pricing campaigns.

Buzzell and Gale would advise market followers to position themselves in a defensible niche. In their view, "resources and quality products are important, but far from sufficient to be highly profitable." On the other hand, one of Stalk, Evans and Shulman's key arguments is that market share is becoming increasingly unimportant. Others have also challenged the outcome of the PIMS research (see for example 8.2 Baden-Fuller & Stopford). Their arguments would include:

- *The effects of economies of scale can be neutralized.* In a hub-and-spoke system, economies of scale are important. But a firm can also develop a competitive formula that is more scale independent, such as point-to-point flights, which only require individual planes to be filled.

- *The effects of risk-averse behavior can be neutralized.* By focusing on price sensitive customers and building up a reliability track record, airlines can overcome this issue.

- *The effects of market leader bargaining power can be neutralized.* By purchasing used aircraft or forming buying consortia, the advantages of the market leaders can be wiped out.

- *The effects of a market leader's blocking power can be neutralized.* By avoiding head on competition when entering the market, a smaller firm can avoid the market leader's retaliation.

- *Resource development is more important than scale.* While a high market share gives a firm the potential to ascend the production learning curve more quickly, it does not mean that the market leader will be capable of developing its intangible resources faster than the smaller firm. In the airline industry the large firms might be less apt at competence development than a smaller firm like Southwest.

2. Analyze the resource base of Southwest. What would you consider to be Southwest's key distinctive resources?

According to figure 5.2 Southwest Airlines' resources can be divided into the following categories:

- Tangible resources:
  - Initial monopoly at Dallas Love Field airport
  - Young, standardized all-Boeing 737 fleet

- Relational resources:
  - Customer loyalty
  - Flexible union contracts
  - Low-cost and high quality airline reputation

- Competencies:
  - Customer service competence (customer knowledge, adaptation capabilities and a customer-oriented attitude)
  - High frequency, high utilization operation competence (scheduling knowledge, aircraft turnaround capability, time-based competition attitude)

Southwest's competencies are what really distinguish the company.

3. What is Southwest's current competitive advantage?

Although Southwest is a no frills airline, it can not be said that the firm's competitive advantage only comes from cost cutting. Southwest has developed an integrated competitive formula, in which a number of characteristics reinforce each other, resulting in a strong competitive advantage. In other words, not one separate element, but the 'configuration of activities' (Porter, 1996) and the underlying resources that are responsible for the firm's competitive advantage. This competitive formula consists of the following elements:

- *Limited passenger service.* For example, no meals and no baggage transfers, yet without the impression of low quality.

- *High frequency, short-haul, point-to-point operations.* The company runs its air operations much like a bus/rail transport company. Planes leave frequently, on time and go directly to the point of destination.

- *High aircraft utilization.* Aircraft are used as shuttles, keeping them in the air as often as possible.

- *Lean, fast ground and gate crews.* To keep airplane utilization high, ground and gate crews must be able to turnaround planes quickly and flexibly.

- *Low cost structure.* Other parts of the company have also been structured to fit with the low cost approach.

So, does this mean that Southwest has a cost-focus strategy? How, then, can it be explained that Southwest won five consecutive Triple Crown awards, signaling a high level of service quality. By striving for low cost and differentiation, isn't Southwest 'stuck in the middle' in Porter's words, or has Southwest found an innovative way to reconcile the conflict between these two demands? We would argue exactly that. Southwest has taken up the challenge of reconciling the tension between the demands of cost and differentiation, and has found a creative synthesis – an innovative competitive formula – that combines the best of both worlds.

4. *How sustainable do you think Southwest's competitive advantage is?*

Underlying Southwest's competitive advantage are the two distinctive competencies identified in the answer to question two: a customer service competence and high frequency, high utilization operation competence. Southwest should be able to retain its competitive advantage if the company's resource-base meets four criteria for sustainability:

- *Value.* Southwest's distinctive competencies must continue to be valuable in the future. In other words, these two competencies must remain important as the industry evolves further and not be outdated by industry developments.

- *Rareness.* It has already become clear that few competitors currently have the competencies that Southwest has. Whether Southwest's competencies will remain rare depends on the next factor.

- *Imitability.* Will competitors be able to imitate Southwest? This will depend on whether competitors are locked in to their current mode of operation (path dependency), whether they really understand what Southwest is doing right and whether they can change their organizations to actually do the same. It could be argued that the fact that Southwest has an entirely different competitive formula makes it more difficult to imitate. For competitors it is very difficult to take just one aspect out of the Southwest context and implement it into their organization. Only if competitors were willing to completely overhaul their entire way of working, adopting the entire Southwest configuration of activities, would Southwest have a true imitator. But for existing competitors, this is extremely difficult. Only for new start-ups is this as a distinct possibility.

- *Substitutability.* A more real threat to Southwest's competitive advantage in the long run is a rival that innovates and creates an even better competitive formula, thereby overtaking Southwest's system. But how long it might take to out-innovate Southwest is anyone's guess.

At this point the professor might want to focus on possible developments in the industry context. Looking ahead to the discussions that will take place in chapter 8, it can be debated how the airline industry might evolve in the coming years or how a proactive company might be able to rewrite the rules of the competitive game. Students can be asked to envision two or three scenarios of what the industry might look like in 5 to 10 years time, to break open the discussion on whether Southwest can rest on its laurels. It is also an interesting angle to ask who the students see as Southwest's major competitor in 10 years time: one of the major airlines, a Southwest clone, or an industry outsider with a new competitive formula (e.g. a *capabilities predator* looking for growth opportunities, such as Greyhound).

5.   What do you think should be Southwest's strategy for the coming years?

There are a number of dimensions along which this question can be discussed:

- *Strengthening the competitive advantage.* Southwest has proven to be an attractive alternative for other means of transportation on short to medium distances. The low airfares and reliable and frequent flights make Southwest's flights a convenient and quick shuttle service between cities. Through innovative ideas that were consistent with Southwest's philosophy, the airline has made air travel about as easy as taking a bus. Ticketless travel and no seat assignment make travel by air rapid and convenient. Customers know exactly what to expect from Southwest - high quality and no-frills. Southwest might be able to strengthen this competitive advantage by further innovation. For example, Southwest could move towards the introduction of monthly passes like in public transportation, or could introduce company subscriptions. However, it is important for Southwest to remain clearly focused. Porter (1996) gives the example of Laker Airways, which began with a clear cost-focus strategy based on no-frills operations in the North Atlantic market, aiming at a price-sensitive travelling public. Over time Laker Airways began adding frills, new services and new routes, blurring the airline's positioning, and eventually leading to bankruptcy.

- *Geographic growth.* The clearest way to leverage Southwest's resource-base is to expand the company into other states. Such a move also makes sense from an outside-in perspective, as these are interesting markets and Southwest would be wise to pre-empt the rise of clones in these areas. Whether Southwest could easily leverage its formula to offer international flights is a matter to be debated.

- *Segment growth.* There might be other market segments that Southwest may want to consider. For instance, small-scale regional routes, long-haul routes, tourist charter routes and cargo routes. In all cases, the issues to be discussed are whether these segments are attractive and competitively important, and whether Southwest has or wants to develop the competencies needed to serve them. Here a discussion on an outside-in and inside-out approach can be useful. From an outside-in perspective it might be argued that Southwest should move into the most attractive segments (e.g. flying corporate planes) and into those segments needed to protect it from advancing competitors (e.g. no-frills charter companies). From an inside-out perspective it might be argued that Southwest should remain focused on those segments matching its competence-profile. Southwest would probably want to put its efforts into growing its current market segment, by increasing peoples' flying frequency and competing against other forms of transport, such as busses and cars (e.g. could you get families out of their cars by offering them family transportation packages?).

- *Diversification.* Stalk, Evans and Shulman argue that "a company that focuses on its strategic capabilities can compete in a remarkable diversity of regions, products and businesses and do it far more coherently than the typical conglomerate can." This is clearly in line with the inside-out perspective. Applied to Southwest, advocates of the inside-out perspective might argue that there is significant potential for the company to leverage it operational and customer service competencies in similar businesses as well. The most obvious candidates for the Southwest approach to no-frills transportation are the bus and rail services businesses. It can be debated whether Southwest could and should attempt to be a capabilities predator in these businesses.

Other Teaching Issues

Besides the topics covered in chapter 5, this case can be used to touch on the following teaching issues:

- *Strategy formation.* Southwest Airlines was born as a low-fare, short distance airline in 1971 from a sketch on a napkin. The big break for Southwest came in 1974 when all other airlines moved from Dallas Love Field airport. This hadn't been deliberately anticipated by Southwest. The question arises whether Southwest's strategy since then has been more deliberate and planned, or whether the company's strategy has emerged 'on the fly' (link to chapter 3).

- *Creating the industry context.* Southwest Airlines has focused on high frequency, short distance, low fare and no-frills flights. The question arises whether the environment has selected Southwest as a fit firm or whether Southwest has created its own fitting environment. In other words, was Southwest just a lucky firm, in the right place at the right time, or has Southwest actively shaped its environment, by bending and breaking industry rules? The most interesting question is how the development of the airline industry will continue in future. Will Southwest be swept along in the tides of history, or will the company determine its own future by creating an industry context to which it is well-suited (link to chapter 8)?

- *The role of organizational leadership.* In the case it was stated that some observers saw succession of Herb Kelleher as Southwest's most pressing problem. Southwest's operations seemed to be a close reflection of Kelleher's outgoing personal style. In 1990 *Business Month* argued that Southwest was too dependent on one man. There is no doubt that Herb Kelleher has played a significant role in steering the company to success and inspiring employees. An interesting point for discussion is whether Southwest will survive Herb Kelleher and whether the firm will need a new charismatic leader as CEO (link to chapter 9).

What Happened after the Case?

Southwest Airlines has continued to grow on the basis of its original no-frills recipe. In 1998 it operated 288 Boeing 737 jets (average age 8.4 years!), flying more than 52 million passengers annually to 54 cities (55 airports) in 28 states. Southwest's top 5 airports are Phoenix, Houston (Hobby), Las Vegas, Dallas (Love Field) and Los Angeles (LAX). Operating revenues have risen to $4,164 million in 1998, with net income amounting to $433.4 million. Southwest Airlines has become the fifth-largest airline in the United States in 1998. The more than 52 million passengers paid an average one-way airfare of $75 in 1998. In the 1998 *Business Week* Global 1000 Southwest Airlines ranked no. 701 worldwide, compared to no. 937 in 1997, based on a market value of $5,955 million. In the first 6 months of 1999 Southwest's share price has risen considerably, giving Southwest a market capitalization in June 1999 of $10,780 million (topping American Airlines and Delta Airlines in market cap, without even having international flights!).

Since 1992, Southwest Airlines has earned the fifth consecutive "Triple Crown" award for its performance, consisting of best baggage handling, fewest customer complaints, and best on-time performance of all major airlines. Moreover, Fortune (January 12, 1998) named Southwest the best company to work for in the United States.

Strategy

What is remarkable about Southwest Airlines is that Herb Kelleher still is the Chairman, President and CEO of the company. Also, his strategy has not changed since 1990. Southwest Airlines is still a low-fare, high frequency, short-haul, no-frills airline-company that operates point-to-point. In that respect the carrier has stuck to its past and has been very successful at that (see exhibit 2). They have also finally received recognition from the stock market (see exhibit 1).

EXHIBIT 1
Southwest (LUV) stock prices July 1998 – June 1999

Further strategic developments since 1994 include the following:

- *Acquisition of Morris.* In 1994, Southwest acquired Morris Airline Corporation, a small Salt Lake City based charter carrier that operated 21 Boeing 737's to 7 cities, with about 2,000 employees. The deal was valued at approximately $133 million (3.6 million shares of Southwest Airlines).

- *Ticketless travel.* In 1994, Southwest Airlines introduced ticketless travel in four cities, to trim travel agents' commissions. In January 1995 ticketless travel was made available system-wide. This made Southwest the first airline to offer this service throughout its route system. Southwest Airlines is convinced that ticketless travel is the wave of the future and that through ticketless travel it can serve its passengers better. Another development in this respect is the sale of tickets via the Internet. In August 1998, Southwest began with internet-only fare sales.

- *Alliance with Icelandair.* Another important development has been the extension of the marketing agreement with Icelandair for travel from Chicago, Providence, Louisville and Cleveland to Icelandair gateways in Europe.

- *Expansion to the eastern US.* Since the end of 1998, Southwest has been rapidly expanding service to the eastern US, its fastest-growing region. It started flying on a number of airports just outside New York (both north and south of the city). This way, it can offer low-fare rides to New York, Boston and Washington travelers, without having to use the congested facilities such as Kennedy Airport, LaGuardia and Newark. This strategy has already worked in Boston, from where it started flying to Manchester in the north and Providence in the south. Southwest is also looking into whether it is possible to do non-stop transcontinental flights (from Islip, just north of New York, to Los Angeles). In November 1998, Southwest had a 'test flight' which seemed successful and might be just 'a shot across the bow to the major carriers' *(CNN Financial News, December 21, 1998).* If this non-stop transcontinental flight really will become a normal scheduled flight, it gives Southwest some breathing space as it 'allows Southwest a little more targeted competitive response if a major carrier makes them mad' *(CNN Financial News, December 21, 1998).* Gradually, it seems that Southwest is becoming (or is) a major airline in the United States.

Southwest Airlines' success

Exhibit 2 gives a selection of consolidated financial data and operating statistics from 1993 to 1998. This table can be used to make a comparison with the data in Exhibit 8 of the original case.

EXHIBIT 2
Southwest Airlines Consolidated Financial Data and Operating Statistics
(Source: *Annual Report 1998*)

	1998	1997	1996	1995	1994	1993
Financial data (x $1000)						
Operating revenues	4,163,980	3,816,821	3,406,170	2,872,751	2,591,933	2,296,673
Operating expenses	3,480,369	3,292,585	3,055,355	2,559,220	2,275,224	2,004,700
Operating income	683,611	524,236	350,835	313,531	316,709	291,973
Operating margin (%)	16.4	13.7	10.3	10.9	12.2	12.7
Net income	433,431	317,772	207,337	182,626	179,331	154,284
Net margin (%)	10.4	8.3	6.1	6.4	6.9	6.7
Financial ratios						
Return on assets (%)	9.7	8.0	5.9	6.0	6.6	6.2
Return on equity (%)	19.7	17.4	13.5	13.7	15.6	16.0
Operating statistics						
Revenue passengers carried	52,586,400	50,399,960	49,621,504	44,785,573	42,742,602	36,955,221
Revenue passenger miles (RPMs) (000s)	31,419,110	28,355,169	27,083,483	23,327,804	21,611,266	18,827,288
Available seat miles (ASMs) (000s)	47,543,515	44,487,496	40,727,495	36,180,001	32,123,974	27,511,000
Passenger load factor (%)	66.1	63.7	66.5	64.5	67.3	68.4
Passenger revenue yield per RPM (¢)	12.62	12.84	12.07	11.83	11.56	11.77
Operating revenue yield per ASM (¢)	8.76	8.58	8.36	7.94	8.07	8.35
Operating expenses per ASM (¢)	7.32	7.40	7.50	7.07	7.08	7.25
Number of employees at year end	25,844	23,974	22,944	19,933	16,818	15,175

As can be judged by comparing 1990 and 1998, Southwest has more than doubled the Revenue Passengers Carried, more than tripled the Revenue Passenger Miles and Available Seat Miles and brought the load factor up from around 60% to over 65%. Also, the Operating and Net Margin have risen significantly, making it a very successful airline. It seems that Herb Kelleher's strategy has worked very well.

Southwest has a strike-free record of 27 years of profits. In an interview *(Organizational Dynamics, Autumn 1994)*, Kelleher revealed that the key to Southwest's long-term health lies in the strength of its organization. This may be the real lesson for other companies - the best way to handle stiff competition and a fast-changing world is to build an organization on two lasting principles. First, to serve customers in the best possible way. Answering the question how it was possible to serve customers best without any frills, Kelleher said: "It's not substantive, not essential. Getting there on time, with your baggage, and with no reason to complain - those are the essentials. But other airlines were into conspicuous display of nonessentials".

The second principle is having fun. This way it does not only motivate the employees (no wonder Southwest was the most attractive employer in 1998) but also makes the flight much more pleasant for the customer. Even in the annual report, Southwest has statements known as fun facts stating for instance the amount of peanut bags (86.9 million in 1998!) consumed in a year on its flights. In a way, Richard Branson (of Virgin) and Herbert Kelleher are a bit alike. Both are very unorthodox, hands-on, fun-loving and employee-committed entrepreneurs who have a great aversion against the big established companies in their industry and truly manage their companies for their customers and employees. The question remains what will happen when Kelleher, who says himself he will never leave because he is immortal, actually does 'depart' (which despite Kelleher's statement will probably be sooner rather than later).

References

Air Transport World, North America Report, February 1994.

CNN Financial News (www.cnnfn.com/fntraveler/9812/21/nyc/), Southwest: Circling giants?, December 21, 1998.

Labich, Kenneth, Is Herb Kelleher America's best CEO?, *Fortune,* May 2 1994.

Lee, W. G., A conversation with Herb Kelleher, *Organizational Dynamics,* Autumn 1994.

Porter, M.E., What is Strategy?, *Harvard Business Review*, November-December 1996, pp. 61-78.

www.iflySouthwest.com (Annual Report 1998).

- *Illustrating the concept of synergy in acquisitions.* Shell expected that the takeover of Billiton would lead to synergies, which would benefit Billiton. This argument is often used to explain the rationale of a takeover, yet actual synergies are difficult to realize. The case is one famous and often used example (link to 6.3 Sirower and 6.4 Campbell, Goold and Alexander).

- *Understanding the concept of parenting advantage.* Shell assumed that it would be a good parent for Billiton. Shell was and is a very successful company, and allowed Billiton to benefit from its experiences and best practices. The case allows for a discussion of the parenting advantage of Shell, and whether Gencor would be a better parent (link to 6.4 Campbell, Goold and Alexander).

Teaching Guideline

This case can be used as an example of a company (Shell) that had found a successful way to resolve the paradox of responsiveness and synergy, but went on to apply its solution to a new business (Billiton) that did not fit in the mould. As it turned out, managing in the oil & gas industry required different skills and management systems than managing in the mining industry. Therefore the synergies that Shell had hoped to achieve, never materialized. Worse, by focusing on the transfer of knowledge, skills and business systems from Shell to Billiton, Shell was able to destroy more value than it created.

We often start by asking students whether they think Shell's acquisition of Billiton was successful. Most students understand that Shell's acquisition of Billiton was not a success, and argue that this is easily understood by the facts. We then point out that Shell is one of the world's best run companies and that most other large oil and gas companies, such as Exxon, have gone though a very comparable cycle of buying and selling off mining companies. We ask why this could occur if the case is so obvious. Generally students find this a much more difficult question to answer, as the logic of the Billiton acquisitions seems quite convincing. Therefore the professor must usually lead students through the case, and press them to critically look at the issue of synergy. It is very useful for students to see that the word synergy is probably one of the most misused words in business English – as Sirower points out in reading 6.3, acquirers will always speak of synergies, but hardly ever at such a concrete level as to make them tangible. But as you look at the details for real synergies, then most of what seems to be synergetic evaporates.

In this light it is interesting to also ask students at some point whether they think that Shell has now learnt its lesson. Shell's recent diversification moves have been heralded as having a close fit with the core business. They have branched out into solar energy, biomass energy, wind energy and electricity generation (see What Happened after the Case? section). The question is whether there is truly synergy to be found between Shell's current activities and these new businesses, or whether the only thing they have in common is the 'energy' theme.

Suggested Questions

1. Compare the corporate strategy perspectives of Shell and Billiton before the takeover. How would you explain the differences?

2. Would you think Shell's acquisition of Billiton is related diversification? Why?

3. With the benefit of hindsight, what was Shell's parenting advantage for Billiton?

4. Will Gencor be a better parent? Why?

Case Analysis

1. *Compare the corporate strategy perspectives of Shell and Billiton before the takeover. How would you explain the differences?*

Shell achieves synergy by aligning the strategies of vertically related business units in oil and gas. The company controls the whole industry value system from exploration to retail of oil and gas products, reducing the consequences of oil price changes and supplier-buyer uncertainties. This vertical integration strategy has proven very effective in the oil and gas industry, and not surprisingly all major oil companies are vertically integrated. Coordinating vertically related businesses is a key factor to success, which is reflected in Shell's management systems and management style. Much time and effort is spent on planning and coordinating activities across business units.

Billiton, on the other hand, operates in a variety of metal businesses, each of which has a different set of dynamics. The industry structure and developments of zinc, for example, are quite different from copper and most other non-ferrous metals. Therefore, Billiton originally managed each business as a relatively autonomous unit, with little horizontal coordination and alignment. In addition, most metal companies are not vertically integrated either, and with good reason. Metals are raw materials for a large variety of products and industries, which makes it impossible for metal companies to control the vertical chain. Moreover, prices and turnover of commodities change dramatically and quickly, which requires quick reactions of mining companies to industry and market changes. Consequently, responsiveness is crucial for mining companies, while the need for coordination is minimal. Hence, for Billiton the portfolio perspective fits best with the nature of the businesses it is in.

2.   Would you think Shell's acquisition of Billiton is related diversification? Why?

Shell noticed important similarities between the oil industry and the metal industry. Both industries:

▪ employ geological and geophysical methods;

▪ process the raw materials to products before they are ready to use;

▪ must mass-ship products in especially constructed ships;

▪ focus marketing and sales on the same clients;

▪ require high capital investments; and

▪ require excellent relations with governments of host countries and diplomacy skills.

The case sums up Shell's three arguments to enter the metals business, which represents it's view on relatedness:

I.   *Also raw materials.* Metals are – like oil, gas and chemical products - raw materials for a wide range of companies and industries;

II.   *Same value-adding activities.* The metals industry explores, exploits, processes, recycles, and sells non-ferrous metals, industrial minerals, and related products, which are exactly the same processes Shell employs on oil, gas, and chemicals;

III. *Knowledge leveraging.* Shell strives for more intense use of its geological know-how, drilling, and technological knowledge, on other fields than oil and gas.

These are serious arguments, shared by most other major oil companies that also entered the mining business. But there are also reasons to argue that both industries are actually unrelated:

I.   *No vertical integration needed.* Vertical coordination and alignment, to the extent that the industry value system can be controlled, is virtually impossible to achieve in mining. Although many mining companies have made serious attempts to get control over the industry column by implementing a vertical integration strategy, mining products are not end products but raw input materials for a large variety of industries. For example, Billiton acquired construction, building, and building materials firms (such as De Vries Robbé in 1969) to create a fully integrated industry column, but these industry sectors represented only a fraction of metals demand. This observation, and the fact that metal-using firms were quite different businesses to operate than mining ones, led to their divestment within a few years.

II. *Industry specific knowledge.* Secondly, a number of key success factors in the metals business were fundamentally different from those in the oil and gas industry. A crucial one is the importance of industry experience, which is reflected in the saying: "One can only talk metals after at least 20 years' work." Job rotation is an exception, the rule is that someone starts in one metals business and stays there. In other words, specific knowledge and industry experience are far more important than broad experience and general knowledge, the key success factors that Shell had learned from the oil and gas industry and realized through job rotation.

III. *Smaller size.* Thirdly, there is the industry size issue. It was argued that the size of Shell's metals division had to become comparable with the other divisions, and that Billiton should account for at least 10 percent of Shell's turnover. In the context of the total metals industry turnover this was an unrealistic goal. The metals industry could never become more than marginal compared to the oil & gas industry.

With the benefit of hindsight we know that the differences between the oil and gas industry and the metals industry outweigh the similarities, and therefore Shell's diversification was unrelated. But would students have done better? And more importantly, would new diversification opportunities at this moment more accurately be classified as related or unrelated?

3.   *With the benefit of hindsight, what was Shell's parenting advantage for Billiton?*

Billiton expected Shell to provide financial strength and technological capabilities to achieve further growth and a stronger position in the metals industry. These were goals that Billiton could not achieve independently. For many years Shell financed large projects in the metals industry, which enabled Billiton to reach these goals. Billiton's current prominent position is to a large extent the result of Shell's parenting advantage, particularly it's financial strength. It is safe to conclude that without Shell Billiton's position would be less prominent.

However, there were many parenting disadvantages as well. Shell's misunderstanding of the business led to frustrated and demotivated personnel and an outflow of experienced and committed managers and metals experts. If Shell managers had not assumed that what works in oil and gas will also work in metals, there would have been a better basis for building a parenting advantage. But, Shell did not listen well enough to Billiton's arguments and did not understood best practices in the metal business. Shell managers were encumbered by a different dominant logic.

So, there may have been better parents than Shell, but also many much worse. The interesting point is that Billiton has benefited much more from Shell that the other way around – the parent seems to have suffered more than the child. There is no doubt that Shell has not reached its main goal, namely that Billiton would quickly become Shell's fourth leg, a metals division of significant size. This goal has never been within reach, and could never have been reached at all. Many years of losses were suffered, and Shell was never able to turn lead into gold.

4.   *Will Gencor be a better parent? Why?*

The answer to this question is still open. There is no benefit of hindsight here, and the 'benefit of foresight' is still to be invented. However, students can be expected to at least touch on the following points:

▪   *Dominant logic.* Does Gencor understand Billiton's business? It seems to be better equipped to support Billiton, considering its background in mining.

▪   *Synergy opportunities.* Does Gencor offer opportunities to create synergy? Given the fact that

Gencor is in the same business, opportunities for achieving economies of scale and the transfer of management competencies seem to be present.

- *Financial position.* Does Gencor offer Billiton the financial backing it needs to operate in this capital-intensive business? One obvious parenting advantage of Shell, its financial strength, seems to be Gencor's weakness.

Other Teaching Issues

The case also raises a number of issues that are relevant to other chapters in the book. These other teaching issues are:

- *Power of the dominant logic.* When Shell applied its systems to Billiton, it was unaware of the biases and assumptions on which its 'best practices' were based. Shell was prisoner of its own dominant logic (link to chapter 2).

- *Planning versus incrementalism.* The case contains a fine description of Shell's planning system, and how it relates to the oil and gas industry. Billiton was more incrementalist, which makes sense in the metals business. This allows for a discussion on planning versus incrementalism (link to chapter 3).

- *Realizing strategic change.* The case can also be used to discuss the link between strategic planning and strategic change. The conclusion of Shell's strategic planning system was that Billiton should adapt to Shell's standard operating systems. This suggests that change primarily reflects internally focused perception rather than externally oriented needs (link to chapter 4).

- *Compliance to the industry rules.* Shell transplanted its systems, based on the rules in the oil and gas industry, to Billiton, assuming that this would be beneficial to the company. Unfortunately for Billiton, the rules in the mining industry were different, rigid and strict. It seems that Billiton became the victim of non-compliance with the industry rules (link to chapter 8).

- *Importance of the organizational context.* Was Shell in full control of adapting Billiton to its organizational context, or were the complex dynamics of Shell and Billiton organizational processes chaotic (link to chapter 9)?

What Happened after the case?

The case runs until 1993. This section describes the major developments at Royal Dutch/Shell, Gencor, and Billiton after 1993. Visit our website (www.itbp.com) for the most up-to-date information and valuable further links.

Royal Dutch/Shell's Corporate Strategy since 1993

- *Overall strategy.* Since 1993, Royal Dutch/Shell has refocused its corporate strategy to become an all-round energy provider. As the company is acutely aware that fossil fuel will run out in the future, Shell wants to broaden its scope from 'oil company' to 'energy company'. This shift is clear in the 1st of the 9 Shell business principals: "The objectives of Shell companies are to engage efficiently, responsibly and profitably in the oil, gas, chemicals and other selected businesses and to participate in the search for and development of other sources of energy. Shell companies seek a high standard of performance and aim to maintain a long-term position in their respective competitive environments".

- *Diversification.* Consequently Shell has branched out into other forms of energy (production), such as solar energy (first sites started operating in March 1999), biomass energy and wind energy. All of these 'alternative' energy sources together with the forestry operations (which they have had for 20 years) have been clustered in the company's fifth core business: Shell International Renewables. The other four businesses have roughly remained the same as in the case, namely Chemicals, Exploration & Production, Oil Products, and Gas & Power. The last one used to be only Gas, but now Shell is using the gas to power the turbines of power stations (for instance in the UK, Mexico, Columbia, the Philippines, China and Namibia). This creates a total solution in electricity generation, from extraction to transportation to building the power station and generating the electricity.

- *Disintegration.* In a move running counter to its diversification, Shell has decided to spin off a large number of its supporting activities into separate business units. Internal financial services have been organized in Shell Capital, consulting services in Shell International Business Consultancy, IT services in Shell Services International and accounting services in Tasco Europe (a joint venture with Ernst & Young). While these units have Shell operating companies as their primary customers, it is the intention that they move more towards serving outside customers in the future as well.

- *Horizontal integration.* While many of Shell's major competitors have moved towards mergers and acquisitions, Shell has so far not participated in this consolidation trend. In September 1998 Shell and Texaco were engaged in talks to merge their European refinery and marketing assets, but these talks were broken off. The only major deal in the oil sector for Shell the past 5 years has been the Shell/Texaco/ Saudi Arabian Oil co-operation in refinery, marketing and lubricants in the US, which was announced in March 1997. Meanwhile, others did succeed in taking over or merging with large companies in the same industry. First, in 1996 British Petroleum (BP) signed an agreement with Mobil to share their European downstream activities. Following that, BP and Amoco announced their full merger in August 1998. Finally, in November 1998 Exxon (70%) merged with Mobil (30%) to become the world's largest (petrochemical) company, surpassing Shell in the rankings. Also the smaller European firms Total and Petrofina announced that they would merge into Total Fina.

- *Restructuring.* On top of this inability to find a suitable partner, Shell announced in December 1998 that mainly due to the low oil prices (under US$ 10 a barrel) and subsequent lower profits:

    - 4,000 jobs would be cut
    - a £2.7 billion write-off would be taken for restructuring, i.e. a new round of consolidation and stricter control of the diverse empire from the center
    - investment levels would be cut by one third
    - eight chemicals businesses representing 40% of Shell's petrochemical portfolio would be disposed of
    - four national head offices would be closed

- *Synergy focus.* The sale of Billiton and a portion of the chemical business seems to indicate that Shell is moving away from its 'raw materials' exploration and production focus. The investments since 1993 in renewable resources and electricity generation seem to be pointing towards a redefinition of the company as 'energy firm'. Whether Shell can realize actual synergies between its historic businesses and these new ventures is open for debate.

Gencor's Corporate Strategy since 1993

- *Unbundling.* Gencor's corporate strategy has been one of unbundling. As one of South Africa's biggest conglomerates, pressures to 'unbundle' have been very large since President Mandela took office in 1994. This is in an effort to create more transparent and international business in South Africa. In November 1993, the first move of the restructuring for Gencor was to unbundle its major industrial assets by distributing shares in Engen, Genbel, Sappi and Malbak to its existing shareholders. That left it to focus on its aim of being a major international mining group, instead of a huge conglomerate. The next step was to acquire assets outside South Africa. In October 1994 Gencor paid $1.144 billion for the Billiton base metals group owned by Royal Dutch/Shell.

- *Billiton floated on LSE.* By the end of 1996 Gencor's chairman Brian Gilbertson had become increasingly convinced of the difficulty of expanding and funding an international mining operation under South Africa's restrictive foreign exchange controls. He subsequently decided to relocate the base metals business to a market with less strict exchange controls. The best way to achieve the company's aims was to demerge the larger base metals business from the precious metals (gold and platinum) operations and list it on a stock exchange outside South Africa. To achieve this, Gencor sold to the new Billiton group all its interests in aluminum, coal, mineral sands, nickel, Samancor (which houses Gencor's manganese assets), chrome and stainless steel - equivalent to 80% of Gencor's net assets. To pay for them Billiton made a share issue to Gencor that was redistributed to Gencor's existing shareholders, giving Billiton a listing in South Africa in addition to its international listing. To give it a strong balance sheet, Billiton simultaneously made an offering of 375 million new shares (app. 25% of total equity, value $1.5 billion) to international investors. As Billiton already had an office in London, the company chose the UK capital - which is in a similar time zone to South Africa. On the same day that Gencor announced the demerger it also announced the merger of Billiton's nickel interests with Australian group QNI. On September 22, 1997 Billiton entered the FTSE-100 index as the UK's 48th largest company, valued at $7.5 billion.

- *Merger with Goldfields.* An additional reason for splitting the base metals from the precious metals (gold and platinum) was that this would allow Gencor to merge the latter with a competitor. In October 1997, Gencor did just that, by merging its gold businesses (excluding some marginal gold mines which they had sold to Randgold earlier) with those of its rival Gold Fields of South Africa. Through this move the merged company, named Gold Fields, became one of the two biggest gold mining companies in the world (the other being Anglogold).

- *What remains of Gencor.* As a result, the number of employees since February 1998 has dropped to 5, from more than 100,000 people 10 years earlier! Thus, in the course of only 12 months, more than a century of development as a traditional mining finance house was brought to an end. Gencor became an investment holding company with stakes in three of the world's finest mining companies: a 59% stake in Billiton (base metals), 47.9% in Gold Fields (gold) and 18.7% in Implats (platinum group metals). The holding company will pass the receipts from the underlying investments directly to Gencor's shareholders. This reduced strategic posture is likely to endure until either a new business initiative is identified, or until Gencor is itself unbundled. However, any such unbundling is unlikely before the year 2002, when obligations to the Indonesian authorities relating to the closure of the Prima Lirang gold mine on Wetar Island expire, and when warranties given to Billiton on its purchase of Gencor's non-precious metals assets have run their course (these warranties are limited to US$ 220 million in aggregate and to five years from July 1, 1997).

Billiton's Strategy, Activities and Profitability

- *Strategic aim.* Billiton has stated that it wants to achieve real growth as one of the world's foremost natural resource groups by taking advantage of high quality acquisition opportunities, by developing its existing international asset base and by pursuing a focused exploration program to create additional value. They have indicated that they want to own and manage a major portfolio of strategic holdings focused in world class metals and minerals businesses, diversified by commodity and country.

- *Main activities.* Billiton has activities in the following businesses:
  - *Aluminum.* Bauxite mining and alumina refining in Brazil, Surinam and Australia and aluminum smelting in South Africa and Brazil.
  - *Steel, ferroalloys and nickel.* A 52.6% stake in Samancor, the world's largest producer of high grade manganese and chrome ore, 100% stake in QNI of Australia which has as a major holding a 98.9% interest in Cerro Matoso, a Colombian ferronickel refining facility.
  - *Titanium minerals.* A 50% interest in Richards Bay Minerals, a joint venture with Rio Tinto. RBM is the world's largest producer of titanium dioxide slag.
  - *Coal.* A 42.3% controlling stake in Ingwe, one of the world's largest coal producers. 100% stake in Coal Mines of Australia.
  - *Base metals.* Copper and zinc mining and processing operations in Canada and South Africa.
  - *Marketing & trading.* Billiton Marketing and Trading is responsible for selling the raw materials produced by Billiton to the market for the highest possible price.
  - *New business & exploration.* Three areas are covered, namely Exploration & Development, to assist Billiton in the exploration and development for commodities outside those covered by the other divisions, Mergers & Acquisitions and Minerals Technology, which researches and develops new technologies.

EXHIBIT 1
Five Years Financial Summary, in US$ million, except per share data
(Sources: Billiton annual reports)

	1994*	1995	1996	1997	1998
Turnover including associates' turnover:	1683	4736	5648	5815	6060
- production operations	1683	3161	4213	4627	49355
- marketing and trading	0	1575	1435	1188	112
Less share of associates' turnover	-303	-411	-455	-529	614
Net turnover	3063	9061	10841	5286	5446
Operating costs	-1314	-3933	-4526	-4658	-4808
Operating profit	1749	392	667	628	638
Attributable profit	177	261	433	537	481
- as % of turnover	10,5%	5,5%	7,7%	9,2%	7,9%
Investments	1221	1585	1220	1059	632
Attributable net assets	1456	1791	1997	3014	4582
Earnings per share	n/a	n/a	n/a	n/a	22.9c
Dividend per share	n/a	n/a	n/a	n/a	10.5c

Years run from July 1 to June 30 of the given year (e.g. 1998 runs from July 1, 1997 to June 30, 1998)

* Beware: 10-month period only (September 1, 1993 to June 30, 1994)!

EXHIBIT 2
Billiton Share Price and MSCI Non-Ferrous Metals Index

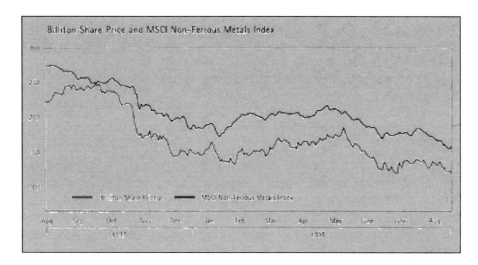

Judging from the above picture, we can conclude that Billiton neither outperformed nor under-performed the relevant index, making it an average market performer. The share-price after August dropped to 103p (end of September 1998) and was around 145p as of March 1999. Also there has been a welcome broadening of Billiton's shareholder base. Immediately after the flotation 22% of the shares were held on the London register. By 30 June 1998 the London register proportion had risen to 37%, and had reached 41% in October 1998.

TEACHING NOTE 12: GRAND METROPOLITAN

Case by David Sadtler and Andrew Campbell

Teaching note adapted by Rob de Wit, Ron Meyer and Melbert Visscher

Case Synopsis

The Grand Metropolitan case provides an excellent opportunity for students to learn about corporate-level strategy. The case describes the history of the company from its beginnings in 1947 through to the appointment in 1993 of George Bull, as the new chief executive. During this period the company has had a number of different corporate level strategies and the case provides sufficient detail for students to consider the merit of each of these strategies, discuss how companies change strategy, and consider what the company's strategy should be for the future. It is suitable for teaching either as an introduction (or summary) session for a segment on corporate-level strategy, or as an extended individual session on the subject.

Teaching Objectives

If used in conjunction with chapter 6 this case can be used to meet the following teaching objectives:

- *Understanding the difference between the portfolio perspective and the core competence perspective*. The history of GrandMet is unfolded in this case, demonstrating how the company moves from an unrelated portfolio of autonomous businesses to a more tightly related group of businesses, sharing food and drinks branding skills (link to introduction and all readings).

- *Understanding corporate value creation*. Having clear insights about how corporate value can be created and having the parenting abilities to create the value are key aspects of corporate strategy. This case allows for a discussion on the issue of composition (selecting businesses where there is an opportunity to create value) and coordination (having the parenting competence to bring the value creation about) (link to introduction and all readings).

- *Understanding the basis of parenting advantage*. Not each corporate center is equally competent in adding value to businesses. The GrandMet case provides examples of both successful and failed corporate value-adding attempts (link to 6.4 Campbell, Goold & Alexander and 6.5 Campbell & Goold).

- *Understanding different corporate management styles*. GrandMet has also progressed through different forms of corporate management. The company has had a holding company structure and financial control, and now seems to be moving more towards a strategic control style. Therefore, this case allows for a discussion on the advantages and disadvantages of a number of corporate management styles (link to 6.5 Campbell & Goold).

Teaching Guideline

The most interesting aspect of the Grand Metropolitan case is that the evolution of the company broadly reflects the evolution of the concept of the multi-business firm. The history of GrandMet runs parallel with the history of corporate management thinking. Each new corporate strategy 'fashion' has had an affect on how GrandMet has been run. Most cases focus on a short period in a company's life span and this makes it impossible to see how the company has evolved and has incorporated new ideas. The GrandMet case embraces a great deal of history and detail about their changing corporate management philosophy. This allows for a discussion on how our understanding of corporate value creation has progressed and how significant the impact of these changing ideas is on an actual firm.

Another important issue that often arises when discussing this case is the role of the chief executive in shaping the future of the corporation. This case seems to suggest that the choice of CEO will largely determine the path of development that the corporation will follow. Students usually like this conclusion as it reduces the complexities of corporate strategy development to the choice of the right 'strong man'. 'With the right captain at the helm, the corporate ship can be steered in the right direction', is often the implicit belief. Of course this issue of 'top-down leadership' is brought forward again in chapter 9, but it is useful to already start discussing it here. Might the role of the CEO in a company with a portfolio strategy be more decisive than in a company following a core competence driven approach? Portfolio restructuring and financial control might be easier to carry out by a small group at the corporate center. A core competence based strategy, on the other hand, requires more extensive strategic control and cross-business coordination, making it more difficult for new CEOs to easily leave their imprints.

As preparation for this case, we often ask students to find out what happened after 1993. This exercise in tracking the firm's further evolution is not too difficult and it makes the discussion at the end of the case more interesting, as the students must do their best to understand the strategic logic of the major moves that have recently taken place. Most students are also more motivated to discuss a company they know (Diageo) than a firm they have never heard of (GrandMet). For this case-updating students can use the links provided at our website (www.itbp.com). For professors a summary of the changes between 1993 and 1999 is given at the end of this teaching note.

Case Questions

1. Identify the eras in corporate strategy at GrandMet. What are the main characteristics of each era?

2. What was the corporate strategy at GrandMet during Max Joseph's chairmanship? Were his insights based on value creation or speculation? What was the role of core competencies during this period? Explain.

3. What kinds of insights and notions of added value formed the basis of Grinstead's corporate strategy?

4. In which ways did the corporate center add value during Sheppard's reign? To what extent does synergy exist amongst the businesses?

5. Which options can be generated for the future regarding GrandMet's corporate strategy?

Case Analysis

1. Identify the eras in corporate strategy at GrandMet. What are the main characteristics of each era?

The corporate strategy eras can be lined up with the identities of the individual chairmen:

- Max Joseph's period embraced two eras. The initial entrepreneurial phase was built on his personal ability to 'sniff out' good property deals and to get them financed. The second period was characterized by financial pressure and restructuring during the 1970s.

- The third era was that of the chairmanship of Stanley Grinstead. The Grinstead era was characterized by diversification. This era seems to have been an unsuccessful one.

- The fourth era in corporate strategy at GrandMet that can be identified is that of the chairmanship of Allen Sheppard. Under his reign GrandMet focused on added value.

2. What was the corporate strategy at GrandMet during Max Joseph's chairmanship? Were his insights based on value creation or speculation? What was the role of core competencies during this period? Explain.

Max Joseph ran GrandMet from a portfolio perspective. The company was built on his personal ability to 'sniff out' good property deals and to persuade his 'city' contacts to finance them. His insight was that money could be borrowed at a lower cost of capital than the returns he could expect from his investments, both in terms of current return and property appreciation. He was largely uninterested in the management of these investments, leaving it in the hands of accountants Ernest Sharpe and Stanley Grinstead.

An important issue is whether Max Joseph's insight was one that concerned value creation (i.e. making something worth more than it was before) or speculation (i.e. guessing that the prices for property would rise). It is possible to argue either way and the discussion should help students understand the difference between value creation and speculation.

Clearly Joseph had valuable parenting abilities in spotting deals and raising finance. The skills of the other two members of the 'triumvirate' can be seen as important in bringing administrative order and financial discipline to a rapidly growing business. Alternatively they can be considered ordinary capabilities, not adding any noteworthy value, but merely administering Joseph's investments.

Max Joseph's abilities can not be viewed as 'core' competencies because they are not held by any of the businesses. They form a competence located at the corporate center. Joseph leveraged this competence by employing it to build and to administer a portfolio of businesses. This difference between parenting competencies as demonstrated by Max Joseph and core competencies as described by Prahalad and Hamel, illustrates the different perspective of Campbell, Goold & Alexander's parenting theory.

The second era in Joseph's tenure was the financially hard-pressed era of the 1970s, when the group came under great pressure. It can be debated whether this was simply a 'natural disaster' that made life difficult for everyone, or whether it represented a flaw in Joseph's concept of buying trading property assets cheaply. The discussion may come to the conclusion that the original idea was good but that he 'got too greedy' and overextended himself, thus departing somewhat from his original conservative and frugal approach to running the business. Others might conclude that there are limits to the number of 'cheap' companies to buy and that successfully running an unrelated portfolio is inherently difficult.

It is not clear that Joseph was creating any value during this era. Rather, the strategy was one of survival, demanding abilities which Joseph, Sharpe and Grinstead did not possess. Nevertheless, either through hard work or luck GrandMet survived.

The demands of survival, however, resulted in some initiatives that laid the basis for GrandMet's strategy in the second half of the 1980s. Allen Sheppard was hired to help generate cash from the beer businesses. He found that it was possible to radically downsize these businesses and generate excellent returns. He developed a team of managers capable of doing this and it was this team that took over the company in 1986.

3. What kinds of insights and notions of added value formed the basis of Grinstead's corporate strategy?

The Grinstead era seems to have been an unsuccessful one. The class should try to determine what kinds of insights and notions of added value formed the basis of Grinstead's corporate strategy. They should include, among other things:

- the notion of geographic balance 'never again will we be totally dependent on the UK, so we will go to the USA';

- the identification of 'attractive industries', and in particular the notion of service industries, which were at that time expected to grow faster than manufacturing industries;

- the notion of diversification and the achievement of financial stability through balance over a number of different business sectors.

While these points fit nicely within the portfolio approach, they assume certain parenting abilities within GrandMet, that in reality were absent. Grindstead's team did not have the parenting competencies to actually acquire and manage this portfolio.

It is important here to stop and to debate the value of the portfolio concepts that drove Grinstead's diversifications. Some students might argue that 'balance' is good or that companies should be investing in attractive industries. The important challenge to give students is 'where is the extra pound note, euro or dollar (i.e. the value created) that results from diversifications driven by this logic?' If there is extra value then it makes sense. If not, then these strategies are most likely to be value destroying rather than value creating: value is destroyed through the premiums paid for the acquisitions. This explains the shareholders' loss of confidence in Grinstead's strategy in the mid-1980s.

Another debate to have with students could be stimulated by asking them what they would have done in Grinstead's place. This will illustrate the crucial importance of having insights about how to create value. Grinstead did not have any clear insights, as he followed the ruling fashion of building a balanced portfolio.

Whatever the conclusions on Grinstead's stewardship of GrandMet's corporate strategy, an explanation is needed for the weak growth in earnings per share during his time. With the benefit of hindsight, it can be seen as the only real low growth period in the company's history.

4.   *In which ways did the corporate center add value during Sheppard's reign? To what extent does synergy exist amongst the businesses?*

The material on Sheppard's reign at GrandMet is rich and detailed and portrays a number of strong notions of how value is created. The case indicates three basic areas:

- The establishment of a performance culture and the nurturing of managerial talent;

- The drive for operating improvements

- Better branding.

It is useful at this point to evaluate how far the Sheppard corporate strategy fits the IDV drinks businesses. The parenting competencies of Sheppard's team are mainly about driving for operating improvements and these do not seem to be a good fit with the needs of the drinks businesses. It is therefore possible to conclude that there are two distinct parts in the corporate strategy - Sheppard's strategy of revitalizing badly managed food and drink businesses, and George Bull's strategy of building a global network of drinks brands and distribution businesses. As a prelude to the appointment discussion, it will be valuable to ask how far there is business and corporate level synergy (i.e. resources that can be leveraged) between these two strategies. The company's public position is that synergy does exist, yet there are few tangible examples of the extra pound note being created.

Further debate can be encouraged by comparing GrandMet's 'Vision 2000' to the analysis of Allen Sheppard's value creating strategy. Vision 2000 was based on a belief that the future would lie in high quality international brands. Yet Sheppard's skills were mainly about driving operational improvements in badly managed companies. The tension between the vision and the skills showed up in practice when GrandMet was looking for acquisitions. Companies like Nestlé, Unilever, BSN and Kraft General Foods were prepared to pay much higher prices for quality branded companies such as Rowntree, Jacob Suchard or Perrier than GrandMet could justify. These companies had more ability to create value from the brands they were buying because of their marketing cultures and global reach.

GrandMet, therefore, ended up acquiring Pillsbury because the company needed revitalizing, a task that Nestlé, Unilever and Philip Morris presumably did not relish.

Further discussion can focus on whether or not retailing is an appropriate part of the portfolio. Despite the company's public statements and the relative success in turning round Burger King, most observers and some insiders do not believe that retailing will be a long-term part of GrandMet's strategy. The parenting skills needed are sufficiently different to make retailing an awkward fit.

5. Which options can be generated for the future regarding GrandMet's corporate strategy?

Whether the class concludes that GrandMet currently has two corporate strategies or not, the company faces some interesting future choices that are well captured by the differences between Ian Martin and George Bull. Ian Martin is a specialist at revitalizing companies and George Bull is skilled at building international brands. The options for the future can be viewed in terms of four different corporate-level strategies:

- *Broad portfolio.* Remain in all current businesses, but give both sectors of the company a large measure of autonomy.

- *De-merge.* Set up two companies making George Bull chief executive of one and Ian Martin chief executive of the other.

- *Turnaround food specialist.* Choose Ian Martin and become the Hanson or KKR of the food industry.

- *Global brands.* Choose George Bull and focus on global brands in food and drink. This implies that some of the less important food activities might be dropped and the company would move more towards building core competencies.

Other Teaching Issues

The case also raises a number of questions that are relevant to other chapters in the book. These teaching issues are:

- *Strategic change.* The transition from Joseph to Grinstead was an evolutionary process, while the switch from Grinstead to Sheppard had more pronounced revolutionary aspects. The question facing the directors as they decide on the successor to Sheppard is whether GrandMet is better served with an evolutionary or a revolutionary shift (link to chapter 4).

- *Competing on brands.* George Bull has built up a global food and drinks business based on strong brands. The question at the business level is whether branding will remain the key success factor in the business. If so, GrandMet might be able to expand 'inside-out' based on this key resource (link to chapter 5).

- *Organizational context.* The value-creating skills of GrandMet seem to depend on a small number of people. Each change in leadership at GrandMet has been accompanied by a significant shift in corporate strategy. Hence, the decisions about the top appointments seem vital. To proponents of the organizational leadership perspective this might be seen as proof that individual top managers can make a big difference. However, advocates of the organizational dynamics perspective might counter that the corporate center might buy and sell businesses like blocks of Lego, but that implementing changes from the top down is much more difficult. This is especially true when the corporate strategy moves from a hands-off portfolio approach to more involved competence sharing (link to chapter 9).

- *Shareholder value.* GrandMet is a corporation that clearly embraces the shareholder value perspective. Its corporate governance structure seems to be well aligned with this choice.

However, might GrandMet's global ambitions be limited by this philosophy? Would continental European and Asian firm's be willing to let themselves be acquired by GrandMet (link to chapter 11)?

What Happened after the Case?

The case ended with the question of who should succeed Allen Sheppard. Allen Sheppard favored Ian Martin and he became the heir apparent. However, at the same time, Sheppard was promoting the vision of global branding. There appeared to be a mismatch between Ian Martin's natural skills and the strategy being articulated. In the event there was something of a mutiny within the company against the Martin choice and Sheppard, in a surprise decision, announced George Bull as his successor. In 1993 George Bull became Group Chief Executive and succeeded Sheppard as Chairman on 1 March 1996. The strategy remained the same. Ian Martin left the company.

The following years were characterized by a continuation of the strategy of divesting non-branded businesses, whilst acquiring strong brands and achieving wider geographic coverage. Cost reduction and restructuring programs, new product development and quality enhancement were important focus points for the strategy of building branded food and drinks businesses with significant international potential. Entering high growth and emerging markets, like China, India, Russia and Latin America, played an important role in achieving organic growth.

The biggest move since the end of the case happened in 1997, when GrandMet merged with another middling branded drinks firm, Guinness, to form a leading firm in the industry. During the first 6 months, the new Diageo was jointly chaired by George Bull of GrandMet and Tony Greener of Guinness. George Bull retired on 31 July 1998 and became non-executive director of Diageo, leaving Tony Greener as sole chairman of the company.

An overview of the most important events is given below. The structure of the Diageo Board on 1 January 1999 is depicted in Exhibit 1. Selected financial results are given in Exhibits 2, 3 and 4.

1993 Sale of Chef & Brewer pubs to Scottish & Newcastle for £736 million. With this move, GrandMet had sold the last of all its hotels, breweries and managed pubs.

1994 Sale of Alpo pet foods for £327 million.

1995 Acquisition of Pet Incorporated in February for £1.8 billion and La Salteña (Argentina) by Pillsbury.

1996 Disposal of Pearle (optical retailers) for £132 million. Also sale of Erasco and Hofmann Menu, national food businesses in Europe, which were operations with low capital returns and limited growth potential. Revitalization of existing brands. Acquisition of Pasta House (Australia) and Frescarini (Brazil) by Pillsbury.

1997 Merger of Guinness PLC and Grand Metropolitan PLC on 17 December 1997. The newly formed company was named Diageo.

1998 Shareholding of 49.6% in Cantrell and Cochrane sold to Allied Domecq meeting a condition for regulatory approval of the Diageo merger by the EU Commission. Disposals of Dewar's and Bombay Gin brands also falls under this condition. Acquisition of Heinz foodservice business.

EXHIBIT 1
Diageo Board of Directors (structure at 1 January 1999)
(Sources: Diageo Annual Report 1998 & Diageo website)

Executive Directors

Tony Greener, Chairman
Appointed to the Guinness Board as non-executive director in 1986. Managing Director of UD 1987-1992; became Chief Executive of Guinness in 1992 and Chairman in 1993. Age 58.

John McGrath, Group CEO
Joined Watney Mann & Truman Brewers (then part of GrandMet) in 1985 and appointed Managing Director in 1986. Appointed to the GrandMet Board in 1992 and became Chairman and Chief Executive of IDV in 1993. Group Chief Executive of GrandMet 1996-1997. Age 60.

Jack Keenan, CEO, UDV
Joined IDV as Chief Executive and was appointed to the GrandMet Board in 1996. Previously spent more than 30 years with the General Foods Group and Kraft Foods International – lastly as Chairman of Kraft Foods International. Age 62.

Dennis Malamatinas, CEO, Burger King Corporation
Appointed CEO, Burger King Corporation in March 1997. He joined IDV in 1989 as Managing Director of Metaxa. Previous positions held include Executive Director and President of IDV Asia Pacific (1995) and President and CEO of The Pierre Smirnoff Company (1991). Age 42.

Colin Storm, Chief Executive, Guinness Ltd.
Appointed Chief Executive, Guinness Ltd. in April 1998. Joined the Guinness Group in 1961. Previous positions held include Managing Director Guinness Great Britain (1997), Managing Director of Guinness Ireland Group (1992) and Managing Director of Guinness Brewing International (1990). Age 59.

Paul Walsh, CEO, The Pillsbury Company
Joined GrandMet's brewing division in 1982 and became CEO of the Pillsbury Company in 1992. Appointed to the GrandMet Board in October 1995. Age 43.

Phil Yea, Group Finance Director
Joined Guinness in 1984 and after leaving in 1988 to join a management buy-in, re-joined Guinness in 1991. Appointed to the Guinness Board in 1993 and was Finance Director 1993-1997. Age 44.

Non-Executive Directors

Robert Wilson, Chairman of Rio Tinto

Bernard Arnault, Chairman and Chief Executive of LVMH and Christian Dior

Lord Blyth, Chairman and Chief Executive of The Boots Company

Sir George Bull, Chairman of J Sainsbury

Rodney Chase, Deputy Group Chief Executive of British Petroleum Company

Peter Job, Chief Executive of Reuters Group

Keith Oates, Deputy Chairman of Marks & Spencer

EXHIBIT 2
Grand Metropolitan Four Year Summary, in £ millions (Source: Annual Report 1996)

	1993	1994	1995	1996
Profit and loss account				
Turnover	8,120	7,780	8,025	8,974
Operating profit before exceptionals	1,042	1,023	1,032	1,108
Share of profits of associates	24	45	48	47
Interest payable (net)	(155)	(123)	(168)	(190)
Profit before exceptionals & taxation	911	945	912	965
Exceptional items:				
- Sale of businesses and fixed assets	(39)	(11)	145	(553)
- Other	(247)	(280)	(137)	(24)
Profit before taxation	625	654	920	388
Taxation	(209)	(197)	(284)	(292)
Profit after taxation	416	457	636	96
Minority interests	(6)	(7)	(35)	(46)
Profit for the financial year	410	450	601	50
Ordinary dividends	(269)	(292)	(312)	(334)
Transferred to reserves	141	158	289	(284)
Earnings per share				
-before exceptional items	29.6 p	32.2 p	29.8 p	31.0 p
-after exceptional items	19.9 p	21.6 p	28.8 p	2.4 p
Dividends per ordinary share	13.0 p	13.95 p	14.9 p	15.9 p
Balance sheet				
Intangible fixed assets	2,924	2,782	3,840	3,884
Other fixed assets	3,538	2,793	2,460	2,249
Other net assets	276	171	515	202
	6,738	*5,746*	*6,815*	*6,335*
Net borrowings	(3,025)	(2,159)	(3,321)	(2,688)
	3,713	*3,587*	*3,494*	*3,647*
Capital and reserves	3,674	3,540	3,103	3,211
Minority interests	39	47	391	436
	3,713	*3,587*	*3,494*	*3,647*

EXHIBIT 3
Diageo Two-Year Summary in £ millions (consolidated profit and loss accounts)
(Source: Diageo Annual Report 1998)

	1997 before exceptional items	1997 exceptional items	1997 Total	1998 before exceptional items	1998 exceptional items	1998 Total
Turnover	12,985		12,985	12,029		12,029
Operating profit	*2,003*	-	*2,003*	*1,942*	*(572)*	*1,370*
Share of profits of associates	196	(24)	172	210	(15)	195
Disposal of fixed assets and businesses	-	(618)	(618)	-	563	563
Merger expenses	-	-	-	-	(85)	(85)
Interest payable (net)	(268)	-	(268)	(302)	(58)	(360)
Profit before taxation	**1,931**	**(642)**	**1,289**	**1,850**	**(167)**	**1,683**
Taxation	(526)	(6)	(532)	(504)	(217)	(721)
Profit after taxation	**1,405**	**(648)**	**757**	**1,346**	**(384)**	**962**
Minority interests	(83)	-	(83)	(83)	-	(83)
Profit for the period	**1,322**	**(648)**	**674**	**1,263**	**(384)**	**879**
Dividends	(654)	-	(654)	(835)	-	(835)
Transferred to reserves	668	(648)	20	428	(384)	44
Earnings per share	32.9 p	(16.1 p)	16.8 p	33.0 p	(10.0 p)	23.0 p

* 1997 (12 months year ended 30 June 1997)
* 1998 (12 months year ended 30 June 1998)

EXHIBIT 4
Diageo Operating Profit Growth per Segment (for the 12 months ended 30 June 1998)
(Source: Annual Report, 1998)

	Operating Profit (in £ millions)	Organic Growth at level exchange
Spirits & Wine	1,070	2 %
Packaged Food	447	9 %
Beer	247	7 %
Fast Food	179	11 %
Total of Continuing Operations	*1,943*	*5 %*

TEACHING NOTE 13: KLM AND THE ALCAZAR ALLIANCE

Case by Ron Meyer, Bob de Wit & Howard Kwok

Teaching note by Ron Meyer and Bob de Wit

Case Synopsis

KLM Royal Dutch Airlines is one of the major international airlines in the world. In late 1992 KLM announced that it was engaging in talks with three other European airlines (SAS, Swissair and Austrian Airlines) to form a strategic alliance, code-named Alcazar. This alliance between the major medium-sized European airlines was intended to create a group strong enough to compete against Europe's big three: British Airways, Lufthansa and Air France. However, the difficulties that needed to be ironed out between the four partners were complex. Alcazar had to deal with two US partners, six national governments, 49 unions and the anti-trust authorities in the US and European Community.

The case describes the industry dynamics motivating the firms to move towards a strategic alliance and details the points of contention between the intended partners. By the summer of 1993 the partners announced the failure of their talks and the stated reasons why the parties decided to all go their own ways. The case concludes with the question of whether KLM should seek new strategic partners, or should move forward on its own.

Teaching Objectives

If employed in conjunction with chapter 7, this case can be used to meet the following teaching objectives:

- *Identifying the difference between horizontal and vertical alliances.* The Alcazar alliance is an example of a direct horizontal alliance. Therefore this case can be used to discuss the differences between horizontal and vertical alliances, as well as the difference between indirect and direct horizontal cooperation (link to introduction).

- *Understanding the spectrum of organizational arrangements between market and hierarchy.* As the Alcazar partners explore the potential value they can derive from cooperation, they must determine the level of integration they wish to pursue. This allows for a discussion on the various organizational arrangements that can be implemented and the different levels of interorganizational dependence that they entail (link to introduction)

- *Identifying the objectives of strategic alliances.* The Alcazar alliance is primarily intended to achieve a higher load factor and lock out new competitors. This allows for a discussion on the variety of objectives that can be pursued by means of alliance (link to all).

- *Recognizing the disadvantages of strategic alliances.* Alliances are quite fashionable, especially in the airline industry. However, the Alcazar partners are forced to recognize that alliances also have inherent disadvantages. These can be discussed using this case (link to all).

- *Understanding the paradox of competition and cooperation.* The Alcazar partners are torn between the desire to pursue their self-interest and to work together towards their joint interest. This case therefore illustrates how alliances combine competitive and cooperative behavior, requiring extra effort to balance the two conflicting forces (link to introduction).

- *Discussing the discrete and embedded organization perspectives.* The main conflict in the case is between KLM and Swissair. KLM sees the alliance as a stepping stone towards a full-scale merger, followed by the creation of a global network including a strong American partner. This view is more in line with the embedded organization perspective. Swissair's stance is more conservative and defensive, seeing Alcazar as a Swiss-like confederation. They see an American partner as necessary, but would like to keep the Americans at arm's length, more in line with the discrete organization perspective. Therefore, the case can be used to discuss both perspectives (link to all).

Teaching Guideline

KLM and the Alcazar alliance is a broad case, touching on many issues (see subject table in the introduction). This makes the case difficult to use at the start of a course, but more useful towards the later stages of a program. However, what is convenient is that the airline business is relatively easy to understand for outsiders. Furthermore, almost everyone has an opinion about airlines, which ensures a high level of interest when discussing the case.

An important feature of the case is that the key event – the breakdown of the Alcazar Alliance talks – is not explained in detail. The probable reason behind the failure is only hinted at. What the strategic agenda was of each party and how expectations among the negotiators could finally not be matched is left to student conjecture. Students often find it difficult to deal with such a case, because the intentions, strategies and negotiation tactics of both sides are not known – they would prefer to find the actual answer in the case. However, the case has be written in such a way that students must work as detectives, figuring out 'motives and opportunity', trying to understand how alliances are formed and why (proposed) alliances sometimes fail. This search for the answer to the question 'why didn't the alliance fly' actually gives students more insight into the process of interfirm relationship building, than if the answer were given somewhere in the text.

One of the tricky issues that the professor must keep in mind when using this case is that some students know a lot about what happened after the case, and will bring this information into the case discussions. We usually press these students to set aside their knowledge of the subsequent events for a moment, to understand what happened in 1993, and to explore what might have happened if the management of KLM had reviewed all of its options carefully. The assignment to come up with some alternatives to KLM's eventual decision usually encourages students to critically evaluate KLM's choices in 1993.

An update on the events in the airline industry after 1993 is given at the end of the case in the 'what happened after the case' section. Visit our website (www.itbp.com) for the most current update on the developments surrounding KLM and its Alcazar partners.

Case Questions

1. What are the 'rules of the game' in the airline industry? What must airlines be able to do to remain competitive?

2. What are the main strategic objectives that can be achieved by means of the Alcazar alliance? What type of structure and functions do the prospective partners have in mind?

3. What are the long-term intentions that each of the partners have with the alliance? Why is KLM so strongly in favor of having Northwest as Alcazar's American partner, while the others remain in favor of Delta?

4. Why do you think the Alcazar talks eventually broke down?

5. What should KLM do now that the 'engagement rings' have been given back?

Case Analysis

1. What are the 'rules of the game' in the airline industry? What must airlines be able to do to remain competitive?

On page 1098 it is explained how competition in the airline industry revolves around three main variables:

- *Low unit cost*. As in any industry, airlines must keep their cost levels down. Exhibit 7 gives the average cost structure in the airline industry. Operational economies of scale are not decisive in this industry. Only increased buying power vis-a-vis aircraft, fuel and service providers are a small advantage of size. Therefore, all airlines are pressed to streamline working practices and to keep wages down.

- *High yield*. In the airline industry yield is defined as the price at which a 'passenger kilometer' is sold. Of course, airlines would like to sell their services at the highest possible price. Common methods are to improve the perceived quality of the service and to lure the least price sensitive business travelers with frequent flier programs. Also important is an airline's ability to refine the art of price differentiation, whereby the same seat is sold to different customers at different prices, depending on their demands and price sensitivity. Here again, size offers few advantages to airlines.

- *High load factor*. In the airline industry load factor refers to the 'occupancy rate'. As in any industry with high fixed costs, airlines must ensure high capacity usage. The lower the unit cost and the higher the yield, the lower the break-even load factor will be. However, a company will only make money if its actual load factor is higher than its break-even rate. In other words, the third key to success is filling its planes (at a reasonable yield). Here the case mentions a number of methods, such as computer reservation systems and frequent flier programs. Most importantly, however, is the use of a hub-and-spoke system, whereby smaller feeder lines provide passengers to fill larger aircraft on trunk routes. By having a large network of linked feeder and trunk lines, coming together in hub-airports, airlines can achieve considerably higher load factors. Smaller airlines are at a disadvantage, as they can only fill their planes with 'point-to-point' customers.

2. What are the main strategic objectives that can be achieved by means of the Alcazar alliance? What type of structure and functions do the prospective partners have in mind?

Using Preece's framework (reading 7.3) it can be argued that the Alcazar partners have two major objectives for the alliance:

- *Leveraging*. The Alcazar partners intend to integrate their operations to gain network advantages. By having more planes feeding into common trunk lines the partners hope to realize a higher load factor. Furthermore, a higher frequency of more evenly scheduled flights could be achieved on routes where the partners now compete, and on marginal lines flights could be integrated to save costs. By having a common network, linking arrival and departure times of connecting flights could also be optimized, leading to better service.

- *Locking out*. Although it was obviously not stated explicitly, the Alcazar alliance was also intended as a defensive measure against the big three European carriers (Air France, Lufthansa and British Airways) and the big four Americans (Delta, American, United and Continental). The alliance was clearly not named after a four towered Moorish fortress for nothing! By becoming the fourth largest carrier in Europe, it was hoped that the group would have a large enough 'protected' home market to withstand the imminent competitive battles after liberalization of the European market.

Structure. Such a fundamental integration of activities creates a very high level of interdependence between the participating organizations. In fact, on the continuum between market and hierarchy, such a move falls just short of a full merger. The main reason for not merging outright was that each airline had obtained landing rights in other countries on the basis of its 'nationality' (landing rights are negotiated between national governments on behalf of 'their' airlines). Therefore the proposed structure of the group would be a joint venture held by the four parent companies in which all operations would be combined. The four 'national' parent companies would retain the landing rights.

Functions. The functions to be performed by the alliance would be the joint marketing and operations of airline services. Initially the four brands would be kept separate, but it was envisioned that eventually these too would be merged together.

3. *What are the long-term intentions that each of the partners have with the alliance? Why is KLM so strongly in favor of having Northwest as Alcazar's American partner, while the others remain in favor of Delta?*

The case does not explicitly mention each partner's long-term intentions and therefore students must analyze the airlines' background and behavior to discover their probable motives. KLM clearly is the odd man out in the group. They have taken a large stake in Northwest, moving beyond the purely symbolic 5% that Swissair and Delta hold of each other. What KLM's stake in Northwest signals, is that KLM sees the transatlantic route as part of its core business and that it intends to work very closely with an American partner to serve this market. In fact, KLM has an option to increase its stake in Northwest, as a next step towards creating a transatlantic airline.

It is not unreasonable to conjecture that KLM's long-term intentions are to build a strong international airline company, serving at least Europe and North America, but possibly growing towards a global network (KLM's corporate planner actually confirms that this was the case). It also seems that KLM envisions an integrated global company, as opposed to a permanent patchwork of alliances. KLM seems to see alliances as a stepping stone towards full merger, instead of a permanent state of affairs. For this reason, a suitable American partner is needed who is willing to blend into an international company, without becoming the dominant party. Of the major American carriers, only the struggling Northwest seemed to fit this profile, as the other majors (United, American, Delta and Continental) seemed too big or powerful to merge with on more or less an equal basis. The Alcazar deal would actually make the European half of a cross-Atlantic alliance larger and stronger that the US half (see exhibits 13 & 14).

In other words, KLM's intentions seem to fit closely with the embedded organization perspective. KLM seems to be highly cooperative in orientation, striving for a strategic partnership with its European and American counterparts. Its intentions are to create a long-term win-win situation for all parties involved.

Swissair, Austrian Airlines and SAS, on the other hand, seem to have a more defensive view of the Alcazar alliance. They seem to define the European market as their core business, which needs to be defended against the big European and American competitors. Their move towards Alcazar seems to be fed by the fear of being left out of the game. They acknowledge the value of an American partner, but have no desire to go further than an arm's length relationship with a company on the other side of the Atlantic. They feel intimidated by the competitive abilities and size of the American carriers and seem fundamentally distrustful about the international ambitions of these US airlines.

Under these circumstances, Swissair, Austrian Airlines and SAS prefer the tactical alliance that Swissair already has with Delta (as the saying goes, 'better the devil you know'). This relationship is a clear form of competitive collaboration, in which both sides are willing to work together as long as there is profit in the short run. There is relatively little commitment and the partnership can easily be jettisoned. This view of the transatlantic alliance fits very closely with the discrete organization perspective.

4. Why do you think the Alcazar talks eventually broke down?

Of course the different conceptions of the transatlantic alliance, as outlined above, were an important stumbling block. The disagreement over the best US partner clearly revealed different views on the future direction of the Alcazar group; to remain a fortress or to become the European part of a global company.

However, a number of other circumstances also contributed to the inability to solve the partnership issue. The most important factors were the following:

- *Dropping pressure.* When the Alcazar talks were initiated, the airline industry was near the bottom of the worst recession ever to have hit the industry. The significant losses suffered by the Alcazar partners focused their attention and created a sense of urgency. It was also believed that the liberalization of the European market would only make matters worse, putting pressure on the airline to cut costs and improve their positions immediately. But as the talks progressed the competitive intensity eased a bit and the cost cutting measures at Swissair and KLM started to show at the bottom line. This lessened the pressure on the Alcazar partners to find a solution 'at any cost'. The current CEO of KLM (then COO), Leo van Wijk, said in 1994 (after the breakdown of the Alcazar talks): "We have two policies - to seek strong internal growth and to find a European partner. We have over-achieved growth in the last couple of years. The partnership strategy was developed at a time when European liberalization was not finalized. A year ago, it looked as if it would take place rapidly but there is now a slowdown in the process, and some people think there is a standstill or a reversal. Against this background, the need to find a partner is not as urgent as a year ago."

- *Doubts about SAS.* While KLM and Swissair were able to trim their cost structure and win new business during 1992 and 1993, SAS slipped further into losses. This unfolding picture of SAS heading for a nosedive led to worries among the other partners. When it became clear that the SAS crew seemed to be revolting against the captain, Carlzon, doubts about SAS's viability grew even stronger.

- *Viable alternatives.* As the talks progressed, all parties involved constantly weighed the Alcazar alliance against other alternatives that they had. Austrian Airlines was actively being courted by Lufthansa, while SAS was also being winked at by the German carrier. Meanwhile, Swissair was considering the opportunity to take a stake in the troubled Belgian airline Sabena, which would also give it the prized foothold in the European Union. Only KLM did not have another suitor on hand, in case Alcazar didn't work out. But then KLM was probably in the strongest position to decide to stay independent, if the Alcazar deal did not meet its intentions.

5. What should KLM do now that the 'engagement rings' have been given back?

Basically, KLM has three alternatives that it should contemplate:

- *Alternative European suitor.* Having courted British Airways first, and then SAS, Swissair and Austrian Airlines, KLM could try to find another European partner. However, if KLM wants to engage in a merger of equals, then Lufthansa and Air France are too large, while others such as TAP (Portugal), Finnair, Air Lingus (Ireland), LOT (Poland), Malev (Hungary) and Olympic (Greece) are too small, remote and/or uncompetitive. Logically, only Iberia (Spain) and Alitalia fit in terms of size and location. However, both airlines are lumbering giants, run for years as government bureaucracies. Much would need to be done to make them an attractive partner for KLM.

- *Transatlantic knot.* KLM could also decide to forego a European alliance and to push forward in the race to build a transatlantic company. Practically, this would mean that KLM and Northwest would speed up their integration process and try to capture a larger part of the cross-Atlantic travel. This process could also be broadened to include an Asian carrier, to cover all three legs of the Triad.

- *Old maid.* It needs to be asked whether all of the mergers and alliances really deliver the scale advantages which in theory they are supposed to do. It could be argued that successful companies such as Southwest and Virgin Atlantic are focused loners, and that life as an 'old maid' isn't as bad as it seems during the current 'dating game'. However, if KLM would opt for a 'go it alone' strategy, there would have to be a clearer picture of the firm's competitive advantage.

Other Teaching Issues

The case also raises a number of issues that are relevant to other chapters in the book. These other teaching issues are:

- *Forming an alliance strategy.* When KLM first developed its strategic plans for the period after liberalization, it selected British Airways as the ideal partner. When these talks were unsuccessful the Alcazar talks were initiated. Now again KLM must develop a strategy for the future. However, the question is whether this strategy formation process can be deliberate, or whether plenty of room must be given to emergentness (link to chapter 3)?

- *Speed and magnitude of change.* In the Alcazar alliance talks all participants seemed to prefer a swift and comprehensive shift to one company. Yet in their relationship with Northwest, KLM has moved slowly and in small steps. This allows for a discussion on the benefits of revolution and evolution in interfirm cooperation (link to chapter 4).

- *Competitive advantage.* The market seems to be demanding larger hub-and-spoke networks and lower costs. Airlines must decide whether to reform themselves to meet these new market requirements, or whether they should build on their historic strengths (link to chapter 5).

- *Low business unit autonomy.* While airlines are often in different lines of business, such as scheduled flights, charters, and cargo, the intertwined nature of their operations makes it difficult to run the company as a portfolio of businesses (link to chapter 6).

- *Industry evolution.* The case describes how most of the players within the industry are convinced that global hub-and-spoke networks are the future of airlines. Most carriers seemed convinced that compliance to the changing rules is the only sane strategy. The question is whether the rules are really as strict as they seem at first and whether there is not ample room for 'choice' (link to chapter 8).

- *Organizational inheritance.* The four way alliance talks involved six governments, more than 40 unions and numerous other stakeholders. Each group had its own interests, while each company had its own history, culture and power structures. The question is whether a four-way merger could ever have been successful under these circumstances. Might it be that most alliances are an easy way out, giving some benefits of size, while avoiding the hard restructuring that a real merger might bring (link to chapter 9)?

- *Global competition?* An important question is whether global scale is really necessary. What are the true advantages of becoming a global airline? Could it be that international diversity might remain high, as customers select national carriers, offering services in their language and meeting their expectations? Might local advertising, local distribution, local regulations and local competitors force airlines to keep a strong local responsiveness (link to chapter 10)?

- *Stakeholders influence.* The Alcazar talks are an interesting example of how companies must manage their many stakeholders, while also asking themselves whose interests they should serve. Each government and union was interested in keeping jobs and prestigious tasks in their own country, while shareholders had most to gain from consolidation at one location. The question can even be asked whether top managers' own interests needed to be served by the alliance (link to chapter 11)?

What Happened After the Case?

The case runs until the beginning of 1994. This section describes the major developments in global alliances in the airline industry, and the alliances of the four members of Alcazar, with the main focus on KLM/Royal Dutch Airlines and its alliance rationale. Visit our website (www.itbp.com) for the most up-to-date information and valuable further links.

Global alliances

- *The nature of alliances.* Since the end of the case, the nature of alliances has changed significantly. In the beginning most of the alliances were marketing alliances with code-sharing and cross-selling of tickets, but at this moment alliances have become more strategic, in the direction of full mergers (see exhibit 1). To get approval for these 'virtual' mergers, airlines 'trade' (in co-operation with their governments) open-skies agreements for exemption of antitrust laws. The KLM-Northwest alliance was the first one to get this antitrust immunity in 1990.

- *Major alliances.* By September 1998 there were over 500 alliances between individual airlines. Four major alliances are currently dominant in the global airline industry. These are Oneworld, Star, Qualiflyer and Wings. These four alliances account for 81% of the total 1.9 trillion Revenue Passenger Kilometers (RPKs) in the global airline industry (see exhibit 2).

EXHIBIT 1
Evolution of Alliances in the Airline Industry (Source: Gellman Research Associates Inc.)

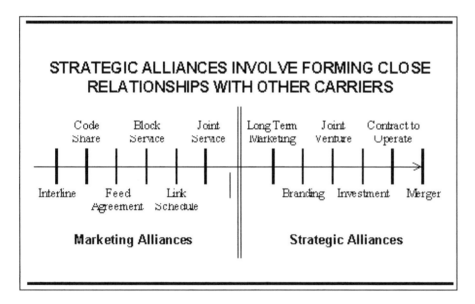

The four major alliances

- *Oneworld.* American Airlines, Canadian Airlines, Japan Airlines, US Airways, British Airways, Qantas, Iberia, and Cathay Pacific.
- *Star.* United Airlines, Lufthansa, Thai Airways, **SAS**, Air Canada, Varig, South African Airways, Singapore Airlines, All Nippon Airlines, Air New Zealand, Ansett and Australia.
- *Wings.* Northwest, Continental, **KLM** and Alitalia.
- *Delta/Qualiflyer.* Delta, **Swissair**, Sabena and **Austrian Airlines**.

All the major alliances comprise of at least one big American carrier together with a few European and other carriers. The Star alliance is the most integrated and most international alliance and combines the largest number of carriers and cultural diversity. Surprisingly, Air France (Europe's 3rd biggest carrier) is not linked to any of the four major alliances, mainly because the French government wants to have some degree of control over Air France, which is not favorable to potential partners. Rumors have surfaced that Air France might link up with KLM and Alitalia in Wings. Otherwise Air France could join the Qualiflyer alliance.

EXHIBIT 2
The Major Airline Alliances in 1998, in Percent of Total Revenue Passenger Kilometers (RPKs)

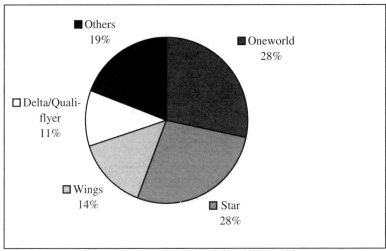

Source: The Economist, September 26, 1998, p. 80

The Alcazar Players

- *Swissair/Austrian Airlines.* In the case, it was said that Swissair needed a big EC partner. However, they did not link up with the mentioned Air France, British Airways or Lufthansa. Instead, Swissair linked up with two smaller carriers, Austrian Airlines and Sabena (in which it bought a 49.5% stake) to create the Qualiflyer alliance. This Qualiflyer alliance teamed up with Delta Airlines, but this relationship is said to be languishing. Strategically, two options surface among industry experts. A link up with Air France, or a link up of the Qualiflyer alliance itself with one of the other three major groupings.

- *SAS.* After the breakdown of the Alcazar talks, SAS gradually distanced itself from its former partners in the European Quality Alliance and started operating an alliance with Lufthansa in January 1996, with SAS handling all Scandinavian passengers and aircraft and Lufthansa the passengers and aircraft at German stations. In February 1997, SAS and Lufthansa Cargo joined forces. In May 1997, the Star alliance was announced. SAS is still operating in this alliance as a major partner and announced a strategic alliance with Singapore Airlines in October 1998.

KLM after Alcazar

- *KLM and Northwest.* The relationship between Northwest and KLM has always been a difficult one. From the beginning, the two American majority owners, Checci and Wilson (former financial experts who bought a 44% stake, now reduced to 20%), and the Board of KLM had different views about how a company should be run. In 1995, Northwest was afraid that KLM was seeking control over Northwest and wanted a standstill agreement, which KLM refused. Northwest then installed a poison pill construction to prevent KLM from exercising its right to increase its stake in Northwest. This resulted in a two-year legal battle. Trust among the two partners further deteriorated, resulting in loss of efficient decision making and indirectly in a loss of potential revenue. The climax of the tussle was the resignation of the three board seats KLM had at Northwest in 1996. In September 1997 KLM agreed to sell back its 20% stake in three phases for $1.1 billion and in return Northwest and KLM signed a 13-year joint-venture agreement. In 1998, Northwest announced it would buy back all the shares at once, thus bringing KLM's stake to 0% three years ahead of schedule. This ended a roller coaster 'marriage', but KLM and Northwest have remained 'friends', as their marketing alliance has been extended.

- *Changes at KLM.* In 1997 KLM CEO Bouw retired and was replaced by the COO Leo van Wijk. This management change had two important results. First, a more aggressive approach to alliances was undertaken (KLM CEO Bouw was said to be too cautious). Secondly, the policy of striving for cross-shareholdings as a means of enforcing commitment was abandoned. These changes opened the door for the deal with Northwest to cut all formal ties and really start working together. It also led to talks with Alitalia. The new management is also pressuring Air France to join the Wings alliance (after that to be renamed Global Wings), to greatly increase the size of the alliance.

- *KLM and Alitalia.* After signing a Memorandum of Understanding in December 1997, KLM and Alitalia reached a formal agreement for an alliance in October 1998. The proposed alliance was intended to result in two joint ventures in the near future, one for passenger transport and one for cargo transport. The KLM-Alitalia partnership is the first alliance with a real multi-hub strategy, i.e. Amsterdam, Rome and the new Milan Malpensa airport. Outsourcing technical services and cabin-personnel to each other will be implemented. Even the exchanging of pilots is envisaged by both airlines, but as it is the last sacred issue in the airline industry, it will probably not be implemented in the near future. At the moment the KLM-Alitalia partnership is the most integrated form of co-operation in the airline business, as a new network organization will be formed that comes closest so far to a full merger.

- *Other KLM ventures.* In recent years KLM has taken 100% control over Air UK (now KLM UK), enlarged their stake in Martinair (a Dutch charter airline) from 50% to 100% (still subject to EU approval) and has taken a 30% stake in the regional Norwegian airline Braathens SAFE, a competitor of SAS. KLM is also allied with Eurowings, a German regional carrier, together with Northwest and Air France.

References

Airfinance Journal, NWA buys out KLM and links up with Continental, February 1998.

Goodnow, J., *Lecture International Business Entry Modes and Strategic Alliances,* Bradley University (http://cyberprof.bradley.edu/~courses/Goodnow).

GRA Inc., *Transportation Advisor,* Volume III, Number 1, January 1993, (www.gra-inc.com/voliii1/voliii1).

KLM website, www.klm.com.

Reed, A., The tumbling of Alcazar, *Air Transport World*, January 1994.

The Economist, One world, few airlines, September 26, 1998, p.19.

The Economist, Mergers in mind, September 26, 1998, p. 80.

Tully, S., Northwest and KLM: The alliance from hell, *Fortune*, June 24, 1996.

Wright Research Center (http://profiles.wisi.com).

TEACHING NOTE 14: THE SALIM GROUP

Case by Hellmut Schütte, Lizabeth Froman and Marc Canizzo

Teaching note by Bob de Wit, Ron Meyer and Melbert Visscher

Case Synopsis

This case provides an excellent example of the role and success of personal networks in economic activities undertaken by overseas Chinese. The case is about the group of companies directly or indirectly controlled by the founder of the Salim Group, Sudono Salim (Liem Sioe Liong in Chinese). In 1937 he arrived in Indonesia from his native province of Fukien (China) almost penniless and managed to build one of Asia's largest business empires through opportunistic expansion. His friendship with Indonesia's President Suharto played a deciding role in the development of the Salim conglomerate. The Salim Group spans dozens of industries around the world. A small group of investors form the hard core of shareholders in most of Liem's businesses. They include Liem's family members, close friends from Fukien province and members of the Suharto clan. The flagship enterprise in the fleet of Salim companies is First Pacific Group of Hong Kong, run by Manuel Pangilinan. The Liem investors retain 65 percent ownership of First Pacific and tight management control.

The challenge presented in this case has to do with the next phase in the Salim Group's corporate development. The group has expanded and internationalized at a high rate, calling into question the effectiveness of the current management style, based on close personal ties between the main leaders within the group. Moreover, Liem has grown older and he must plan for his succession to ensure future continuity. A key issue in the case is whether the next generation of company leaders can continue to operate in the same manner as before, or whether they need to reform the way the group is managed. Is the 'bamboo network' a relic of the past or a key ingredient of the group's strength in the future?

Teaching Objectives

If used in conjunction with chapter 7, this case can be used to meet the following teaching objectives:

- *Understanding the structure and workings of non-hierarchical business groups.* This case gives the opportunity to explore the concept of the Bamboo network as an example of a non-hierarchical form of business organization. Culture plays an important role in explaining the differences of the conception of networks in different parts of the world (link to introduction, 7.2 Jarillo and 7.5 Weidenbaum & Hughes).

- *Understanding strategy making and management control styles within multi-company networks.* Corporate centers play an important role in the success of multi-company networks. Strategically minded central firms view the boundaries of the organization differently. Network partners are seen as an integral part of the organization. This contrasts with the neoclassical view of collaboration as a different form of competition. Depending on the approach to networks different management styles will be adopted (link to 7.4 Lorenzoni & Baden-Fuller).

- *Analyzing the resources needed to manage multi-company networks.* Managing multi-company networks will involve more than just the allocation of financial resources. Managerial competencies will need to be brought in to steer the networks' operations to success. Relational resources play an important role in the networks of overseas Chinese. Commitment to a network will come from a long-term relationship and trust, not just from a capital infusion (link to introduction and 7.5 Weidenbaum & Hughes).

- *Discussing the advantages and disadvantages of multi-company networks.* As became apparent in the introduction of chapter 7, different views exist concerning the merits of networks. Evaluating advantages and disadvantages often involves certain levels of subjectivity and cultural differences. Discussing possible advantages and disadvantages can provide more insight in the differing perspectives on network level strategy (link to all).

Teaching Guideline

If there is one case in this book that challenges Western conceptions of 'proper' business management and 'successful' corporate diversification strategy, then it is the Salim case. To understand the basic concepts of overseas Chinese networks, students need to understand that this particular type of networking is characteristic of the overseas Chinese way of organizing economic activity. Overseas Chinese networks are, for the most part, personal networks (*guanxi*), built on reciprocal obligations. These networks are organized on the basis of kinship or other mutual ties, like being born in the same region. Hamilton (1991) argues that cultural and historical developments lie at the root of *guanxi*. He refers to cultural influences like Confucianism and the role of trust in Chinese society as the cause of this type of networking. Many of these networks seem to have developed in the laissez-faire economies of Southeast Asia. The Bamboo Network (reading 7.5) by Weidenbaum and Hughes explains this phenomenon further.

It is very useful to first start class discussion by taking some time to reflect on Chinese culture and the backgrounds of the overseas Chinese who started these networks, before launching into the case. If the class has students from different cultural backgrounds, the next step can be to ask them what types of social networks exist in their countries and whether these affect the way business is conducted in their country. The implicit model that many students have, especially if they are from North America or northwestern Europe, is that organizations and business are largely depersonalized and mechanistic. It is often assumed that 'face-less' economic efficiency dictates organizational structures and processes, and that relationships within and between organizations are largely functional. But if pressed to think about the role of personal and social ties within their country, students can often come up with examples of organizations that do not fit the mechanistic stereotype. Examples might come of family businesses, cooperatives, church-centered companies, Keiretsu-like groups and 'old boys' networks.

Finally students can be asked to compare the overseas Chinese conception of business networks with the prevailing conception of business networks in their own country. Students can be asked to make a list of the advantages and disadvantages of each type of network. Students will quickly come to the conclusion that culture and historical developments play a deciding role in the formation of different types of networks. The most important learning objective is to get students to understand that inter-firm relationships are not only about economics, but also about people. And nothing is so culturally diverse as the way in which people form relationships in different countries. Without an understanding of these personal and social links between (groups of) people, it is difficult to understand the relationships between organizations.

The section "What Happened after the Case" provides interesting material to put the Salim Group, in the light of the Asia crisis and the overthrow of President Suharto of Indonesia. Students can be asked to what extent the network played a role in Salim's survival during the crisis, or whether the group's links to the Suharto clan is actually Salim's Achilles' heel. Would the Salim Group have been able to survive the crisis without the help of the network, or was it actually a millstone around the group's neck?

Case Questions

1. How can the corporate strategy of First Pacific Company be described? How does the company create value?

2. How is the First Pacific Group managed and what are the roles of the corporate center?

3. How does Liem Sioe Liong manage the Salim Group and which resources does he bring in to further expand the group?

4. What are the advantages and disadvantages of building a business empire as Liem Sioe Liong has done?

5. What advice would you give Anthony Salim to further improve the prospects of the Salim group and to keep the group on track to becoming Indonesia's first multinational?

Case Analysis

1. How can the corporate strategy of First Pacific Company be described? How does the company create value?

At first glance, corporate strategy at First Pacific comes close to the portfolio perspective described in chapter 6. First Pacific has autonomous business units in four areas: banking, telecommunications, marketing & distribution and real estate. Growth has been largely accomplished through opportunity-driven acquisitions in each of these areas. However, it can be argued that First Pacific's business units are not as autonomous as one would expect in a true 'portfolio' company. First Pacific does have decentralized operations management, but still retains a high level of centralized decision making. As the case mentions, First Pacific has been described as a one-man show with Manny Pangilinan as a financial genius and admired visionary.

Thus, First Pacific can be described as an investment type conglomerate, but not in the traditional Western sense. The portfolio perspective focuses on the leveraging of financial resources and emphasizes financial synergies. First Pacific also has this focus, backed by strong deal-making abilities and the professional management of Pangilinan's central team. The major difference with the traditional Western conglomerate is that First Pacific also adds value by leveraging its relational resources. Each company purchased by First Pacific is given access to the network of relationships that the other units have built up, and can make use of the *guanxi* that Liem has acquired. In other words, each First Pacific business can tap into the company's core intangible resource – *guanxi*.

2. How is the First Pacific Group managed and what are the roles of the corporate center?

Manny Pangilinan, the trusted advisor of the Liems, manages First Pacific through active involvement in all of the company's businesses. First Pacific's top management includes heads of each division, but is dominated by a group of Filipino bankers who have been selected by Pangilinan himself. Top managers hold important equity positions in the companies that they manage, thus sharing First Pacific's goal of increasing shareholder value.

Pangilinan's active involvement in all parts of the company does not fit with the financial control approach that would normally be expected in a 'portfolio' company. He does not give the business units full independence to set their own course without interference from the corporate center. On the contrary, Pangilian keeps up to date on all developments, influencing decisions where necessary, much more like a family type of business. His role is to support the business units in their strategy development, and to mobilize the company's relational network when useful. In other words, the role of the corporate center is not only financial, but includes the active use of contacts, favors, reputation and power to get deals done. The corporate center is a spider in a web of relationships that can be used to facilitate sales activities, to gain access to new customers, to encourage joint ventures, to ease government regulations, to discourage active competition, and to 'catch' new acquisition candidates. To add value in this way, the corporate center must be actively involved in the business of all of its divisions.

3. *How does Liem Sioe Liong manage the Salim Group and which resources does he bring in to further expand the group?*

The Salim group is a non-hierarchical form of business organization. Like many 'bamboo network' firms, it consists of cross-holdings of privately owned, family-run, trade-oriented firms. The Liem investors, including family members, close friends and members of the Suharto regime, are the shareholders of most of Liem's businesses. The Liem investors retain tight management control over the firms within the group. Equity not held by the Liem family is placed in friendly hands. Most new overseas investments by the Liem family are not undertaken directly by the Salim group, but rather through foreign-based associates.

Liem manages the business through the allocation of resources, especially intangible resources like information and relations. Small numbers of managers are placed at the head of individual businesses and are frequently rotated around the group, assuring that the loyalty of management is to Liem and not to the separate businesses. It is evident that in this context trust plays an important role. Earlier it became apparent that trust lies at the basis of *guanxi*. The high level of trust makes decentralization of subsidiaries' operations possible, while relations are managed and resources allocated centrally. The strategy of all the affiliates is overseen by a small group of Executive Directors that are close to Liem.

Opportunity-driven investment behavior, and Liem's and Anthony's deal-making capabilities, have in part led to the large growth of the Salim group. Another important factor in the successful growth has been the relation network. Control of markets and competition has been achieved through cross-ownership arrangements with other Indonesian-Chinese tycoons and by special monopoly-like benefits from the Suharto regime. Personal contacts, trust, history and mutual gain play a vital role in this respect. Finally, it must also be pointed out that Liem's ability to select the right people, and to put them in the right place at the right time, has contributed greatly to his success.

4. *What are the advantages and disadvantages of building a business empire as Liem Sioe Liong has done?*

Any form of organization has advantages and disadvantages *compared to* alternative organizational arrangements. Therefore, a distinction needs to be made between advantages and disadvantages compared to 'hierarchy', and when compared to 'markets'. Some major advantages when compared to hierarchy are the following:

- *Lower governance costs.* A network like Liem's makes less use of contracts, formalized plans and written reports. These hallmarks of bureaucratic formalization are less necessary in an organization functioning on the basis of personal relationships. Moreover, there is much less need for layers of management, leaving more room for horizontal coordination and self-organization with the network.

- *Greater flexibility.* Companies within the group can work together where advantageous and can join forces with other companies where useful. This gives the firm much more flexibility than in vertically integrated companies.

- *Lower capital investment.* Working through joint ventures, small shareholdings and alliances is often much cheaper than through mergers and acquisitions.

Some major disadvantages when compared to hierarchies are the following:

- *Risk of opportunism.* The lack of contractual basis opens up the risk that network partners might act opportunistically, to the disadvantage of the other network companies. Some companies might also show less commitment when problems arise and might abandon their partners prematurely.

- *Lack of central decision-making.* Especially when complex, high investment projects need to be undertaken, the lack of strong central decision-making can be a burden. Each network partner might be just a bit too independent to force them into a centrally directed project.

Network forms of organization must also be compared to market relationships, as the other major alternative. Some major advantages when compared to market relationships are the following:

- *Lower transaction costs.* A high level of trust and long term commitment within a network lowers the need for contracts, policing, hedging and courtroom battles. The long period that firms work together also allows for investment in the relationship and the avoidance of switching costs.

- *Easier access to capital through network.* Raising capital for risky projects is often much faster and less costly when network partners trust each other. Also, less energy needs to be spent on impressing financial analysts, and more competition-sensitive information can be kept secret.

- *Faster decision-making.* As there is a higher level of trust among the network participants, new initiatives can be started without extensive negotiations and confidence building at the beginning of joint activities.

- *Locking out competitors.* By aligning their strategies, network partners can make it more difficult for competitors to expand and for new entrants to get a foothold in the market.

Some major disadvantages when compared to market relationships are the following:

- *Lock-in.* The responsibilities that a firm has towards its network partners might inhibit development, even external market parties would be preferable suppliers or buyers. Historical obligations and close ties might actually hold a company back from exploiting new opportunities that would require more freedom of action. Furthermore, a company might be much less competitive, because its network partners are the weak links in the value chain.

- *Less exposure to outside knowledge.* By sticking with the same partners for a long period of time, the company will gain fewer opportunities to acquire new knowledge. In particular, it is generally more difficult to get foreign companies involved in the network.

5. *What advice would you give Anthony Salim to further improve the prospects of the Salim group and to keep the group on track to becoming Indonesia's first multinational?*

The Salim Group is very dependent on the Indonesian and Southeast Asian markets. Anthony has already shown his willingness to venture into Europe and the United States. Moving into Europe and the United States will mean that network relations will lose importance since Anthony will need to adhere to common business practices in other parts of the world. Anthony is trying to gain international credibility by professionalizing management and using non-Indonesian holding groups as acquisition and growth vehicles. Furthermore, Anthony is looking to divest smaller holdings and to take greater control of key businesses.

Apparently, Anthony is trying to find a balance in organization between the networked Salim Group on the one hand and more Western-style conglomerates on the other. It seems that he wants to use these conglomerates to expand operations outside Southeast Asia. In this way the Salim group will not be directly involved in overseas investments, but will play a role behind the scenes. Maybe this will make it possible for the network to co-exist with more Western-style operations.

When answering this question a variety of options exist. But students will at least want to take the following issues into account:

- *Organizational model*. Is the 'bamboo network' model of organization a relic of the past, or does this mode of organizing economic activity hold promise for the future?

- *Geographic scope*. Can and should the Salim group branch out of Southeast Asia, or is this asking for trouble?

- *Business scope*. Should the Salim group stay involved in such widely diverse lines of business, or narrow its focus? Is the age of the conglomerate definitively over in Southeast Asia (see the recent break up of Korea's Daewoo), or will such business empires remain a dominant feature on the economic landscape?

Other Teaching Issues

- *Strategy formation*. As Anthony puts it: "The formation of the Salim Group was by accident, not design. Our growth was driven by opportunities available to us." Nevertheless, the building of the network was not something that just occurred. This provides for interesting discussions on the deliberateness and emergentness of strategy formation (link to chapter 3).

- *Corporate level strategy*. The strategy of Salim's flagship enterprise First Pacific Group comes close to the portfolio perspective. However, the First Pacific Group is more than just an investor exercising financial control. The First Pacific Group has proved to be very good at leveraging relational resources. This can be seen as a core resource of First Pacific (link to chapter 6).

- *Organizational leadership*. This case provides for an interesting discussion on the topic of organizational leadership versus organizational dynamics. The Liem investors exercise tight informal control over the group's operations. However, the development of the network can be seen as an evolutionary process where history plays an important role in the behavior of the network partners (link to chapter 9).

- *Internationalization of networks*. The Salim group has achieved fast international expansion through a decentralized approach and opportunistic investments. But for the Salim Group to become Indonesia's first truly multinational company, more clarity needs to be created about cross-border relations. Will all foreign acquisitions be run on a local-for-local basis, or does Salim want to strive for some sort of cross-border synergy (link to chapter 10).

- *Principle-agent issue*. The goal of the First Pacific Group is to increase shareholder value, with the shareholders being for the large part the Liem investors. A part of the tension between shareholders and stakeholders has been solved by giving top management significant shareholdings. The First Pacific Group is therefore a good example of how a far-flung company can be controlled by making the 'agents' partly 'principals' (link to chapter 11).

What Happened after the Case?

The case runs until 1992. It ends with Anthony Salim's intention to build a Pan-Asian company. The goals mentioned are: (1) streamlining the Group's holdings, (2) consolidating the family's control at the expense of the other Liem investors and (3) strengthening his company's balance sheets. Although little information is available about the Salim Group itself, the following text will describe the developments within the main holding of the group, the First Pacific Group, the impact of the Asia crisis and what has become of Anthony's goals.

The Salim family. As family patriarch, Sudono Salim (82), better known as Liem Sioe Liong, is still the chairman of the Salim Group. His son, Anthony Salim (49), is president and CEO of the Salim Group and is responsible for daily operations. Although Pangilinan runs First Pacific, he owns only 3 percent of it. The Salim family and three associated families control 54 percent. But company executives say the Salims let Pangalinan run the show. All they ask is that he keeps in contact by phone with Anthony Salim from time to time. Though the Salims control the single largest stake, they do not have the largest number of votes or the biggest influence on a day-to-day basis at First Pacific. This is a good example of the new management style Anthony is implementing.

The Asia crisis. As the economic crisis has unfolded in Southeast Asia, Indonesia has been one of the countries that has been hit hardest. This has had an enormous impact on the Salim group. The following items are important in this context:

- *The Chinese in Indonesia.* There are over thirty major conglomerates in Indonesia. Their emergence was spawned by a series of deregulation measures in the 1980's. Indonesian-Chinese make up a mere 3% of the population, but hold about 75% of the country's wealth and control the majority of these conglomerates. Salim Group has found itself under attack from politicians anxious to appease popular pressure to break the hold of ethnic Chinese conglomerates on the economy and distribute their assets to indigenous groups.

- *Liem Sioe Long and Suharto.* Liem Sioe Long, founder of the Salim group, is the Suharto family's longest standing Chinese associate. While Liem is not exactly lacking business skills, his friendship with Suharto has certainly helped his cause. During the riots in May 1998 an angry mob wrecked Liem's mansion in Jakarta and torched his portrait. Ever since, Liem has reportedly left Indonesia and remains in California while Anthony runs the business. According to Forbes Magazine, Liem's personal fortune dropped from an estimated US$4 billion in February 1998 to US$1.7 billion after Suharto's fall.

- *Salim and Indofood.* A run on the deposits of Salim's Bank Central Asia (BCA) in the weeks following the riots, almost led to the collapse of the bank. Billions were pumped into the bank by the authorities to avoid collapse. To pay back this rescue operation Salim has had to sell stakes in many firms to the Indonesian Bank Restructuring Agency. Selling stakes in its businesses to foreign firms has been the group's strategy to cope with its troubles. However, the recent political crisis has all but devastated Salim's business interests in Indonesia. As a countermove, the Salim Group has sold Indofood to its own subsidiary, First Pacific, and Japan's Nissin Food Products. This will allow Indofood to make use of the packaging expertise of Nissin, but more importantly it will shelter Indofood from some of the political uncertainties it would have had to face as an Indonesian company.

First Pacific Company. Due to Anthony's restructuring plans and the necessary responses to the Asia crisis, the new structure of First Pacific has changed significantly, as can be seen in exhibit 1. Further developments are detailed below:

- *First Pacific on the move.* Drawn into the Asian crisis with debt topping US$2.9 billion, the company looked to be on the brink of insolvency. Instead the conglomerate - with controlling stakes in 18 companies spanning Asia, the US and Europe - divested four prized assets and emerged with US$2.3 billion in cash. The key asset sold was Holland-based Hagemeyer N.V., which garnered US$1.7 billion. It is interesting to note that at one moment the value of the Hagemeyer stake, traded on the Amsterdam exchange, was worth more than the value of the whole First Pacific Company, listed at the Hong Kong stock exchange! Flushed with cash, First Pacific retired some US$1.2 billion in debt, injected US$552 million into four Asian subsidiaries and went on an acquisition spree.

- *Positioning.* With the sell-off, First Pacific is positioning itself to be the primary investment vehicle for Western fund managers, whom it reckons will return to Asia in droves in a few years. Surrounded by an international team of young executives, the managing director Pangilinan is trying to manage First Pacific according Western business norms and he is intent on building a reputation as a trustworthy and high quality business.

- *New strategy at First Pacific.* Until recently First Pacific had invested largely in start-ups and built them up into profitable companies, mostly in trading, property, finance and telecommunications. Since the crisis it has come up with a new strategy: buying into established corporations with huge turnovers and divesting mature companies that have peaked in their markets.

- *Profit and turnover of First Pacific.* Exhibit 2 shows that profit before exceptionals and turnover have decreased heavily during the last two years, of course due to the major divestments at the end of 1998.

EXHIBIT 1
The Structure of the First Pacific Group as of April 30th 1999:

Consumer	Property	Telecommunications	Banking
Darya-Varia	**First Pacific Davies**	**PLDT**	**First Pacific Bank**
Indonesia (89%)	Asia, UK (100%)	Philippines (17%)	Hong Kong (41%)
Berli Jucker	**Pacific Plaza Towers**	**Smart**	**PDCP Bank**
Thailand (84%)	Philippines (85%)	Philippines (51%)	Philippines (28%)
Metro Pacific	**Bonofacio Land**	**Escotel**	
Philippines (85%)	Philippines (56%)	India (49%)	
Indofood	**Landco Pacific**	**Metrosel**	
Indonesia (51%)	Philippines (51%)	Indonesia (35%)	
		Shenzhen Merchant Link	
		China (60%)	
		Fujian Telecom	
		China (25.5%)	

Suggested Further Readings

Hamilton, G. (ed.) (1991), *Business Networks and Economic Development in East and Southeast Asia*, Hong Kong, Centre of Asian Studies/University of Hong Kong.

Redding, S.G. (1990), *The Spirit of Chinese Capitalism*, Walter de Gruyter, Berlin.

EXHIBIT 2
First Pacific Profit and Turnover, 1991-1998

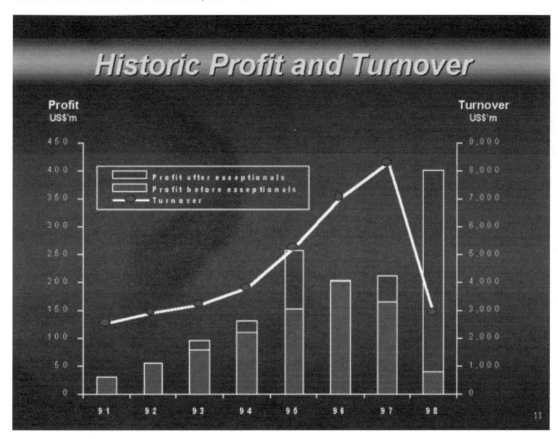

TEACHING NOTE 15: THE CHAMPAGNE INDUSTRY

Case by Karel Cool, James Howe and James Henderson

Teaching note by Pursey Heugens and Ron Meyer

Case Synopsis

Champagne is probably the most prestigious wine in the world. The association with festivity, the impressive history of the wine houses, and the fact that only the wines from a tiny region near Reims, a city in northern France, may actually be called champagne, all add to that prestige. However, fame alone is seldom a guarantee for future success, and in fact the industry faces a few very serious threats. Paradoxically enough, the greatest threat to the champagne industry are probably the players from within the industry itself. From its earliest days, the production of champagne has been divided between two different groups: the *récoltants* who grew the grapes, and the *négotiants*, who fabricated and sold the champagne. By 1993, there were 15,000 registered grape growers, who together controlled 87 percent of the vineyards in the Champagne region. The *négotiants* or champagne houses numbered 261. Together, they produced 145 million bottles of champagne in 1992.

Due to this great number of parties, trying to establish some form of co-ordination within these groups is almost a mission impossible, let alone establishing it between both groups. Moreover, or probably consequentially, the players within this industry have to cope with internal conflicts of interest. The community of champagne houses cannot afford to dilute their image by selling a lot of cheaper, lower quality wines. At the same time, it is lucrative for each champagne house individually to maximize its output of such *petits champagnes*. The grape growers should by and large limit their total supply of grapes, both to secure that only high quality grapes are being produced and to make sure that supply does not surpass demand. Unfortunately, each individual *récoltant* can make a surplus profit by maximizing output. The conflicts between growers and houses (grape prices) are even more obvious. To cope with these internal problems, both groups have unified themselves in a body that represents their collective interests – the Comité Interprofessionel du Vin de Champagne (CIVC). This body resolves the internal conflicts by setting the grape prices, and by limiting the quantity of grapes that may be grown per hectare – consequentially restricting the champagne output.

On top of the internal conflicts, the champagne industry faces competition from other sparkling wines, such as Spanish (Catalan) *cava*, Italian *spumante*, German *sekt*, and a number of substitutes from the 'new' wine producing countries, such as the United States (California), Australia, and a number of South American countries.

In September 1989, the CIVC failed to reach an agreement that satisfied all parties for the first time in almost 50 years. Moreover, due to the increasing quality of other sparkling wines, the champagne industry faced the fiercest competition ever. The case ends in 1993, when the members of the CIVC met to discuss the crisis that resulted from the failure to compromise. This meeting was going to be critical to the future of the champagne industry. The question was whether the future of the champagne industry was malleable, or whether the industry was to be swept along in the uncontrollable tides of history.

Teaching Objectives

If used in conjunction with chapter 8, this case can help to meet the following teaching objectives:

- *Analysis of industry structure.* Very detailed information on all of the competitive forces in the champagne industry is discussed in this case. This makes it possible to discuss how these forces shape the nature of competition in the industry (link to 8.1 Porter and 8.4 Hamel & Prahalad).

- *Multi-level analysis*. This case provides opportunities for a discussion on multi-level analysis. Appropriate (aggregation) levels of analysis are the individual growers and houses, their respective clusters, the (French) champagne industry, and the global sparkling wines industry (link to 8.3 Hannan & Freeman, and 8.4 Hamel & Prahalad).

- *Identifying the forces of environmental selection*. This describes trends and developments beyond the control of the individual organization that might actually cause environmental selection. It can be discussed how the process of environmental selection of fit and unfit firms takes place (link to 8.3 Hannan & Freeman, and 8.5 Arthur).

- *Identifying the importance of industry creation*. Due to the open end of the case, it is possible to discuss a broad range of corporate level and network level strategies, aimed at proactively changing the rules of the game in the champagne industry. This allows for a discussion on the process of creating a new industry environment and on the question to what extent the champagne industry is malleable (link to 8.2 Baden-Fuller & Stopford, and Hamel & Prahalad).

- *Explaining the importance of inter-firm coordination in industry creation*. The champagne industry consists of numerous players, of which most are relatively small. Coordination between the players is therefore of utmost importance. This allows for a discussion on the importance of network-level strategies in industry creation (link to chapter 7).

- *Distinction between compliance and choice perspectives*. Finally, the main issue of this chapter can be raised, namely the malleability of the industry. It can be debated whether an organization's survival mainly depends on its compliance to industry pressures, or on its ability to break with industry recipes and to create new rules (link to all readings).

Teaching Guideline

Most students have a working knowledge of the product manufactured by this industry and therefore a 'bubbly' discussion quickly erupts. We have found, however, that many students find it a rather challenging case for two very different reasons.

First, students like to think in terms of industry creation, but usually do this by suggesting the introduction of new technologies that can entirely change the rules of the competitive game. However, in this case new technologies are not the issue, so many students are at a loss. It might take some effort to impress upon them that shaping an industry can take on many forms.

A second, more challenging issue is that students often have difficulty placing themselves in the position of a manager of a French champagne company. To understand much of the rivalry, conflict and potential for cooperation, students must be able to understand the psyche of the industry managers. These managers are almost exclusively French; few have had formal business training, are strongly loyal to the industry's traditions, and have a long history of mistrust and conflict. Most students tend to determine the strategy to be followed from their own point of view, not from the perspective of the industry incumbents.

Yet, if these two points are kept in mind, the case is a very valuable, as none of the strategic options is obviously the best one. Both the industry evolution and industry creation perspectives can be persuasively argued on the basis of this case.

Suggested Questions

1. If you were allowed to name three characteristics to describe the champagne industry, which three would you choose? Explain why these characteristics can be seen as weaknesses, as well as strengths.

2. This industry shows the signs of some deep-rooted conflicts of interest. What potential conflict exists between the individual grape growers? What is the potential conflict one might find amongst the wine houses? What is the primary conflict to be found between growers and houses?

3. Consider the industry evolution perspective. What are the internal industry forces to which the individual players must comply? What are the external developments with which the champagne industry must cope?

4. Consider the industry creation perspective. How can a unified champagne industry compete with its strongest competitor - other quality sparkling wines?

5. Think about new year's eve – ten years from now. You and a couple of friends have decided to throw the best party in the new millennium yet. Do you think that champagne will be the best wine to buy? Considering your answers to previous questions, what are your reasons to believe so?

Case Analysis

1. If you were allowed to name three characteristics to describe the champagne industry, which three would you choose? Explain why these characteristics can be seen as weaknesses, as well as strengths.

The actual question here is about the distinctiveness of the champagne industry. Numerous answers are obviously possible, but among the most frequently mentioned ones will probably be:

- *Image of luxury and festivity*. Probably no other product in the world is so often associated with good times and prosperity as champagne. This image is so strong that it can almost be stated that the direction of causality has been inverted. A good party does not ask for champagne, but occasions that allow for champagne tend to turn into good parties.

- *Reputation for quality*. Sparkling wines from the champagne region are expensive. Although their luxurious image is a strong explanation for the premium prices, this is not a completely adequate answer. The connotation of good quality these wines bear is also an important factor.

- *Strong brand names*. The names of the champagne houses and especially the brand names of the wines are probably the most important strategic assets of this industry. Names like Moët et Chandon and Dom Perignon are among the best-known brands in the entire wine industry.

- *Unique location*. The Champagne region near Reims is not an agricultural area of impressive size. In fact, it is relatively small if one compares it with other regions where grapes for sparkling wines are grown. But it is the only region in the world whose wines are allowed to carry the champagne name.

- *Craftsmanship*. The Northern part of France is not exactly the best place in the world to grow grapes, due to the rough terrain and the frequently harsh weather conditions. Furthermore, the champagne method of making sparkling wine involves a very delicate and difficult process. Trained under such conditions, the growers and houses of the Champagne region have developed superior craftsmanship for making wines of constant high quality.

- *Vertical disintegration*. The champagne industry is characterized by a rather sharp distinction between grape growers and wine makers. Although such divisions of labor are not uncommon throughout the wine industry, a lot of wine makers tend to control their own vineyards.

- *Low concentration*. The industry has its share of large wine makers, but its most distinctive trait is the strong fragmentation of the grape growers and wine makers. The overall industry concentration level is very low.

CASE 15: THE CHAMPAGNE INDUSTRY **165**

These are only some distinctive traits of the champagne industry. During class discussions, more and other characteristics will obviously be mentioned. The point is not to make a complete analysis of the champagne business, but to show that the characteristics of an industry can be its most obvious strengths and at the same time its principle weaknesses. For example, a strong brand name can be a highly regarded asset, but the vulnerability of brands makes it dangerous to build an empire on a name. Another example is that the relatively high level of vertical disintegration makes the champagne industry lean and competitive on the one hand. On the other, it is a source of conflicting interests and of low mutual loyalty. An analysis like this highlights the paradoxical nature of strategy, and shows the intrinsic limitations of strategic tools such as SWOT analyses and scorecards.

2. *This industry shows the signs of some deep-rooted conflicts of interest. What potential conflict exists between the individual grape growers? What is the potential conflict one might find amongst the wine houses? What is the primary conflict to be found between growers and houses?*

In every non-monopolistic industry, competitors battle for market share, for superior resources, and for control over formal standards and informal norms. Even in monopolistic industries we can witness clashes between monopolists, buyers, and suppliers, and obviously between monopolists and the state. In other words, every industry has its share of (potential) conflicting interests. Yet, seldom are such deep-rooted and institutionalized patterns of conflict encountered as in the champagne industry. Three potential conflicts are the most striking:

- *Growers vs. growers.* The first potential conflict of interest to be discussed here is an 'intra-sector' conflict. Grape growers have their own internal clashes. In order to guarantee the high quality of grapes, growers should limit their output per hectare/acre. The fewer grapes that are grown, the better they become, because the remaining grapes get more than their fair share of sun, nutrients, and attention. Growers should also restrict their output in order to keep market prices at an acceptable level. If the supply of grapes vastly overruns demand, prices tend to become so low that it is hard for everyone to make a living. Although it is favorable for the community of grape growers as a whole to restrict their output, every individual grower has an incentive to maximize his output. However, such 'rationally egoistic' actions do hurt the interests of the community of growers.

- *Houses vs. houses.* The second conflict under discussion is also an 'intra-sector' clash. Wines exist in all qualities, and the same holds true for champagne. On the one hand, there are premium brands that represent the most expensive wines in the world, while on the other there are the low quality *petit champagnes*, competing for shelf-space with lower quality *cavas* and *sekts* in the supermarkets. The community of champagne houses cannot afford to dilute their image by selling a lot of these cheaper, lower quality wines. At the same time, it is lucrative for each champagne house individually to maximize its output of such *petits champagnes*.

- *Growers vs. houses.* The third and final conflict to be discussed here can be found between houses and growers. Apart from any weak or strong ties that might bind representatives of both sectors together, there is one important link between both groups: grape prices. These prices form a root of conflict. The growers need to sell their output, and they will try to maximize their prices while doing so. The houses, on the other hand, need grapes grown in the Champagne region as input for their wines, but they will try to minimize prices. Without appropriate countervailing powers, this situation can easily escalate into a form of 'cut-throat' competition.

These three potential clashes can be further explored by referring back to game theory models discussed in 2.3 Hua Ho & Weigelt.

3. Consider the industry evolution perspective. What are the internal industry forces to which the individual players must comply? What are the external developments with which the champagne industry must cope?

It is possible to view the development of the champagne industry as an autonomous process, to which firms must adjust or risk being selected out. The industry evolution perspective is compelling in this respect, especially if we consider that the champagne industry consists of a large number of relatively small players. We will start with an evaluation of intra-industry pressures:

- *Increasing concentration.* The champagne industry has become more and more concentrated, especially among the largest players in the industry. The consolidation race has a number of implications for smaller players that would like to maintain their autonomy and that are considering a change in strategy. First of all, due to the quality differentials among the various wines, buying other brands is a form of diversifying risk. In times of economic prosperity, the more expensive wines will sell relatively well, while recessions and slumps favor *petit champagnes*. Second, increased scale has a number of advantages, such as production efficiencies, pecuniary economies, increased bargaining power, and the like. Smaller companies have to comply with pressures of this kind.

- *Increasing conflict.* Since the late 1980s, the champagne industry has experienced more conflicts than ever before. The role of the CIVC has deteriorated, while the concentration movement has gained momentum. During informal negotiations, old deals were terminated and the individual players failed to induce each other into new ones. The companies in the industry will have to comply with this new mentality or pass away.

One important factor complicates the analysis. The champagne industry is not a stand-alone business, but it is embedded in the much larger global sparkling wines industry. Hence, there are also a number of forces that operate at this higher level to which the players in the champagne industry must comply:

- *Increase in output.* Over the last couple of decades, the worldwide sparkling wines industry has grown dramatically. Traditional producers of sparkling wines, such as the Catalunya region around Barcelona, and southern Germany and Northern Italy have increased their outputs. In other regions all over the world, such as California, South Africa, Australia, and Chile, new sparkling wine cultures have developed. The players in the French champagne industry must to comply with this increasing output.

- *Increase in quality.* Life used to be easy around Reims. The sparkling wines from that region were certainly not the cheapest in the world, and the local wine makers also did not produce a whole lot of it as compared to other regions in the world. But at least they could claim to make the *best* sparkling wine in the world, and there are always people willing to pay premium prices for superior products. Unfortunately, the quality levels of wines from other regions have increased dramatically. The French wine makers will have to learn to live with the fact that the best sparkling wines of the world are not necessarily champagnes.

4. Consider the industry creation perspective. How can a unified champagne industry compete with its strongest competitor - other quality sparkling wines?

It is true that new producers of sparkling wines have entered the scene, and it is also true that the quality of the non-champagnes has risen to great heights. Yet, according to the industry creation perspective, if the champagne industry gets competed away by these external parties, this is possible because they have let it come this far themselves. The champagne industry has a number of strategic assets – brand names, the generic 'champagne' name, a reputation for quality, favorable associations, and the like – which cannot be copied or superceded easily by external competitors.

If we adopt the industry creation perspective, the question is not *whether* the champagne industry can prosper by competing with other producers of sparkling wines, but *how* they can. The answer to this question is not straightforward, but two directions can at least be given:

- *Cherish strategic assets.* The assets mentioned above should be cherished. They need to be managed with care and consideration – not exploited too quickly and only with short-term results in mind. This implies that the champagne industry must keep on investing in improvements in methods of production, protect its festive image, and prevent erosion of its high-quality image.

- *Overcome internal trouble and strife.* This industry is vulnerable to internal conflicts. Although it is up to the class to find specific strategic solutions to the internal industry conflicts, we will discuss three potential solutions here:

  - *Consolidation.* The first approach is to strive for industry consolidation. Overall concentration is low, and the number of parties is high, and the resulting potential for 'self-destructive' competition is large. By reducing the number of parties, it might be easier to counter the threats facing the industry. Even if short term cut throat competition broke out, some individual firms might be able to improve their position and emerge from the battle stronger than before (this approach coincides with the discrete organization perspective in chapter 7).

  - *Self-regulation.* Just as Odysseus asked his crew to tie him to the mast in order to withstand the lure of the Sirens' song, so firms in the champagne industry could ask to be bound to rules to avoid the lure of 'cut throat' competition. For instance, the growers could decide amongst themselves to voluntarily limit the quantity of grapes they grow. The champagne houses have the opportunity to restrict their output of *petit champagnes*. The growers and houses combined could agree to compromise on grape prices. Such measures of self-regulation could allow the champagne industry as a whole, and its individual constituents, to make a living (see the embedded organization perspective in chapter 7).

  - *Government intervention.* The champagne industry is one of France's national symbols. This makes it likely that the French government will intervene in the industry if it becomes threatened. One possibility is to do so by imposing formal rules on the industry. Another is to subsidize the industry or its products. The champagne industry is also one of the main employers in the northern part of France. It is therefore likely that the European Community would also offer agricultural support to keep the people of the region at work.

The role of a body such as the CIVC must be seen in the light of the second solution. It can prove to be an important intermediary party, mediating between the several battling parties in the industry. Arguably, perhaps the most important function of the CIVC is its role as an institutionalized meeting point for industry members. An institution such as the CIVC offers opportunities for monitoring and sanctioning over and above those of the more or less anonymous market.

5. *Think about new year's eve – ten years from now. You and a couple of friends have decided to throw the best party in the new millennium yet. Do you think that champagne will be the best wine to buy? Considering your answers to previous questions, what are your reasons to believe so?*

This question is meant as a stimulus for class discussion, rather than for presenting any single best answer. However, to stimulate an interesting discussion, it is important to have a more or less balanced distribution of supporters of each perspective in the classroom. If the supporters of the industry creation perspective enjoy a majority, one should stress the factors underlying industry evolution (concentration and conflict within the champagne industry, and increasing output and quality among the non-champagne sparkling wine industry players). However, if the people in favor of the industry evolution perspective gain the upper hand, typical creation features (cherishing strategic assets and overcoming internal trouble and strife) should be emphasized. If it is possible to find a balance between both perspectives in terms of adepts in the classroom, one can prevent the discussion moving to a premature consensus.

Other Teaching Issues

During the discussion of the case questions, various teaching issues have passed in review, including the lead topic of industry malleability. Although this latter topic is at the core of this case, there are also some peripheral topics worth discussing, in particular:

- *Strategy formation within networks of firms.* While the focus in chapter 3 was on strategy formation within a firm, this case introduces the additional complexity of strategy formation within a network of firms. Yet again the question is that of deliberateness and emergentness (link to chapter 3).

- *Strategic change in a traditional industry.* At the end of the case, students might have an idea how the problems in the Champagne industry might be attacked; yet the question is whether this should be approached in a revolutionary or evolutionary fashion. Radical and swift change might be necessary to break resistance, but it might also be the death of this tradition bound industry (link to chapter 4).

- *Critical review of industry structure analyses.* For advanced classes only, this case is well suited to a critical review of industry structure analyses. After all, where does one draw the line? One can make a good five forces analysis of the champagne industry, and still be left with an uncomfortable feeling. Does the champagne industry belong to the global sparkling wine industry, or are these arenas separable (link to chapter 5)?

- *Network level strategy.* This case shows the need for strategies that surpass the boundaries of the individual firm. The various conflicts of interest that are present in this industry cannot be solved adequately at the firm level. In fact, in such problems, there is a clear gap between individual and collective (strategic) rationality (link to chapter 7).

- *Organizational inertia.* Although there is much agreement that something must be done, many of the conditions of organizational inertia are also present (link to chapter 9).

- *A strong home base.* All players in the champagne industry are clustered around Reims. On the one hand this seems obvious, since 'Champagne' is simply the name of the region. Yet, on the other hand, it is not that obvious that a disproportionate share of the world's greatest sparkling wines come from this particular region. This suggests the existence of a 'champagne diamond', according to the concept introduced by Porter (link to chapter 10).

- *Organizational purpose.* As with so many agricultural sectors, growing grapes is not only a business, but also a way of life. Companies therefore play an important social role in the Champagne region communities. In setting out a new path for the industry, the question is how the purposes of economic profitability and social responsibility to workers and the local communities might come into conflict (link to chapter 11).

What Happened After the Case?

The case runs until March 1993. It ends with the agenda issues of the extraordinary meeting of the CIVC. This meeting had to deal with the question: "What to do with the surplus and can we agree upon a three-year plan for the good of the whole champagne industry?" Although little information about the industry is available, this section will describe the major developments in the market and agreements made in the champagne industry. Visit our website (www.itbp.com) for the most up-to-date information and valuable further links.

Agreements in the Champagne Industry

Unfortunately, we do not have the actual content of the agreement made in 1993. However, three years later, in 1996, a renewed agreement was accomplished. With the Third Millennium less than four years away at that time, the Champenois made some important decisions. The first and most important, adopted in April 1996, concerns the relationship between Champagne's two main groups, the Champagne houses and the Champagne growers. The second decision concerns the aging of Champagne wines prior to shipping.

The partnership between the two major groups was based on a framework for the next four harvests, in the period 1996-1999. Its main elements are:

1. *Price.* As in 1992, the reference price for the grapes stayed at 24 FF per kilo in the *grands crus*. (The price varies with the rating of each *cru*, from 80 to 100% in the *grands crus*). A small annual adjustment will be possible based on economic elements gathered by CIVC, such as inflation, etc.

2. *Contracts.* In 1992, the percentage of the growers' production that they had to sell to the Champagne houses was officially 53.2%. However, new contracts are not bound to a percentage. All new contracts are to be made individually between Champagne Houses and Growers.

3. *Grapes/Hectare.* In 1992, the maximum allowable yield of grapes per hectare was limited to 11,900 kilos. This limit was negotiated with the French government agency responsible for the certification of the various wines in France (*Institut Nationale des Appelations d'Origines*). In 1996, an annual yield of 10,400 kilos of grapes per hectare was negotiated, allowing the production of 65 hectoliters of Champagne wines per hectare.

4. *Reserve stocks (blocage).* In 1992 all grapes over 9000 kg per hectare, up to the maximum of 11,900 kg per hectare could be stored. In the new agreement the *blocage* rules are as follows: It is possible that all or portions of the wines held in *blocage* could become available in case of a deficient harvest. In this case, this special reserve would have to be replenished with wines of quality from the following harvest(s), with the objective of maintaining a quality reserve equivalent to half a harvest at least. This system of *blocage* and *deblocage* will be fine-tuned to allow all the growers to better master their crops in the future.

5. *Transparency.* From now on, all transactions in the market are monitored by and under the auspices of CIVC. CIVC is responsible for informing all the parties about the volume and the prices of these transactions.

The second agreement concerned the aging process of wines. According to this decision, multi-vintage Champagnes bottled after 1996 had to be aged for a minimum of 15 months after bottling, instead of 12 months. Bottling usually takes place in the spring following the harvest, and cannot be performed before January 1st. In fact, most Champagne producers already age their classic wines 2-3 years. For vintage Champagnes produced with the grapes of one harvest exclusively, the minimum aging required by law has become 3 years from the bottling date, instead of 3 years from the harvest date. Many Champagne producers age these wines 4-5 years minimum before they release them.

Developments in the Champagne Industry

Although general information about the whole industry is not easily accessible, this part will discuss three major developments in the industry using information from the key market player LVMH:

- *More and better substitutes.* The annual global output of sparkling wines is expected to continue to grow. Existing regions are expanding, and new wine regions are quickly coming on stream. Moreover, the quality of the non-champagne sparkling wines will continue to increase. This implies that the champagne industry will face more and better substitutes.

- *Limits to output.* At the same time, the champagne industry has nearly reached its maximum output. The region around Reims is simply too small to produce more grapes. Subsequently, the champagne industry is destined to lose market share in a continuously growing market. This means that the players in the industry will have to critically review their ways of competing. Focusing on high quality and high margin niches seems to be the most obvious approach.

- *Cyclical nature of the Champagne market.* Focusing on high value-added products has a downside. People tend to buy more luxury products in times of economic prosperity, and less during economic slumps. The champagne industry is cyclical already, but the *petit champagnes* also sell relatively well during leaner times. A focus on more expensive brands is likely to increase the level of cyclicality in the industry.

- *Market growth.* The CIVC expects that the supply will continue to grow with 5% a year as shown in exhibit 1.

EXHIBIT 1
Champagne Production 1950-1998 (Source: CIVC)

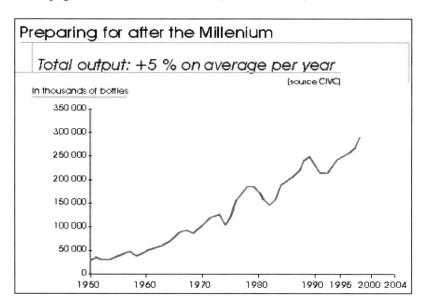

LVMH and the market

To overcome the threat of decreasing sales because of substitutes like 'sparkling wines' LVMH focuses on the following strategy and uses the following tools towards the next century.

Strategy:	Tools:
• *Premium brands*	• Excellent products
• Short list of leading brands	• Lean organization
• Adding value for the clients	• Organizational structure by houses
• A real business	• Efficiency & cost control

To overcome the threats mentioned earlier, LVMH trusts the strength of its leading premium brands and its 'houses' structure. The most important recent takeover, the acquisition of Krug by LVMH in January 1999, is intended to further build on the 'houses' approach. Diversification and an increase in marketing expenditures are also being used to win market share and to fight other sparkling wines. The following figure shows which products LVMH has recently introduced. Moreover it is interesting to see that these products have gained importance over the last years in terms of sales.

EXHIBIT 2
New Product Introductions by LVMH since 1995

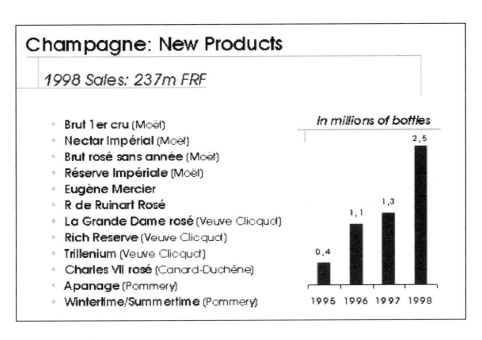

TEACHING NOTE 16: NATIONAL BICYCLE INDUSTRIAL CO.

Case by Suresh Kotha and Andrew Friend

Teaching note by Pursey Heugens and Ron Meyer

Case Synopsis

The National Bicycle Industrial Co. (NBIC) is a subsidiary of the Japanese industrial giant Matsushita, and one of Japan's leading bicycle manufacturers. In 1987, the company introduced an innovative production system, called the Panasonic Ordering System (POS). The distinctive characteristic of POS is that it uses mass-customization techniques, aimed at offering an almost infinite variety of feature combinations, derived from a relatively small number of modularized options. For customers this means they can select a frame in the shape, size, and color of their choice, and can add on a large number of the additional features. For NBIC, the techniques are an opportunity to accommodate to the wishes of the customer while trimming costs and keeping the complexity of operations at a manageable level. The aims of NBIC with POS were twofold. First, the firm wanted to increase the amount of high value-added products it could offer. Second, the company wanted to differentiate its high-end Panasonic brand from competing products.

There have been three categories of reactions to POS. First, NBIC enjoyed extensive media coverage after the introduction of its mass-customization system. Within a span of two years, NBIC was featured in magazines such as Fortune, the New York Times, and the Washington Post. A second, potentially related, response was an increase in the company's sales. Before the introduction of POS, NBIC's market share was languishing behind its two competitors in the high-end segment, Bridgestone and Miyata. Yet within a few years after the introduction of POS, the market share of Panasonic improved dramatically. A third reaction was that competitors started to imitate POS. Nonetheless, they were unable to duplicate all aspects of the NBIC strategy, mostly because the targeted market segment was to small to justify investments in additional capacity. However, whether POS will be the ticket to a bright future for NBIC remains to be seen. Both exports and domestic sales were flat in the early 1990s. The question for NBIC in the future is whether the high-end market is only a profitable niche, or whether it is the first step towards a stronger position in the broader bicycle market.

Teaching Objectives

If used in conjunction with chapter 8, this case can be used to meet the following teaching objectives:

- *Understanding industry development.* This case describes the structure of the bicycle industry and how NBIC is attempting to change the rules of the competitive game. This allows for a discussion on how industries change and what the sources of change can be (link to all readings).

- *Discussion on the importance of industry structure.* The profitability of all bicycle manufacturers seems to be under pressure. This would suggest that when it comes to profitability the industry's structure matters, not the individual firm's behavior. Of course, industry creationists could argue that low profitability merely indicates that the firms are not innovative enough (link to 8.1 Porter and 8.2 Baden-Fuller & Stopford).

- *Discussion on paradox of compliance and choice.* The case describes a major innovation in the bicycle industry, which raises the question of whether this move will change the rules of the competitive game for all industry players. Importantly, this case is open-ended enough to generate a debate on whether industry rules can truly be created by individual firms (link to all readings).

- *Difficulties and risks of rule breaking.* NBIC's move has been costly and not without risks. This case allows for a discussion on what it takes to actually rejuvenate an industry, and what risks are involved (link to 8.2 Baden-Fuller & Stopford and 8.4 Hamel & Prahalad).

- *Developing industry foresight.* NBIC might have been able to improve its competitive position through mass customization, but the question is whether it can continue to shape its industry. Does the company have a vision of where the industry could be headed or be led? The case gives ample opportunity to discuss the issue of industry foresight (link to 8.4 Hamel & Prahalad).

Teaching Guideline

The National Bicycle Industrial Company case is easy to use, as students can readily understand the basic issues at hand in the bicycle industry. What also makes the case interesting is that most students don't know what eventually happened to NBIC. This leaves the case open-ended enough for a real discussion to take place.

Our experience is that most students are quite enthusiastic about the concept of mass-customization. We like to discuss mass customization, as it is a very concrete example of how to create a synthesis between two opposites (as also described in the Honda case). Mass customization is a creative solution to the tension between mass production and custom building. However, this does not necessarily mean that it is the sure-fire competitive advantage that will propel NBIC towards global success. Yet, most students do think that NBIC should be able to change the competitive rules of the game. They tend to cheer for the innovator and to be overly optimistic about the chances of success. It is, therefore, somewhat disappointing for them to find out that NBIC was not successful – but it is a worthwhile lesson for them to understand the pitfalls, limitations and risks of being the innovator. For the professor it is good to know why NBIC failed (see the section 'What Happened after the Case?'), as this helps to slowly nibble away at the students' enthusiasm for NBIC's rule-changing attempts.

Suggested Questions

1. Analyze the structure of the bicycle industry and identify NBIC's main competitors. Which main market segments exist? What are the 'rules of the game' in these respective segments?

2. What are the principal strengths and weaknesses of mass-customization production systems in general, and the Panasonic Ordering System in particular?

3. Consider the industry creation perspective. How can NBIC use the mass-customization system to change the rules of the game in the bicycle industry? Which issues does NBIC need to resolve?

4. Consider the industry evolution perspective. What are the forces internal to the industry that might block NBIC's attempts to change the rules of the game?

5. What do you think the bicycle industry might look like in ten years time? What advice would you give NBIC to shape (or adapt to) this future industry structure?

Case Analysis

1. Analyze the structure of the bicycle industry and identify NBIC's main competitors. Which main market segments exist? What are the 'rules of the game' in these respective segments?

Main competitors. Within the bicycle industry, only a few global companies exist. There are only a limited number of countries in the world where first-class bicycles are manufactured. Everyone who wants to ride a very special bike must turn to brands from these countries. Oddly, the leading countries vary according to the type of bicycle being produced. Most of the top brands in road-racing bikes are strictly European. Italy is by far the world's largest exporter in the top segment, with famous brands as Colnago (the global market leader in road racing), Pinarello, Bianchi, Basso, and many more. France is runner up, with brands such as Look, Vitus, and Peugeot. Belgium (Eddy Merckx, Diamant) and The Netherlands (Giant, Gazelle) also enjoy a favorable position in this product category. Yet, when it comes to mountain bikes (MTB, also known as All Terrain Bikes, ATB), virtually all of the established names have their origins somewhere along the West Coast of the United States, where the MTB was 'invented' in the 1970s. Famous brands are Klein, Gary Fisher, Cannondale, Scott, Trek, Merlin, and American Eagle. Over the last decade a sizable increase in the number of brands in the upper segment coming from the Pacific Rim can be witnessed. The manufacturers from this region produce road-racing bikes, as well as MTBs. Although many of the brands that stem from this region are aimed at the middle segment, some products have reached a quality level that almost matches the American and European premium brands. Especially the Taiwanese brand Giant and the Japanese brands Panasonic and Miyata are highly regarded.

Competitive groups. In most countries, the bicycle market can roughly be divided into three segments. First, there is a mass market for relatively cheap bicycles, meant for children and for transportation purposes. In the mass segment, price, distribution and brand loyalty are important competitive factors. There are obviously quality differences in this segment, but the customers in this part of the market tend to be rather price sensitive. Much of this mass-market is dominated by local brands, as brand loyalty and transportation costs keep all but the cheapest imports out. The second segment is that of medium priced recreational bicycles. For consumers in this segment quality, variety and fashion are more important, but price remains a dominant issue.

In the premium segment, completely different rules apply. Most bikes in the top segment are meant for 'serious' recreational purposes, or for competition. Under such circumstances, emotion plays a much larger role than for buying a bike to ride to the shopping mall or in the park. Price is only the second or third criterion on which a buying decision is based. Also important is that in this segment almost no complete bikes are sold. Most of the premium brands mentioned above are frame makers, rather than bicycle manufacturers. Cycling enthusiasts will first buy a frame (which usually amounts to 35% to 50% of the value of the complete bike) at a local retail shop. Then they make a selection of parts, mostly after close deliberation with their retailer, other specialists, or their peers. This deep-rooted consumption pattern is one of the most powerful explanations for the relatively low penetration of the Asian brands in the top segment. Asian companies consider themselves bicycle manufacturers, not frame designers.

Rivalry amongst existing competitors and new entrants. In addition to the points mentioned above, it can be concluded that competition is rather fragmented and generally locally oriented. Product differentiation is relatively low, and innovation slow. Entry into the mass-market part of the industry is possible for manufacturers from low cost countries. Entry (mobility) into the higher segments is more difficult, due to the importance of branding and distribution infrastructure.

Structure of, and power in, the value system. In the value system an important distinction must be made between vertically integrated manufacturers and specialists. The vertically integrated manufacturers produce the bicycle frame, as well as many of the bicycle parts. However, there are also many companies that only make frames, while others only make parts, while yet others only assemble bicycles. At all stages of the value system the industry is fragmented and few manufacturers have significant bargaining power. The same is true for the distribution system, where there are many wholesalers and retailers, but no dominant parties.

2. *What are the principal strengths and weaknesses of mass-customization production systems in general, and the Panasonic Ordering System in particular?*

Most mass-customization production systems are relatively new, but they are all based on the well-established principle of modularization. A product is broken down into a (limited) number of components or modules. For each component, a restricted number of alternatives are sought. These alternatives can be used interchangeably. Ideally, each module makes a viable combination with every other module, even if chosen at random. Thus, a large number of possible outcomes (combinations of modules) exist. Mass-customization production systems in general show a number of distinct advantages:

- *Enhancing consumers' choice.* Mass-customization systems have the potential to enhance the level of choice for customers. Through the sheer endless number of combinations the modularization system can make, almost every need for differentiation can be met.

- *Complexity and cost reduction.* Forced by competitive pressures, companies may sometimes feel the urge to extend the number of products in a particular product line. Such extensions are usually followed by an increase in complexity of organizational processes – logistics, record keeping, marketing and sales, and the like. Furthermore, more products, with short production runs, usually mean higher unit cost. Modularization is a way of complying with competitive pressures on the one hand, while keeping the cost level and organizational complexity manageable on the other.

However compelling these advantages might sound, mass-customization also has a downside:

- *Replication and imitation.* As argued above, mass-customization systems are based on relatively simple principles. Moreover, it is impossible to legally protect a complete production system, since such systems cannot be captured under patent laws. The consequences are that mass-customization systems are relatively easy to replicate or imitate. The only ways of protecting a system against imitation are trying to maintain secrecy, or positioning the system itself in a way that full-scale entry is unlikely to be profitable (by aiming at relatively small niche markets, for example).

- *Production inertia.* Key to making mass-customization systems a success is making sure that every component fits all others. This need for interchangeability is at the same time the seed for production inertia. New components can often not be added to the system, because their introduction would lead to high changeover costs or incompatible modules.

The above strengths and weaknesses of mass-customization systems in general apply to the Panasonic Ordering System as well, but there are also some additional ones. We will start with a discussion of the strengths of POS.

- *Novelty.* NBIC was the first manufacturer of bicycles that developed and implemented a system of mass-customization. This novelty has given the company a lead that competitors had to make up for.

- *Value added.* As mentioned in the case, the new production system increased the number of high added value products of NBIC. Therefore, the system could represent a valuable contribution to average margins and corporate performance.

- *Establishing the brand.* It is mentioned in the case that the production system got a lot of positive media attention. It seems that the Panasonic bicycle brand has benefited greatly from such positive associations as novelty, consumers' choice, and technological superiority.

Unfortunately, POS has some distinct disadvantages as well:

- *Consumer education.* Customers that want to use POS will have to go to a local retail shop and order the appropriate modules. The level of decision-making involved should not be taken lightly, especially since it requires a considerable amount of knowledge on behalf of the customer. This minimum required level of knowledge could become a major burden if NBIC wants to extend its activities to other market segments.

- *Expensive.* Mass customization systems may be cheaper per product than hand-built or hand-assembled products, but they are definitely more expensive that mass-fabricated products. In the cost-sensitive market segments, the cost level could become a serious constraint.

- *Export.* POS may have become a success in Japan, but it is hard to replicate that success overseas. First, the characteristics of the bicycle market differ from country to country, and it will be hard to develop one system to cover all countries. Second, for most countries delivery time could become a major issue, as it takes weeks for products to be sent from Japan to other countries.

3. *Consider the industry creation perspective. How can NBIC use the mass-customization system to change the rules of the game in the bicycle industry? Which issues does NBIC need to resolve?*

These are the issues that are essential for NBIC, if they are to be successful at breaking the rules of the game in the bicycle industry:

- *Barriers to imitation.* One of the principal weaknesses of mass-customization systems is that they often can be copied quite easily, as they are based on fairly simple principles. There are two ways to overcome this weakness. First, NBIC can try to install legal barriers to imitation by patenting crucial parts of the system. However, patenting production systems is extremely difficult. An alternative is to manage the underlying firm capabilities with care. By continuously making investments in their development, a company can at least maintain the favorable gap with competitors.

- *Delivery time.* Above it was mentioned that one of the major weaknesses of the mass-customization system is the long delivery time, especially to foreign markets. NBIC will have to find some way to shorten delivery time (e.g. faster transport, local production) or they will have to convince customers to accept long delivery time (e.g. snob appeal, encourage advance ordering).

- *Local presence.* Premium quality bikes are not bought by mail-order. Measuring the customer in order to buy the appropriate size of the frame, choosing the right parts, adjusting the height of the seat-post and steering bar, and providing after-sales service are complex tasks that require the expertise of a genuine professional. Therefore, a company that wants to sell high quality bikes needs to have access to a chain of local retailers, capable of delivering the required service.

- *Partnerships with parts suppliers.* In the top-segment, there are two firms that control the market for bicycle parts: Shimano of Japan and Italy's Campagnolo. A firm that is serious about selling premium quality bikes must maintain favorable relationships with both of these companies. Although the products they make are perfect substitutes, most customers simply prefer one brand to the other. In order to sell a lot of premium bikes, access to the products of both companies must be guaranteed.

- *Extension to other segments.* The high quality segment of the market is highly profitable – but it is only a niche. To fundamentally change the rules of the game, NBIC will have to transfer the mass-customization system to the broader market. However, NBIC does not seem to have any clear ideas on how to move beyond their current niche.

- *Strong brands.* The high quality segment of the bicycle market is dominated by global brands, while local brands rule the middle and lower quality mass-markets. Therefore, mass-customization techniques are not a sufficient condition to gain a favorable position in the market. NBIC also needs to build or acquire strong brands in order to exploit their system to the fullest.

Students may come up with a variety of different ideas on how to resolve these issues. Normally, we summarize these ideas on the board before moving to the next question.

4. *Consider the industry evolution perspective. What are the forces internal to the industry that might block NBIC's attempts to change the rules of the game?*

There are four major forces that may block NBIC's bid to change the rules of the competitive game. These are the following:

- *Customers.* NBIC is assuming that customers will be attracted to the new concept of the mass-customized bicycle. Yet it is not at all clear that bicycling enthusiasts will be drawn to this concept. As stated earlier, most European racing cyclists are used to assembling their own bicycles together with the retailer, and may not be interested in the Panasonic 'prefab' concept. The recreational cyclists might not be enthusiastic about the higher cost and long delivery times, effectively blocking NBIC's move into neighboring segments.

- *Distribution channels.* NBIC will need to find a significant number of retailers willing to do the measurements and feature selecting, that are required to actually sell the mass-customized bicycles. In Japan they already have some distribution, but this is not strong enough, while outside the country they have no network yet. It remains to be seen whether retailers can be found with the needed skills and whether specialized bicycle retailers are at all interested in the POS system.

- *Suppliers.* Only 35% to 50% of the value of a bicycle is made up by the frame. The rest of the value stems from the bicycle parts. Especially the large parts makers have strong bargaining power and often supply retailers directly, giving them a strong market position. These suppliers might not be inclined to help NBIC to shift the market towards mass-customized bicycles, because this would weaken their own position (they would no longer supply consumers directly).

- *Competitors.* How will competitors react towards the POS system? Will they imitate it? Will strong local competitors try to pressure retailers into keeping NBIC out? Will competitors push down their own production costs, so that NBIC's products become prohibitively expensive? A broad range of counter measures can be discussed that might thwart NBIC's moves.

5. *What do you think the bicycle industry might look like in ten years time? What advice would you give NBIC to shape (or adapt to) this future industry structure?*

This open-ended question is meant to stimulate a class discussion on the topic of industry foresight. Until now the students have had to respond to the possible change in the rules of the game, triggered by NBIC's introduction of the POS. Now students are asked to think ahead themselves and to envision a number of possible future states themselves. In this discussion the issue will continuously be whether the strategist must try to *predict* the unfolding industry structure (the determinist industry evolution perspective) or whether future industry structures can be *invented* (the voluntarist industry creation perspective).

Other Teaching Issues

Besides the issues of industry creation and evolution, this case can also be employed to discuss the following issues:

- *Creativity and mental maps.* Breaking the rules of the game depends to a large extent on overcoming engrained beliefs about how companies should compete (industry recipes). This links back to the discussion in chapter 2 on logic and creativity. This case also illustrates, however, that not only the company strategists are limited by their current beliefs. Customers' and distributors' mental maps with regard to bicycles and the industry can also be very difficult to change, effectively inhibiting innovation in the industry (link to chapter 2).

- *Capabilities-based competition.* This case extensively describes the Panasonic ordering and production system. It is rare to see such a detailed description of the links between production and strategy. Therefore, it is very tempting to devote some time on a discussion on the links between production and strategy, and especially to the development and deployment of production capabilities. Furthermore, it is interesting to discuss how NBIC's strategy is now built around the exploitation of this capability. Finally, it can be discussed whether NBIC's resource-base might lead to a sustainable competitive advantage (link to chapter 5).

- *Vertical networks.* As discussed in the case analysis, NBIC is dependent on suppliers and retailers for the successful execution of its strategy. Both must be tempted to cooperate with NBIC, while their interests are not fully in line with the interests of NBIC. This allows for a discussion on managing interdependence relationships in the value system (link to chapter 7).

- *The international context.* Consumer tastes in bicycles are far from homogeneous. Some regions clearly favor racing bikes, whereas other regions prefer ATBs (All Terrain Bikes). In some countries the bicycle is the most popular means of transportation, while it is considered nothing more than a children's toy in others. In other words, the bicycle industry is an appropriate vehicle to discuss issues surrounding globalization and localization (link to chapter 10).

- *Diamond model.* It is remarkable that there are only a few places in the world where first-class bicycles are manufactured. There is a very distinct ATB-cluster in California, USA, and there is a racing bike cluster in Northern Italy. These clusters may stimulate a discussion on national diamonds (link to Porter, chapter 10).

What Happened After the Case?

The case runs until 1993, and stops just at the moment that NBIC is encountering some difficulties in establishing its position. After 1993 the most important developments have been the following:

- *Withdrawal of the Panasonic brand.* NBIC tried to establish the Panasonic brand in a number of Western European markets in the early 1990s. Unfortunately, the introduction was not an instant success. After a number of unsuccessful years, the brand had to be withdrawn from most of the new markets. The reasons were twofold. First of all, Panasonic tried to sell complete bicycles in the upper segment. Deep-rooted consumption patterns in this segment – buying frames rather than bicycles – were the cause of customer reluctance. Second, the Panasonic brand is well known in most European markets, but only as a consumer electronics brand. Most people associated Panasonic with VCRs instead of ATBs.

- *Growth of the American bicycle industry.* Due to the rise of the ATB, the global bicycle industry has witnessed healthy growth over the last decade. Yet this growth in the top-segment mostly benefited the traditional ATB manufacturers, located in the US. NBIC has not been able to capture its share of the increase, due to the low international penetration.

- *Segmentation.* The distinction between the mass-market and the high-end segment is still very present in the bicycle industry. NBIC has failed to bring its mass-customization strategy to the mass market. Their low number of retail outlets and disinterest among consumers are seen as the primary reasons for this failure.

TEACHING NOTE 17: TELÉFONOS DE MÉXICO

Case by Robert Hoskisson, Jennifer Alexander, Tom Blackley, Linda Chen, Dru Ubben, John Economou, Sewardi Luis, and Richard Martinez

Teaching note by Bob de Wit, Ron Meyer and Melbert Visscher

Case Synopsis

This case describes one of the most fundamental and drastic changes in the history of Teléfonos de México (TELMEX), Mexico's state-owned telephone services company. In September 1989 the president of Mexico announced the privatization of TELMEX. The objective of the privatization was to radically improve telecommunications services in Mexico. In 1990 the Mexican government sold all of its TELMEX shares to a Mexican-led consortium, which also included France Télécom and Southwestern Bell. An agreement with the Mexican government gave TELMEX the power to be the exclusive long-distance service provider in Mexico until the end of 1996. After this date competitors would be allowed in the Mexican market and TELMEX would be required to connect competing networks with its local networks at government approved rates.

   To avoid losing too much share of the liberalized market, TELMEX's executive committee has only a short period of time to transform the old monopolist into a competitive contender. The question in the case is not only what the new TELMEX should look like, but also whether a transformation is possible at all. And if so, should change be imposed top-down by the organization's leaders, or is change more likely to happen through chaotic processes of self-organization?

Teaching Objectives

If used in conjunction with chapter 9 this case can be used to meet the following teaching objectives:

- *Identifying sources of inertia.* TELMEX is facing drastic changes now that the market is set to open up to competition. Yet, the TELMEX organization does not seem to have the ability to fluidly adapt itself to these new circumstances. This allows for a discussion on sources of inertia (link to introduction and 9.5 Rumelt).

- *Understanding the role of organizational leadership.* As TELMEX enters the newly turbulent waters, the company's executive committee will be challenged to set a course for the future. They will need to determine their approach to achieving a strategic reorientation, taking into account their powers, as well as the limits to their abilities (link to introduction, 9.1 Christensen et al and 9.3 Bourgeois & Brodwin).

- *Understanding the role of organizational dynamics.* Transforming a formerly state-owned company as it enters a highly competitive environment means that top management will have to deal with cultural, political and learning constraints. This case allows for a discussion on how managers can deal with such chaotic factors, while not letting the organization get stuck in the mud during the process (link to introduction, 9.2 Stacey and 9.4 Johnson).

- *Insight into the paradox of control and chaos.* The threat of competition has evoked rapid technological and organizational changes within TELMEX. Yet it is doubtful whether these changes will be sufficient to survive in a liberalized market. The question is whether top management has the ability to impose change on the organization and whether it should want to impose change top-down (link to all).

Teaching Guideline

The Teléfonos de México case can be a difficult case to teach, as the telecommunication industry has a complex structure and is in a constant state of flux. The number of strategic questions raised by the case is enormous, yet students will find they do not have enough industry knowledge to make the necessary recommendations.

However, as an example of organizational transformation, the case does very well. To most students the three blows sustained by TELMEX are very clear: privatization, liberalization and rapid technological change. These set the stage for the question of how an elephant can be made to dance, when it has been caged all its life.

As an introduction to this case it can be very useful to first discuss the privatization of state-owned companies in general. Students can be asked to name an example of a privatized company they know and to ask themselves whether the privatized company went on to become a success. It can be very helpful to collectively list the factors that students believe have helped some companies to emerge successfully from the privatization process, while other companies wither away. This question helps to focus students' attention on the specific challenges faced by companies being privatized. A follow up question could be to ask the class for an example of a local company that is still government-owned, and then to ask students what type of problems they would expect if this company were to be privatized.

Case Questions

1. What are the major competitive challenges facing TELMEX? How strong is the pressure on TELMEX to change?

2. How capable is TELMEX of changing? What might be TELMEX's major sources of inertia?

3. How would you get TELMEX prepared for the period of deregulation after 1996 if you were to take the organizational leadership perspective?

4. How would you get TELMEX prepared for the period of deregulation after 1996 if you were to take the organizational dynamics perspective?

5. Given the above analysis, what would you do to get the organization in shape for the competitive battles ahead?

Case Analysis

1. What are the major competitive challenges facing TELMEX? How strong is the pressure on TELMEX to change?

In a positive sense, TELMEX is faced with two competitive challenges that can lead to further growth and profitability:

- *Market extension.* Currently, Mexico is 'under-phoned', leaving much room for extending basic service to a wider segment of the population.

- *Market penetration.* Mexicans also make use of relatively few telephone products and services, leaving ample room for growth.

Yet, there seem to be more threats on the horizon than opportunities. TELMEX needs to deal with the following four challenges to its position:

- *New entrants.* After 1996 new entrants can be expected to come into the Mexican market with aggressive share-buying tactics. Most of these new competitors will be international telecommunications giants.

- *Strengthening business buyers.* As internationally operating companies seek global suppliers of telecommunication services, TELMEX will see its bargaining positioning vis-a-vis these clients weaken.

- *Rapid technological developments.* While telecommunications have always required a high level of technical sophistication, the recent technological developments have made the industry more high tech and require companies to rapidly upgrade their technological competencies and physical infrastructure.

- *Unstable domestic economy and currency.* TELMEX will need to deal with a domestic market that shows signs of instability and must compete against foreign competitors who can enter the Mexican market relatively cheaply.

What makes all of these factors especially challenging, is that change will be discontinuous. All issues will lead to radical changes in the Mexican telecom industry in a very short period of time. Furthermore, the scale of change need by TELMEX is large – both in terms of financial cost and organizational restructuring. Taken together, this makes the pressure on TELMEX to change very high.

2. *How capable is TELMEX of changing? What might be TELMEX's major sources of inertia?*

Given TELMEX's organizational inheritance as a state-owned monopoly, it is not unlikely that they will need to overcome some major inertial forces. In reading 9.5, Rumelt identifies five key sources of inertia. TELMEX does not seem to suffer from the first two sources of inertia, distorted perception and dulled motivation. The company's perception is acute and motivation sharp, as can be witnessed by the executive committee's program of large-scale improvements of TELMEX's operations and technology. However, the other sources of inertia mentioned by Rumelt might actually be holding TELMEX back:

- *Speed and complexity.* The speed and complexity of the changes faced by TELMEX are tremendous. This might inhibit the organization in responding effectively to the competitive challenges.

- *Reactive mind-set.* Furthermore, a *reactive mind-set* might prevail in a company that was state-owned not so long ago and which was known for a lack of market orientation. Even though the executive committee might have the right vision and strategy, it still depends on the lower layers of management for implementation of the necessary changes.

- *Vested values.* In the state-ownership period, TELMEX was a utility, with an internal, technical focus, in which customers were not high on the priority list. To be competitive in the new market conditions, TELMEX's cultural values must change to an external, service-orientation, but this might be very difficult for many managers to internalize.

- *Vested interests.* In the old TELMEX, bureaucracy was a way of life and many managers had got their jobs on grounds other than their managerial abilities. It is clear that as the company transforms itself, some departments and individuals will lose out, and therefore might oppose any change.

- *Embedded routines.* As the old TELMEX operated in a relatively stable environment for so long, it is not unlikely that deeply ingrained routines have developed within the company.

- *Capabilities gap.* The "new" TELMEX might require specific expertise in the field of marketing or in the field of corporate strategy. If these are not or insufficiently present, this could inhibit the transformation process.

3. *How would you get TELMEX prepared for the period of deregulation after 1996 if you were to take the organizational leadership perspective?*

Getting TELMEX prepared for the period of deregulation would involve finding a strong leader to push through the necessary changes, according to the organizational leadership perspective. This leader's task would be to create the conditions under which decisive action could be taken and to ensure that resistance to change would be overcome. According to Christensen *et al* (reading 9.1) this leader would have three roles to perform:

- *Chief architect of organizational purpose*. The leader of TELMEX would be responsible for setting the course for the company for the coming years and allocating resources so that these strategic objectives could be met.
- *Organizational leader*. Furthermore, the leader of TELMEX should be focused on getting the selected strategies implemented. The leader would be in charge of pushing changes through, both by setting people's tasks and by evaluating their progress.
- *Personal leader*. Finally, the leader of TELMEX should have the skill to articulate the necessity of the changes being implemented and should have the ability to persuade and motivate individuals in the company. This role recognizes the importance of getting lower management levels motivated to act pro-actively in the change process.

A proponent of the organizational leadership perspective might also point to the different styles leaders can use in the organization. Bourgeois & Brodwin (reading 9.3) have identified five leadership approaches. In principle, each approach might be applicable in TELMEX to prepare the organization for the period of deregulation. Nevertheless, the leader should take firm control to overcome the identified inertia.

4. *How would you get TELMEX prepared for the period of deregulation after 1996 if you were to take the organizational dynamics perspective?*

Proponents of the organizational dynamics perspective would argue that TELMEX's executive committee actually has little freedom to shape the organization's future. In this respect Johnson (reading 9.4) would probably argue that the strategic choices TELMEX's executive committee makes, are just shaped by the cultural web that TELMEX is entangled in. Trying to impose change top-down would probably just ignite political infighting and would lead to passive resistance by many of the adversely affected. TELMEX's leadership might be able to make some impressive (yet predictable) plans, but they would get stuck trying to force the organization to implement them.

A proponent of the organizational dynamics perspective would argue that at best the company's leadership could help to create circumstances that will improve the chances of new strategies evolving. These circumstances could include some of the following:

- *Relinquishing control*. First, the executive committee would have to give up the idea of being the brains of the organization. They would have to see their role as strategy process regulators, not as the designers of new strategy. Letting go and allowing things to happen is probably the best option the executive committee has.

- *Encouraging initiatives*. The executive committee would have to encourage individuals and groups to be intrapreneurial, launching new ideas and experimenting with new services. These initiatives would compete against each other and the most viable would be given further support and commitment as they slowly proved themselves.

- *Provoking multiple cultures*. To prepare for the new competitive circumstances, TELMEX would need to get in more outsiders to break through the cultural consensus within the company. By increasing the firm's 'genetic diversity' the quality of strategic discourse could improve and the chance of creative ideas would be larger.

- *Widespread strategic thinking abilities*. As all employees should be involved in the process of spontaneous self-organization, they could benefit from more training in the area of strategic thinking.

- *Encouraging learning and risk-taking.* Old recipes can only be challenged if there is room for discourse, experimentation and learning. Employees should be encouraged to participate in self-organization processes and to learn explicitly, instead of being punished for not focusing on short-term results and for engaging in risky innovations.

Letting the organization find its own way in the state of bounded chaos might also neutralize a few sources of inertia that have to do with the cultural web Johnson described. Vested values, vested interests, embedded routines and a reactive mind-set can only be defeated by the employees themselves, not by the organizational leader 'bulldozing' over any resistance.

5. *Given the above analysis, what would you do to get the organization in shape for the competitive battles ahead?*

Here students can come up with many answers, trying to find a balance between control and chaos. Their answers should at least touch on the following points:

- *Role of the organizational leader.* How much control should the organizational leader try to exert in trying to change the company? Should the transformation be a one-man show, maybe backed by an army of external consultants, or should the focus be on being a supportive leader, helping others to develop the business? In this context, it can even be asked who this leader should be.

- *Methods for overcoming inertia.* Now that TELMEX is forced to change by the imminent threat of competition, they need to deal with cultural sources of inertia. The TELMEX employees will need to understand why certain changes in operations and behavior are necessary. Motivation is very important in periods of such drastic changes. Sufficient support needs to be realized at the operational level in order to secure implementation successes.

- *Managing alliance relationships.* In order to prepare itself for intense international competition the company needs to learn more about international markets, needs to acquire expertise in the area of new services, and needs to be able to serve international customers. The strategic alliance with Sprint might prove to be the right vehicle to acquire these items, but the alliance must be developed further to ensure mutual commitment and investment in the relationship.

Other Teaching Issues

The case also raises a number of questions that are relevant to other chapters in the book. These teaching issues are:

- *Strategy formation.* This case provides for an interesting discussion on the emergent or deliberate nature of strategy. TELMEX's executive committee seems to have set a clear direction for the company and apparently has mapped out a clear course of action to make TELMEX an able competitor in a liberalized arena. However, others might argue that management would be wise to adapt to unfolding circumstances, experiment and build political support in a more incrementalist way (link to chapter 3).

- *Strategic change.* TELMEX is faced with the most dramatic changes in its history. The privatization of the company has rocked the organization and significant changes can be expected in future. The question is, however, whether revolutionary change should be pushed through quickly, or whether the company should move at a fast but more stable pace, giving the company more time to transform in a more evolutionary fashion (link to chapter 4).

- *Building competitive advantage.* Coming from a protected position, TELMEX must now determine its competitive position and distinctive competencies. As the telecommunication industry seems like a commodity business, in which only price is important, it is interesting to discuss how TELMEX might be able to differentiate itself (link to chapter 5).

- *Defining the new industry rules.* As the telecommunication industry goes through a total transformation, it can be discussed whether telecom companies must comply with the evolving rules, or whether they have the power to influence the developments in their industry (link to chapter 8).

- *The responsibilities of a privatized company.* TELMEX was founded as a government-owned corporation to provide telephone services to the Mexican population. Its current concession emphasizes its responsibility to the Mexican public. Yet, the new competitive situation places a high emphasis on being more profitable and responsive to the demands of its shareholders. The question is how responsible privatized companies are, or should feel, with regard to the public good (link to chapter 11).

What Happened after the Case?

The case ends as TELMEX joins into a partnership with Sprint Corporation by means of a non-equity strategic alliance in December 1994. Since then the following major developments have taken place:

- *Further development of alliance with Sprint.* With its monopoly position set to expire within two years, this alliance was intended to help TELMEX improve its operations and services, and to serve a wider group of internationally-operating corporate clients. In terms of new services, the alliance with Sprint allowed TELMEX to introduce Virtual Private Network, Frame Relay Global Service, International Private Services and Videoconferencing. The relationship with Sprint has also brought TELMEX into Global One, the international partnership, which also includes Deutsche Telekom and France Télécom. This partnership offers a wide range of voice and data services for businesses, telephone companies and large international customers. In February 1997, TELMEX filed an application with the US Federal Communications Commission (FCC) to operate long-distance services in the US through the strategic alliance with Sprint. The application was approved half a year later. TELMEX would first focus on the Hispanic population in the US as a first step to further international growth. In 1999 TELMEX purchased a 55.5% stake in Topp Telecom Inc., a US cellular phone services company.

- *Major restructuring.* An extensive reorganization of the company was carried out over 1995. Operations and commercialization were decentralized into 10 new Regional Divisions and two new Corporate Directors were appointed to manage policies and strategies. Marketing, Sales, Communications, Legal and Human Resources Departments also were reorganized. In 1996 TELMEX's old commercial offices were upgraded to turn them into modern Telecommunications Services Centers.

- *New service.* Since 1994, TELMEX has introduced numerous new services, including phone cards (TELCARD telephone credit card, LADAFÓN prepaid card and LADATEL prepaid cards), value-added digital telephone services (e.g. Call Waiting service, Three-Party Calling service, Follow-Me service, Caller ID, Call Forwarding), and prepaid cellular telephones (the popular Sistema Amigo).

- *New businesses.* TELMEX has also moved more aggressively into related telecommunication services. UNINET is TELMEX's Universal Network (introduced in January 1996) that offers domestic and international multi-protocol transmission services with high routing and package switching capacities. IDP (Internet Directo Personal) was introduced in April 1997. TELMEX is the most important Internet access provider in Mexico with over 146,000 subscribers and a growth rate of 325% in 1997. In 1998 TELMEX purchased 18.9% of Prodigy Communications Corporation, a US Internet services provider.

- *Adaptation to foreign competition.* In 1996 TELMEX carried out all the work necessary for new long-distance operators to establish interconnection beginning on January 1, 1997. TELMEX invested 562 million dollars in this process and it required full-time participation of more than

500 company employees. In accordance with the agreement, Mexico's 60 major cities would be interconnected in 1997, 40 more in 1998 and an additional 100 in 1999 and 2000. In 1997 TELMEX experienced the effects of intense competition in the long-distance market. However, 75% of the customers in the 60 cities that were opened to competition in 1997 decided to remain with TELMEX.

EXHIBIT 1
TELMEX Financial Data Highlights, in millions of Pesos with purchasing power as of December 31, 1998 (Source: Annual Report, 1998)

FINANCIAL RESULTS	1998	1997	1996	1995	1994
Total Revenues	78,241	72,025	72,791	73,167	77,813
Cost of Sales and Services	17,136	16,833	16,591	21,675	23,341
Commercial, Administrative and General Expenses	15,507	14,135	14,690	12,495	11,928
Depreciation and Amortization	15,719	14,284	15,598	13,197	9,447
Total Costs and Expenses	48,514	47,081	50,251	47,368	44,716
Operating Income	29,727	24,944	22,541	25,800	33,097
Net Income	16,401	15,242	15,922	16,312	20,939
Total Assets	153,873	151,586	153,290	178,139	200,415
Total Debt	30,052	30,531	18,332	28,871	28,149
Stockholder's Equity	105,898	104,651	122,453	138,513	147,148
Total Debt/Capitalization (%)	22.1	22.6	13.0	17.2	16.1
STATISTICS					
Communities with Telephone Service	24,711	24,691	20,694	20,688	20,572
Access Lines in Service[1]	9,927	9,254	8,826	8,801	8,493
Cellular Customers[1]	2,113	1,112	657	399	306
Kms. of L.D. Circuits in Service[2]	133	113	96	87	82
Domestic L.D. Minutes[2]	9,077	8,232	7,867	7,294	6,746
International L.D. Minutes[2]	3,286	3,768	3,558	3,055	2,622
DATA PER SHARE (pesos)					
Earnings per share	2.08	1.81	1.74	1.61	1.98
Book value	13.71	12.89	13.80	14.35	14.02
Market Value at Year-End	24.40	22.75	12.98	12.36	10.24
Nominal Dividend per Share	0.700	0.525	0.350	0.300	0.250
Outstanding Shares[2]	7,724	8,118	8,875	9,654	10,499

[1] In Thousands
[2] In Millions

TEACHING NOTE 18: CARTIER

Case by Sumantra Ghoshal, Francois-Xavier Huard and Charlotte Butler

Teaching note by Bob de Wit and Ron Meyer

Case Synopsis

The Cartier company was established in 1817 when Pierre Cartier opened a shop in the Marais, Paris's artisan quarter, where he sculpted powder horns and decorative motifs for firearms. Pierre was succeeded by three generations of Cartiers, until Robert Hocq and then Alain Perrin took over the company. Currently Cartier is the world's leading luxury products firm, with a market share of approximately 4%. It is the leader in luxury watches (which represent 46% of Cartier's turnover) and deluxe leather goods (10% of turnover) and second in jewelry (25% of turnover). Furthermore, Cartier is well known for its lighters, pens and perfume.

The Cartier case does not deal with one specific issue, but sketches the way that the company operates and it outlines the challenges that the company is facing. All of these challenges at Cartier seem to have one aspect in common; namely that they require the firm to balance conflicting demands. For instance, it is crucial to Cartier's success to retain its exclusive image, while maximizing sales in the meantime. Hence the company must cope with the delicate balance between exclusiveness and sales volume. Likewise the company must balance tradition and innovation, publicity and mystery, focus and diversification, and control and creativity.

It is the balancing of this last pair of extremes that seems to be the most important factor for Cartier's continued success. According to Alain Perrin, Cartier's current president, creativity is the essence, the very soul of Cartier. The company creates new products that do not follow a trend, but set it - customers follow Cartier, not the other way around. The company has also created innovative promotional events and has used non-traditional approaches to marketing and distribution. All of these mould-breaking activities require a measure of organizational chaos. On the other hand, Perrin feels that "if you decentralize creativity too much it is no longer creativity, it's a mess ... the final decision must come from one man". Hence, striking a balance between creativity and control is a key strategic issue for Cartier.

Teaching Objectives

If employed in conjunction with chapter 9 this case can be used to meet the following teaching objectives:

- *Understanding of organizational inheritance.* Cartier is a company with a long history and a proud heritage. This inheritance is the basis of Cartier's strength, but it is also the source of potential inertia. The case makes it clear that an organization's culture is the carrier of its competencies, but simultaneously the major barrier to innovation and change (link to introduction and 9.4 Johnson and 9.5 Rumelt).

- *Understanding of managerial initiative.* Managers do not only 'manage' the current organization, but they also lead the organization through processes of transformation. The Cartier case illustrates how managerial initiative can lead to a break with the inherited past and to the creation of new organizational structures and processes (link to introduction and 9.1 Christensen et al.).

- *Discussion on the importance of organizational leadership.* The Cartier case can be used to discuss the role of strong leadership, in particular in organizations where creativity and innovation are important. Is strong leadership necessary to be creative or is strong leadership the most important barrier to creativity (link to 9.1 Christensen et al. and 9.2 Stacey).

- *Discussion on the importance of organizational chaos.* The Cartier case offers a number of examples of organizational processes that can not be tightly managed and directed. The question is which processes are and should be left lightly controlled, and what form of control should be used under these circumstances (link to 9.2 Stacey and 9.3 Bourgeois & Brodwin).

- *Discussion on control and chaos.* Overall, the case can be used to explore the paradox of control and chaos. It is debatable whether Perrin as the organization's leader really has the freedom to determine the firm's strategy. It can be argued that he and Cartier are prisoners of the organization's past. How much control does Perrin really have and how much control should he strive for? To what extent is organizational chaos constructive or destructive (link to all readings)?

Teaching Guideline

The Cartier case is a rewarding, yet difficult case to teach for a number of reasons. First, as Cartier and Perrin are so successful, students are quickly inclined to be too uncritical, or they even exhibit a bit of hero worship. Therefore, it is often up to the professor to be the devil's advocate. Second, the case does not limit itself to one specific issue, nor does it have a clear problem definition - on the contrary, it is a rather general description of how the company is run. Students are often at a loss as to what to concentrate on. Here the instructor has a more difficult task than normal in trying to keep class discussion focused. Third, the topic of the organizational context is often one of the more difficult subjects to deal with, in particular for students with relatively little organizational experience.

It might be useful to start the case discussion by asking students what type of person and manager Alain Perrin is and whether they would like to work for him (even a show of hands at this point is fun to get things polarized). As Perrin is such a central figure in this case, an analysis of his character and management style are useful for setting the stage for further debate. This analysis could even be structured by using the Christensen et al. reading, looking at Perrin's personal and organizational leadership roles, and his role as architect of organizational purpose. By asking who would like to work for Perrin, it will quickly become clear that having a strong, direct, impulsive and omnipresent leader as Perrin also has its downsides and that many people do not appreciate working with such a person. The advantages and disadvantages of such 'strong' leadership can be surfaced, and be used as input for the following discussion.

When working with a multicultural group it is particularly interesting during the discussion to focus on the fact that individuals from different cultures view the importance of strong leadership, participation, stability and chaos quite differently. Therefore, the balance that each student will strike between control and chaos will not only reflect their personal preferences, but also their cultural background.

Case Questions

1. What has been the basis of Cartier's competitive strategy since Robert Hocq took over as CEO? What type of organization has been created to pursue this competitive strategy?

2. Describe Alain Perrin's leadership style. To what extent does he control the strategy of Cartier?

3. Is there a threat that Cartier's current success will become the seed of its own destruction? If so, in what way would you change Cartier's strategy process, management style and organizational culture to avoid this negative scenario?

4. To what extent do you believe Alain Perrin should control the strategy of Cartier?

5. In what way will Cartier need to adapt its strategy to the industry context in the coming years? Or could Cartier actually shape its industry context? Does your strategy content advice fit with the organizational context?

Case Analysis

1. What has been the basis of Cartier's competitive strategy since Robert Hocq took over as CEO? What type of organization has been created to pursue this competitive strategy?

Cartier existed as a relatively small entrepreneurial firm, driven by creativity, up until the 1960s, when weak management and Cartier family discord seem to have led the company to lose its sense of direction. This crisis was finally solved by the sale of Cartier to Robert Hocq. He was able to achieve profitable growth by defining the market he was aiming for and by setting up a new organization. After his sudden death (and after 2 years of presidency by his daughter Nathalie), this high-paced evolutionary growth was carried on by Alain Perrin, who has been president since 1981.

Competitive strategy. Both Hocq and Perrin understood the importance of a *strong brand*, especially for luxury goods. Products come and go, but the brand must be eternal. People do not primarily buy jewellry, watches and perfume because they are technically superior or nicer, but because of the product's image. This implies that brand management is an essential task within Cartier. Brand issues mentioned in the case include exclusivity (vs. sales volume), focus (vs. diversification) and mystery (vs. publicity). In a nutshell, Cartier wishes to exploit its image, without killing it.

      To build and exploit a strong brand it is important to have a clear vision of the image the company wants to project and to ensure that all activities contribute to the long-term health of the brand. A legend can only be kept alive if it has a personality, which can be communicated and followed - by its products and the atmosphere created, Cartier gives direction to the tastes of the upper class. Cartier must lead consumers and therefore itself needs clear leadership. After all, creating and maintaining a consistent and appealing image is not something that can be done 'by committee'. With any work of art, whether it is a painting, a building, a movie or an image, *artistic direction* must be in one hand. Especially where the market is fickle and an intuitive grasp of what the market will accept is important, a leader providing clear direction can be the difference between failure and success (just think of Steven Spielberg in the motion picture business).

What Hocq and Perrin also understood was that building a stable luxury brand image demands constant *product renewal and innovation.* Cartier's luxury goods are fashion items and consumers demand change for the sake of change. Success therefore depends on the company's ability to be a trendsetter, which means that the company must continuously be creative and innovative. The company must constantly create new products, new fashions and new marketing campaigns. Organizationally this means that the company constantly needs to challenge existing ideas, it must be able to tap into new ideas wherever they are found and it must quickly transform itself to have the ability to bring these new concepts to the market. In other words, there must be room for creative chaos.

Organizational form. So, taken together, in the Cartier organization strong personal control by the chief executive is combined with "calculated chaos". Within Cartier, Perrin is omnipresent, directly supervising all of the important decisions. He himself refers to this as an "active executive". Characteristic of this form of management is that there are few middle management and staff positions or at least few with much power - the CEO establishes direct links with the operating employees. In a large organization such as Cartier this is difficult to keep up, so Perrin has surrounded himself with a number of trusted advisers, who work as his eyes and ears. These advisers operate beside the regular line organization, offering Perrin a parallel source of information and thus more power to directly control the organization. "Under Perrin, absolutism lives on in France".

Yet on the other hand he realizes that creativity is the lifeblood of the organization and that this is only possible in a state of disequilibrium, where existing ideas are challenged, people come into conflict with one another and new concepts emerge over time. There he also sees the need for "calculated chaos". Skilled experts combine their efforts in multidisciplinary project teams to create novel products and campaigns. Everyone participates in the act of creation - every new product involves all 200 people working at Cartier International. This requires a high degree of informal communication, freedom of expression and a willingness to discuss crazy ideas.

2. Describe Alain Perrin's leadership style. To what extent does he control the strategy of Cartier?

As follows from the previous analysis, Perrin is only partially in control of Cartier's strategy. He is not the master planner who single-handedly formulates the company's strategy, divorced from the organizational context (Bourgeois & Brodwin referred to this as the commander approach). Perrin's role is far more complex, as he tries to combine control and chaos:

- *Managing bottom-up "calculated chaos".* One of Perrin's ways of making strategy at Cartier is to manage a bottom-up process and to judge the outcomes (Bourgeois & Brodwin refer to this as the crescive approach). Perrin organizes the circumstances under which new concepts can emerge from within the company. He is the premise setter and referee in a situation of calculated chaos (Stacey would call this bounded instability), where everyone can challenge old ideas, brainstorming is permitted and novel concepts can be brought forward. This highly participative approach is needed to enlist each individual as a source of information and ideas, and to avoid getting stuck with a fixed company recipe. On the one hand, such chaos requires the willingness to accept challenge and conflict (as Stacey puts it "to move toward an explosively unstable equilibrium (disintegration)"). On the other hand, there must also be a strong motivation to work together toward a common goal ("to move toward a stable equilibrium (ossification)"). Perrin manages this calculated chaos quite tightly, to ensure that conflicts do not lead to paralysis and creativity does not result in a mess. However, he can only guide the creation process, not determine what is created (he is fully in charge, not fully in control).

- *Elements of top-down "absolutism".* In many other circumstances, Perrin prefers to make important strategy decisions together with his small group of advisers. These decisions are implemented top-down using Perrin's powers of position (line authority and control by advisory group) and personality (expertise, forcefulness, omnipresence and attentiveness). In this way Perrin is able to exercise quite a bit of control over the organization (Bourgeois & Brodwin refer to this as the collaborative approach).

It can be concluded that, as the organization's leader, it is Perrin's intention to combine direct control and controlled chaos. However, from an organizational dynamics perspective it can be argued that Perrin is less in control than he thinks. As is argued in the introduction to chapter 9, even strategies 'freely' devised by a chief executive are often forcefully, yet often unknowingly, influenced by the company's internal circumstances (strategy follows organization). The question is to what extent Perrin is the captive of Cartier's cognitive, cultural and political fabric (9.4 Johnson) and even the captive of his own strategic recipe. Nothing can be concluded with certainty based on the case information, but it could be argued that Perrin might have been captured by his own success - having been successful, he might not dare to stray from the formula he has found. This point, however, will be picked up in the following question.

3. Is there a threat that Cartier's current success will become the seed of its own destruction? If so, in what way would you change Cartier's strategy process, management style and organizational culture to avoid this negative scenario?

This phenomenon of a company's prolonged success ultimately leading to its own failure has been called the Icarus paradox by Danny Miller (see further readings section). It can often be witnessed that organizational success leads to the strengthening of the cultural web, which inhibits the organization's ability to change in future (9.4 Johnson). This phenomenon is something that every successful company must fear. In particular, successful companies must take care that the very factors that have lead to the success are not 'enshrined' in the organizational culture and therefore made undebatable. So, what are Cartier's success factors, which might become the seeds of its own destruction in the future?

- *Success of its exclusive branding*. Of course, in the luxury business image is everything. However, could Cartier be relying too heavily on its exclusive image? Some images and brands go out of style, are boycotted (Perrier), are associated with drug dealers and pimps, or are hit hard by economic recession (Porsche). Images are fragile, especially where customers are fickle and without long-term loyalty. Does Cartier's further international expansion therefore not hold an enormous risk?

- *Success of its distribution*. Cartier has had a particularly strong distribution system, with shops and concessions around the world. But where is the limit? If Cartier products are widely available in every country around the world, will this not spoil some of the Cartier mystique and exclusivity?

- *Success of its diversification*. In the same vein, the pressure on Cartier to exploit its brand may lead to pasting it onto too many goods.

- *Success of its strong leadership*. This is probably the most significant threat. Cartier's success is largely due to Alain Perrin himself - his market intuition and strategic decisions have made Cartier what it is today. However, there is a threat that Perrin will make himself too important within the company. As absolute power corrupts absolutely, Perrin could become exaggeratedly autocratic or could take the organization on a personal ego-trip. Perrin might award himself too many powers and not pay enough attention to encouraging the development of other strong managers that would be willing to challenge his orthodoxies. In the long run this would leave the organization without a broader base of management talent and vulnerable to the continued presence of just one person.

What could be done to combat these threats? Focusing on the latter threat, the following points could be discussed:

- Self-reflection and adaptation by Perrin,

- More room for chaos over control

- More delegation of power to operating companies

- Strong management development program

- Bring strong outsiders in

- Use semi-autonomous watch company (e.g. Piaget) as management breeding ground and pilot company, partially outside of Cartier culture and Perrin's influence

4. *To what extent do you believe Alain Perrin should control the strategy of Cartier?*

Based on their answers to the previous questions, students must evaluate whether Perrin's approach to making strategy is the most appropriate under the circumstances or whether he needs to increase or decrease his control. Here three issues are important for the discussion:

- *Is there really room for strategic innovations?* Do students believe that Perrin's approach allows for enough innovation and the real challenging of established ideas? Or is all of Perrin's talk about 'calculated chaos' just window-dressing for a very absolutist - presidential, in the French sense - type of leadership? Can creativity truly be stimulated in a company with such a strong-willed person at the top or are employees encouraged to bring forward new ideas as long as they are in accordance with the ideas of the boss?

- *How can Perrin retain direct control as the organization grows further?* In an organization of 200 people, Perrin already had difficulty retaining control, relying on close advisers to keep his grip on the firm. But as Cartier grows and diversifies further, the span of control issue will become even more pressing. It will become increasingly difficult for Perrin to directly control the strategy of all of the company parts. The question is how the strategy process at Cartier needs to be adapted. Especially now that Cartier has gone full-scale into watch manufacturing, it needs to be determined how the management of these activities needs to be blended in with the way the rest of the company is run.

- *What will happen if Alain Perrin is no longer head of Cartier?* What would happen to Cartier if Perrin were killed while crossing the rue Francois 1er? According to Perrin himself, not very much: "anybody could be Alain Perrin at the head of Cartier". But is this true? Is Perrin just "any good manager" or has he made himself indispensable - actually even modeling the company to reflect himself? It was argued that to be successful in the high fashion business a strong sense of direction and a strong CEO seemed to be important - are there plenty of younger managers ready to take his place. Or has he by his very own management style obstructed the rise of other strong personalities that could fill his shoes? If the answer to these questions is that Cartier is too dependent on Perrin, does this entail that Perrin should lessen his control?

5. *In what way will Cartier need to adapt its strategy to the industry context in the next coming years? Or could Cartier actually shape its industry context? Does your strategy content advice fit with the organizational context?*

Here a wide variety of strategic issues can be brought forward for further discussion. In each case the professor should ask whether the strategy put forward by the students fits with the organizational context. Some important points could be:

- *Competitive positioning.* Porter would probably describe Cartier as a differentiated focus company. In chapter 5 the risks of this generic strategy are mentioned as being: Imitation or greater differentiation from competitors, basis of differentiation becoming less important to consumers, losing cost proximity, decreasing attractiveness of the industry and new competitors subsegmenting the industry. Does Cartier face any of these threats? How could Cartier strengthen their position and the industry? (link to chapter 5)

- *Limits to growth of Cartier brand.* How much stretch is there in the Cartier name? How far can the brand be extended across countries, across products and across market segments (further down market) before the brand is damaged?

- *Horizontal integration.* Cartier International has sought most of its growth externally, by adding other brands to its family, such as Piaget, Baume et Mercier and Yves Saint Laurent. Is this a direction that Cartier should pursue? What advantages does it have? Does it enhance Cartier's market power or cost position? Does it leverage and contribute to the firm's competencies? What are its disadvantages? (link to chapters 5 & 6)

- *Backward integration.* Cartier has vertically integrated into the production of lighters, pens and watches. Is this a good idea? What are the advantages (reliability, quality control, and efficiency) and the disadvantages (inflexibility, capital investment, and alien manufacturing culture)? Is manufacturing a key Cartier competence? Should it become one? (link to chapters 5 & 6)

- *Forward integration.* Cartier has also vertically integrated into distribution, by setting up Cartier shops around the world. Is this a good idea? What are the advantages (secured market access, enhanced bargaining power, more market information) and the disadvantages (difficult to control, channel conflicts, capital investments)? Is distribution a key Cartier competence and should it be one? (link to chapters 5 & 6)

- *Diversification.* Should Cartier move into other products beside jewelry, watches, leather, lighters and pens? They have already dabbled in perfume and scarves - is this the logical limit? What are Cartier's competencies that could be leveraged by moving into other products? What are the dangers of such moves? (link to chapter 6)

- *Limits to growth of Cartier organization*: How far can the company grow further without Perrin losing his control and without losing creativity?

Other Teaching Issues

The case also raises a number of issues that are relevant to other chapters in the book. These other teaching issues are:

- *Nurturing strategic thinking.* In the case much attention is paid to the issue of creativity in determining Cartier's future strategic moves. However, the question must also be asked whether there is enough room for more rigorous analysis within the firm. Or is 'being creative' just an excuse for avoiding some disciplined rational thinking (link to chapter 2)?

- *Deliberate or emergent strategy.* To what extent can Cartier actually draw up long term strategic plans in an industry where innovation and creativity play such a dominant role (link to chapter 3)?

- *Managing corporate strategy*: As discussed in question 5, Cartier is now involved in a number of different businesses. What is the best corporate management style to suit their range of businesses and what are the pitfalls of this style (link to 6.5 Campbell & Goold, chapter 6)?

- *Hollow corporation putting on weight.* Cartier has traditionally outsourced much of its non-strategic activities, along the lines of 7.4 Lorenzoni & Baden-Fuller. Yet recently the company has changed course, by integrating both forward and backward. How does this compare to the arguments put forward in chapter 7?

- *Managing cooperative relationships.* Cartier works together with YSL and Ferrari, and might establish more cooperative relationships in the near future. What is their motivation, what form should they take and how must these relationships be managed (link to chapter 7)?

- *International competitiveness and global strategy.* France is the home base for most of the leading luxury goods producers in the world. Is this coincidence, or another example supporting Porter's diamond model? If so, what consequences does this have for Cartier's worldwide strategy (link to Porter, chapter 10)?

What Happened after the Case?

Since the case was written in 1992 there have been only a few important developments at Cartier:

- *Formation of Vendôme.* The owner of Cartier, Richemont, together with Rothmans, has reorganized their portfolio of companies, splitting the tobacco and luxury products. All producers of luxury goods (Cartier, Piaget, Mont Blanc, Dunhill and Karl Lagerfeld) have been grouped in a new company Vendôme, to be run by the former head of Cartier's jewelry division, Joe Kanoui. Vendôme is 70% owned by Richemont and is valued at FF3 bn., with Cartier representing about FF2.1 bn. (Cartier was sold for FF160 mn. in 1984!). Within Vendôme all companies will retain their autonomy (Financial Times, 23-26 June 1993). The reorganization has been criticized as few cost savings have been made and there is little evidence of sales increases. Profits have increased only modestly (*Financial Times*, 2 July 1994).

- *Purchase by Richemont.* In November 1997 Richemont, the owner of 70% of the stock of the Vendôme luxury group placed a bid for the remaining stock. The stock price was suffering, partly due to the turmoil in the Asian markets, (it dropped from a value of 550p to 320p). Richemont is now full owner of Vendôme Luxury Group. Analysts now praise the purchase, which at the time was not seen as wise. Thanks to a recovery in the Luxury Goods market, Cartier has been enjoying record sales for the past 3 years partly due to new jewelry lines.

- *Further growth.* Cartier now has over 200 shops worldwide, and is continuing to expand. Cartier has continued with same strategy that has proven successful for all but a few years in the middle of the 90s. There has been some diversification (leather), but that is all. They have come with innovative new collections that have been highly successful, especially their 150th anniversary collection. Cartier is the major earner within Vendôme, and compensates for poor performing companies like Alfred Dunhill (Richemont annual reports)

EXHIBIT 1
The Richemont Group Structure

BRITISH AMERICAN TOBACCO (23 %)	VENDÔME LUXURY GROUP (100%)
Following the merger of Rothmans International and British American Tobacco, which became effective on June 7 1999, Richemont acquired a 23.3% effective interest in the enlarged British American Tobacco.	CARTIER ALFRED DUNHILL MONTBLANC PIAGET BAUME & MERCIER VACHERON CONSTANTIN
HANOVERDIRECT (49 %)	LANCEL HACKETT
Direct Retailing	SULKA CHLOÉ SEEGER JAMES PURDEY & SONS PANERAI

TEACHING NOTE 19: SAATCHI & SAATCHI WORLDWIDE

Case and Teaching Note by Ron Meyer

Case Synopsis

In 1986 Saatchi & Saatchi became the largest advertising agency group in the world. The corporation also owned a sprawling portfolio of communication services companies and consulting firms. Its share prices had skyrocketed from £25 in 1980 to more than £500 by 1987. Boldly Charles and Maurice Saatchi attempted to acquire two British banks, but at this point the company started to unravel. Within three years the company was at the brink of insolvency and Saatchi & Saatchi's entire strategy was being reevaluated.

This case ends in 1991 with two key strategic questions that need to be answered. First, does Saatchi's 'one-stop communications shopping' concept make sense, or is there little added value to having a wide range of communication services within one corporation? Second, does Saatchi's 'global marketing' concept make sense, or are there too few customers that are really in need of global campaigns?

Teaching Objectives

When used in conjunction with chapter 10, the Saatchi & Saatchi Worldwide case can be employed to meet the following teaching objectives:

- *Identifying the pressures for global standardization, coordination and integration.* The case describes how the Saatchi brothers believe that their clients will increasingly demand cross-border standardization and/or coordination. In other words, as Saatchi's clients globalize, so must Saatchi - however, the question is whether there will be many companies that will feel the pressures for global standardization and/or coordination. The case therefore allows for a discussion on globalization pressures felt by both Saatchi and its clients (link to all readings).

- *Identifying the pressures for local responsiveness.* Likewise the case can be used for a discussion on the pressures for local responsiveness felt by Saatchi and its clients (link to all readings).

- *Discussion on the balancing of globalization and localization.* Once the pressures for a global approach and for local responsiveness have been determined, the case can be used to discuss how these conflicting demands can be reconciled in an international strategy (link to Prahalad & Doz).

- *Discussion on the management of international organizations.* One of the most difficult strategic issues in the international context is finding an organizational form that will work. The Saatchi case is a good example of an international firm struggling to find the organizational configuration that will give it the best balance of globalization and localization benefits. The case therefore allows for a discussion on the advantages and disadvantages of various alternative organizational forms.

Teaching Guideline

The Saatchi & Saatchi case is a fairly accessible case for almost any group, because most people have a relatively good understanding of the advertising service and the dynamics of the advertising industry. The case also creates enthusiasm, as the advertising industry is quite 'sexy' and Saatchi & Saatchi has had a controversial reputation. The case is also quite appropriate when discussing the topic of globalization, as few companies have been such outspoken supporters of global strategy as Saatchi & Saatchi.

One of the key points when teaching the Saatchi & Saatchi case is to encourage students to take a more balanced view of globalization and localization. Hardly any industry is entirely local or entirely global, but normally encounters a mix of conflicting pressures - globalization is not a matter of black and white, but of various shades of gray. Nor is it really a dichotomy between global (worldwide) and local (national), as some industries face pressures to integrate at a regional (e.g. Southern Africa) or continental level (e.g. Europe), while other industries need to be responsive at the sub-national (e.g. Quebec) or even municipal level. It is also almost impossible to treat every market segment and functional area as being equally globalized or locally responsive. Students must be willing to disaggregate the industry into groups or segments and the firm into functions or activities, and to judge each element independently. The first two questions are intended to force students to be more specific about whether they think the advertising industry is global or not.

Often, especially if students have had little exposure to international business issues before, it is useful to start class with a general discussion on globalization. An idea is to ask students what proportion of industries they believe are already entirely global (I usually ask for a show of hands to the question "who thinks that more than half are global"). This polarizes and excites, and it surfaces many of the preconceptions students have about the globalization phenomenon. A rough idea of the number of companies with a relatively global strategy is a first step to establishing how many companies are in need of cross-border advertising campaigns, which is the focus of question 1.

Case Questions

1. Is advertising a global business? Where would you place advertising on the integration-responsiveness grid? Is this true for all segments of the advertising business?

2. Are the pressures for global integration and local responsiveness equally strong for all functions/activities? Where would you place the major value-adding activities of an international advertising agency in the IR-grid?

3. Do you think that a straightforward global strategy makes sense for Saatchi & Saatchi Advertising Worldwide? If not, what type of strategy would you suggest?

4. What type of organizational structure does Saatchi & Saatchi Advertising Worldwide need and how can this structure be made to work? In particular, what type of human resource management do you think is needed?

5. How can Saatchi & Saatchi Advertising Worldwide be linked to the other companies in the Saatchi & Saatchi Worldwide portfolio to create synergy? Do you believe that Saatchi's concept of total communications is a viable way of pulling the portfolio together? What alternatives do you see?

Case Analysis

1. Is advertising a global business? Where would you place advertising on the integration-responsiveness grid? Is this true for all segments of the advertising business?

Any classification of the advertising industry in general would be too sweeping to be useful. Therefore it is necessary to identify the various segments of the advertising business that encounter different types of global integration and local responsiveness pressures. This segmentation can be quite sophisticated, but for classroom purposes the identification of four product-market segments is usually sufficient. These are:

I.   Local companies (from municipal to national level) requiring local advertising
II. Regional (from binational to continental level) and worldwide (from multi-continental to global level) companies requiring local advertising

III. Regional and worldwide companies requiring regional advertising
IV. Worldwide companies requiring worldwide advertising

When judged according to the pressures outlined by Prahalad & Doz, this leads to the grid positions as given in exhibit 1.

EXHIBIT 1
Estimation of Globalization Pressures on Advertising Market Segments

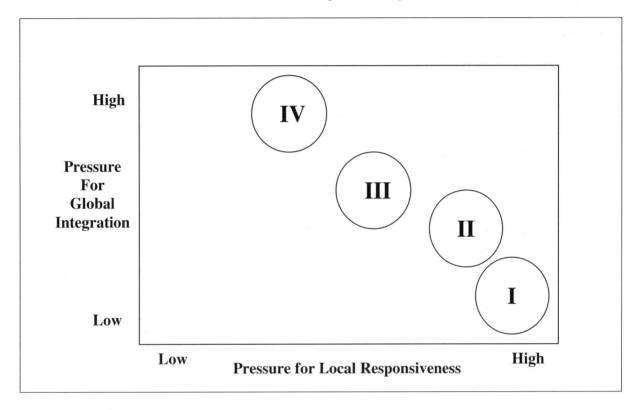

Of course these positions are rough estimates, but what they help to clarify is that the 'globalness' of the various segments of the advertising business differ quite significantly. Segments 1&2 are relatively locally responsive, while segments 3&4 require a combination of global integration and local responsiveness.

An important next step is to address the question of how large each segment is and how fast cach is growing/dccrcasing. Not much data is available to cstablish this, but based on case exhibit 11 it seems fair to estimate that segment 1 is the largest (approximately 40-60% of the market), followed by segment 2 (20-40%), segment 3 (10-20%) and segment 4 (1-3%). How fast each will grow depends on whether you agree with advocates of the global convergence perspective (e.g. Levitt) or with proponents of the international diversity perspective (e.g. Douglas & Wind). If the supporters of the global convergence perspective are right, it can be expected that segments 3 and especially 4 will grow quickly. Initially this growth will be at the expense of segment 2 (locally responsive multinationals moving toward more globally integrated strategies), but in the long run also quite significantly at the expense of segment 1 (local companies losing out to global competitors). If the proponents of the international diversity perspective are right, any shifts will be marginal. And for every company or industry that becomes more globally oriented, others will emerge that are more locally oriented.

2. Are the pressures for global integration and local responsiveness equally strong for all functions/activities? Where would you place the major value-adding activities of an international advertising agency in the IR-grid?

No. Here too a disaggregate view reveals large differences in the pressures felt by different functions and activities. In exhibit 2 the primary activities of an advertising agency - advertising development ("production"), advertising execution ("assembly & distribution") and account management ("marketing & sales") - are placed in the IR grid, differentiating between segments 2 and 4.

EXHIBIT 2
Estimation of globalization pressures on advertising activities

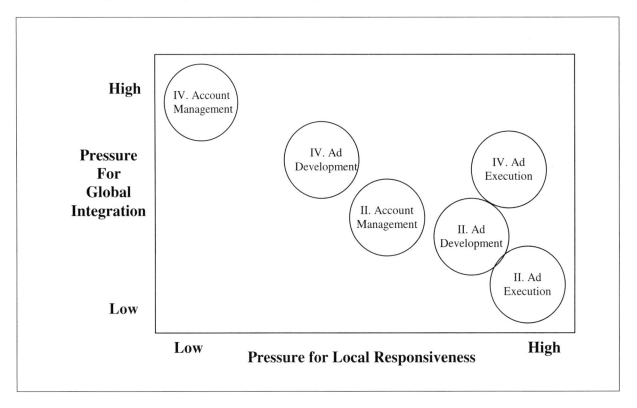

For segment 4 worldwide accounts must be managed centrally, with only a little adaptation to local subsidiaries of the worldwide account. The designing and general development of advertising campaigns must also be highly coordinated, but with a good deal of concern for the specific requirement of different markets around the world. The advertising execution, for instance the choice of media, frequency of ads, timing of the ads and the adaptation of details to local peculiarities (e.g. language, paper size) must also be coordinated, but must simultaneously be highly locally-responsive.

For segment 2 the overall need for cross-border coordination is much lower. Account management does require medium cross-border coordination, as these regional/worldwide companies will often prefer to have one advertising agency internationally, or at the least might be open to international cross-referencing (company ABC France might recommend Saatchi to ABC Germany). There might also be a bit of advantage in cross-border coordination for advertising development, particularly in borrowing successful ideas that have proven themselves in other countries. Execution, however, is entirely locally responsive.

Of course, the conclusion that must be drawn is that any classification of a segment as global or local must not lead to an undifferentiated approach. A more specific appraisal of each activity and sub-activity is required to determine the most appropriate strategy and organizational approach.

3.   Do you think that a straightforward global strategy makes sense for Saatchi & Saatchi Advertising Worldwide? If not, what type of strategy would you suggest?

No. The reason for Saatchi's difficulties can be seen in a nutshell by looking at exhibit 1. Only segment 4 would benefit from a relatively straight forward global strategy, although even there exhibit 2 suggests that some functions still require a high measure of local responsiveness. The problem is that this segment is quite small (1-3%), and despite potential high growth, will never become large enough to support such a huge agency. Even segment 3 (in particular pan-European and pan-NAFTA advertising) is not large enough for Saatchi to fully dedicate itself to. Saatchi also needs clients from segments 1 and 2 to remain a mainstream advertising agency. Hence, a simple global strategy is out of the question, as Louis-Dreyfus has seemed to acknowledge when he took over the helm in 1990.

So, what are the options open to Louis-Dreyfus? Although students might come up with a variety of ideas, the most obvious ones are the following:

A.   *Global strategy by focusing on segments 3 & 4.* The company could be shrunk or split and become a niche player only serving segments 3 & 4 with a relatively simple global/regional strategy.
+   Clear positioning and image
+   Relatively simple organization to run
-   Customers might fear lack of local responsiveness
-   Turnover might be too small to pay for office network
-   Downsizing painful, costly and bad for image

B.   *Locally responsive strategy by focusing on segments 1 & 2.* The company could dump its global advertising strategy and refocus on local responsiveness.
+   Clear positioning and image
+   Relatively simple organization to run
-   Totally contrary to organizational culture and mission
-   Painful loss of face in market
-   Loss of 'big name' MNC customers might lead to defection of local customers
-   Loss of potential growth segments

C.   *Multi-focal strategy by horizontal coordination.* This is basically Saatchi's current approach. Each local agency is fairly autonomous, but work together on a project by project basis, initiated by the Worldwide or Regional Account Directors.
+   Each agency remains fairly autonomous, motivated and responsive
+   WADs and RADs can assure coordination on a project by project basis
-   Difficult to get all agencies working together
-   Matrix organization with two bosses, split loyalties, unclear career paths
-   Lack of specialization on local or cross-border campaigns

D.   *Multi-focal strategy by vertical differentiation.* An alternative would be to have a clearer split between segments 1 & 2 on the one hand and segments 3 & 4 on the other hand. For segments 3 & 4 Saatchi could pursue a relative global approach and for segments 1 & 2 a locally responsive approach, but this would entail splitting up the organization into two divisions, namely a local and a global advertising division. The WADs/RADs would run the global business more forcefully, but personnel could still be stationed at the local agencies.
+   Clear differentiation of target markets and responsibilities
+   Simpler to develop consistent culture and human resource policy
+   More responsive to worldwide and regional accounts that prefer one boss
-   Partial loss of local autonomy and motivation
-   Conflicts between divisions about accounts
-   Overspecialization, loss of local know-how by global division, lack of learning between divisions, domination of headquarters culture

4. *What type of organizational structure does Saatchi & Saatchi Advertising Worldwide need and how can this structure be made to work? In particular, what type of human resource management do you think is needed?*

Assuming that the discussion will turn to option 3, 4 or a related option, the organizational structure to be sought must be some type of multi-focal organization. In the terminology of Bartlett and Ghoshal, Saatchi would have to strive for a transnational solution, balancing global and local pressures. A number of the organizational forms that could be debated would be:

- *Locally dominated matrix structure*. This structure closely resembles what Saatchi already has and corresponds with option 3. The local agencies are the main organizational building blocks and cross-border coordination for regional or global clients is mainly achieved by means of regional or worldwide account directors. These WADs/RADs can influence and negotiate, but do not have the hierarchical power to punish or reward to ensure that cross-border coordination takes place.

- *Lead-country matrix structure*. This structure closely resembles the previous one, except that the role of the WAD/RAD is not played by someone from headquarters, but is assigned to a lead agency (e.g. Britain) that has the responsibility for achieving coordination across borders

- *Bifocal matrix structure*. In this matrix structure the geographic component (national agencies) would dominate when it concerned clients from segments 1 & 2, with minimal cross-border coordination focusing on trading ideas (coordination by means of internal advertising and informal information exchange), learning effects (coordination by means of centralized conferences and education) and leads (coordination by regional boards and informal contacts). For clients from segments 3 & 4 the headquarters WADs/RADs would dominate, with local agency personnel primarily responsible to them during the length of a project/campaign. In other words, the WADs/RADs would have formal hierarchical power.

- *Dual structure*. A variation on the previous structure would be the case where the WADs/RADs would be further empowered by having permanent dedicated staff in most of the main agencies, instead of staff on assignment. This would actually mean the creation of two parallel structures (one local for segments 1 & 2 and one global for segments 3 & 4), both with clear lines of authority, incentives and career paths. A particular advantage of this structure is that it avoids the matrix problem of having two bosses.

Making any of these actually work will require what Bartlett & Ghoshal refer to as 'flexible integrative processes'. Managers will need to have the ability to see strategic issues from both the global and local perspectives. Some points that could be discussed here are:

- Necessity of cross-border management exchanges or even career paths
- Necessity of cross-border learning by means of training and conferences
- Necessity of cross-border networking by means of informal contacts
- Internationalization of headquarter personnel - should Saatchi lose its British identity (following the global convergence perspective) or is this actually part of its competitive advantage (following 10.4 Porter)?

5. *How can Saatchi & Saatchi Advertising Worldwide be linked to the other companies in the Saatchi & Saatchi Worldwide portfolio to create synergy? Do you believe that Saatchi's concept of total communications is a viable way of pulling the portfolio together? What alternatives do you see?*

This question is a matter of corporate level strategy and therefore must be approached by going back to the literature in chapter 6. Two perspectives on corporate level strategy were presented - the portfolio and core competence perspectives. Both approaches would emphasize a different type of synergy that Saatchi & Saatchi Worldwide could aim for:

- *The portfolio perspective.* From a portfolio perspective, Saatchi should strive for financial synergies - money should be transferred from cash cows and dogs to question marks and stars, while also spreading risk. From this perspective Saatchi is in pretty poor shape, as there is very little money to be reshuffled and risk is concentrated in a number of cyclically related businesses (link to 6.1 Hedley). Nor are the businesses typically the kind that fit well with a financial control style by the parent company (link to 6.5 Campbell & Goold). This alternative need therefore not be further pursued.

- *The core competence perspective.* From this point of view, Saatchi should be built around a common set of competencies. The term "total communications" seems to suggest that all Saatchi's businesses have a common competence, namely communications, however, this is not the case. First, the label "communications" hides many different marketing services that don't really have much to do with communication (e.g. market research, media buying). Second, communication is so diverse and communication knowledge is so difficult to codify and transfer that making it into a core competence would be extremely difficult. Finally, the organization has voluntarily split itself up into rivaling advertising agencies to ensure customer confidentiality, making the building of a joint core next to impossible.

It seems more likely that Saatchi would try to find a type of balance between synergy and responsiveness, by taking a view somewhere in the middle between the portfolio and core competence approaches. One of the most obvious ways of creating value would be to transfer skills or share activities between its businesses. This seems to be the route that Saatchi has taken. The activity shared is the acquisition of new clients. The corporation actively seeks cross-referral opportunities between its businesses, and it projects an image of "one stop shopping" toward potential new clients. The pros and cons of this strategy are:

- \+ Simple linkage requiring very little coordination
- \+ Especially uncertain and unsophisticated customers may prefer to be cross-referred or have one stop shopping
- \- Reluctance to cross-refer if the quality of the other business unit is not trusted or not known well enough
- \- Reluctance to cross-refer if there is no incentive
- \- Most customers prefer to shop to get the best
- \- Many customers want to spread their dependence
- \- Many communication services are decided upon by different sets of decision-makers

Cross-referencing and one stop shopping will probably result in a number of extra accounts and extra services provided. However, the question is whether this added value will be higher than the extra costs of having the various business units within one corporation (cost on headquarters staff, cost of coordination and control). Furthermore, all this cross-referencing does not create any synergy between Saatchi & Saatchi Advertising, Backer Spielvogel Bates and the corporation's other independent agencies.

Linkages that could be given more emphasis could be joint media buying (to achieve quantity discounts and a better package) and transfer of market know-how (e.g. personnel exchange). A further linkage that might be of importance is the umbrella of the Saatchi group's name. Especially the group companies might profit from their link to a leading advertising agency.

In short, there do not seem to be a lot of opportunities for creating synergy within Saatchi's array of businesses. But, while there seem to be few convincing arguments for keeping the corporation together, there also seem to be no pressing arguments for a corporate split either. Which route to pursue is a point for further discussion. It might be useful to end the discussion with the question of which corporate management style (link to Campbell & Goold) would best fit Saatchi & Saatchi Worldwide.

Other Teaching Issues

Beside the topics covered in chapters 10 and 6, this case can also be used to touch on the following issues:

- *Basis of competitive advantage.* It can be asked what the bases of competitive advantage are in the advertising industry. To what extent is competitive advantage a matter of positioning (e.g. importance of brand name) and to what extent a matter of developing capabilities (e.g. ability to be creative) (link to chapter 5)?

- *Creating a global industry.* A key question in this case is whether an advertising industry player, such as Saatchi, can actually influence the development of the industry. Can Saatchi by its very actions create or increase a global market segment, or must it just adapt itself to the developments taking place (link to chapter 8)?

- *Organizational leadership.* Saatchi is a company with a strong leader. Some would argue that this is the company's strength, while others would argue that it is actually the company's Achilles' heel. With the benefit of hindsight, it can seen that strong leadership can sometimes have some disadvantageous effects on an organization (link to chapter 9).

- *Corporate governance.* As most students will know, the Saatchi brothers came into conflict with the company's shareholders and were forced to resign. This was a rare case of shareholder activism and holds out a mixed message on how effective shareholder action can be. This may lead to a discussion on the question of how corporate governance should best be organized (link to chapter 11).

What Happened After the Case?

The case runs until 1991. This section describes the major developments at Saatchi & Saatchi after this period and looks at what happened to Maurice and Charles Saatchi after 1991. In particular we have focused for the globalization ambitions after the end of the case. Visit our website (www.itbp.com) for the most up-to-date information and valuable further links.

- *No more Saatchis at Saatchi & Saatchi.* In 1993, Charles Scott took over the CEO position from Robert Louis-Dreyfus who became CEO of Adidas. At the end of 1993, Charles Saatchi handed in his resignation, to "become honorary president of the company and… to concentrate on his creative role for the group." In December 1994, Maurice Saatchi was fired by the Board as Chairman of Saatchi & Saatchi after mainly American shareholders pressed for his removal. This was because of the continuous bad performance of the company and a £5 million remuneration package (including options) he wanted for himself. Particular shareholders were less than happy with his extravagant remuneration package, particularly because the share-price dropped from £50 to £2 in seven years. Together with the fired Maurice Saatchi, four top-executives (Jeremy Sinclair, David Kershaw, Bill Muirhead and Simon Dicketts) left Saatchi & Saatchi as well to join the New Saatchi Agency (see below for further details).

- *Change of name to Cordiant.* In January 1995, Saatchi & Saatchi Advertising Worldwide changed its name into Cordiant. In 1996, Charles Scott became Chairman and appointed Bob Seelert as Chief Executive.

- *Battle in court.* After being fired, Maurice Saatchi started a campaign against the company he once headed as Chairman. In May 1995, an out-of-court settlement ended this 'war', with Maurice Saatchi as the virtually complete winner. He was allowed to continue using the Saatchi name, although he had to change the name from New Saatchi Agency into M&C Saatchi Agency. In return Cordiant dropped its lawsuit seeking a share of Maurice and Charles' $40 million settlement with Adidas Chairman Robert Louis-Dreyfus for giving up a stake in the sports clothing company (Cordiant had argued that the brothers were mixing corporate and personal business). The issue of how soon ex-Saatchi executives could break loose of their contracts and begin working for Maurice was also resolved. They could start at the end of May 1995. Cordiant also agreed to drop a $50 million U.S. lawsuit it filed against Mr. Muirhead, its former North American CEO, claiming a breach of contract and alleging theft of company records. Legal action over Maurice's right to use the Saatchi name in Australia was also dropped. For its part, M&C Saatchi agreed "not to solicit or act for Saatchi & Saatchi, Bates or Zenith Media clients or employ their staff, other than those who have already moved, until 31st December 1995." This promise came after M&C Saatchi had already pried $210 million in business away from Saatchi & Saatchi Advertising, including British Airways, Qantas Airways, Dixons consumer electronics, Gallaher's Silk Cut cigarettes and Mirror Group Newspapers. Dozens of ex-Saatchi staff had already joined M&C Saatchi by that time.

EXHIBIT 3

World's Leading Agency Brands, Ranked by 1997 Worldwide Gross Income in US$ mn
(Source: Advertising Age)

1	Dentsu	1,927
2	McCann-Erickson Worldwide	1,451
3	J Walter Thompson	1,121
4	BBDO Worldwide	987
5	DDB Needham Worldwide	920
6	Grey Advertising	918
7	Euro RSCG	883
8	Leo Burnett Co	878
9	Hakuhodo	848
10	Ogilvy & Mather Worldwide	838
11	Young & Rubicam	781
12	Publicis	625
13	Ammirati Puris Lintas	621
14	D'Arcy Masius Benton & Bowles	607
15	*Bates Worldwide*	520
16	Foote, Cone & Belding	511
17	*Saatchi & Saatchi*	**490**
18	TBWA International	476
19	Bozell Worldwide	404
20	Lowe Worldwide	300
21	Carlson Marketing Group	285
22	Wunderman Cato Johnson	280
23	TMP Worldwide	264
24	Rapp Collins Worldwide	260
25	Asatsu	230

- *Improving Cordiant's financial position.* With a £126.6 million rights issue in November 1995, Cordiant tried to restore the group's control over its own finances, lost after the Saatchi brothers borrowed heavily to finance their massive acquisition spree in the 1980s. The issue not only allowed Cordiant to clear most of its debt (which stood at £700m in 1990), it also enabled the renascent group to negotiate cheaper borrowings in the future and pay its first dividend in six years in 1997. For clients, it allowed Cordiant to let go of the past and redefine the company culture.

- *Split up.* In December 1997, Cordiant officially spun-off its major business units into separate companies, Saatchi & Saatchi Worldwide and Bates Worldwide. Both companies became a 50% shareholder in Zenith Media, the third major separate business unit. The primary reason given by Cordiant for the demerger was to allow Bates to compete for client work it was denied because some Saatchi clients insisted on a groupwide "no client conflict" policy (for instance Bates could not pursue Unilever business, because of Saatchi's work for Procter & Gamble). Saatchi & Saatchi became listed on both the London and the New York Stock Exchange.

- *What's left of Saatchi & Saatchi.* After selling off its Siegel & Gale subsidiary in June 1998 for £20 million, Saatchi & Saatchi is at present an international holding company with operations in advertising, marketing, and communications. Its namesake advertising agency, which generates about 85% of the company's sales, has about 160 offices in more than 90 countries and serves clients such as Procter & Gamble, Toyota, DuPont, and General Mills. The company also owns Cliff Freeman & Partners ad agency. In addition, Saatchi & Saatchi provides worldwide marketing communications services and media services through Rowland Worldwide, a 70% interest in The Facilities Group, and a 50% stake in Zenith Media Worldwide.

- *Strategy at Saatchi & Saatchi.* Judging from the number of countries in which Saatchi & Saatchi is present (32 in the case, now over 90), the company has continued to internationalize. This points towards a strategy of globalization in a geographic scope sense. The significance of true global coverage as a way of giving clients the service they need is highly emphasized. However, the extent of cross-border coordination has not increased. Saatchi's mission is "to be revered as the hothouse for world changing creative ideas". With this mission also came the decision to drop the word 'Advertising' from their name and to describe themselves as an ideas company. The company has become more corporate, but less charismatic. According to some it is now more stable and much more likely to be around in five years time.

- *Profitability at Saatchi & Saatchi.* For the full year to December 1997 the company generated sales of £378 million (£375 million in 1996) and a pre-tax profit of £27.8 million (£16.5 million in 1996). For the first half-year of 1998 Saatchi & Saatchi reported sales of £193 million (£183 million in the 1st half of 1997) and a pre-tax profit of £20.6 million (£7.6 million in the 1st half of 1997).

M&C Saatchi Agency

Immediately after he was fired in December 1994, Maurice, together with his brother Charles and four top executives of the former Saatchi & Saatchi, started an advertising company called the New Saatchi Agency. In May 1995 this company was renamed M&C Saatchi Agency. As mentioned above, M&C Saatchi took away some important clients from Saatchi & Saatchi as well as 39 staff members. Heavily reliant on their former clients, M&C Saatchi had to open up a number of new offices fast to retain those clients. In addition to that, M&C Saatchi was very actively looking for new accounts. By the end of 1995, non-Cordiant accounts already made up 35% of total business. At the moment, the company has its headquarters in London and main offices in New York, Sydney, Melbourne, Auckland, Hong Kong, Singapore and Dubai, with total billings amounting to £195 million. The main clients (of the 29) are British Airways, Dixons, HSBC, ANZ Bank and Asprey. Maurice and Charles Saatchi are no longer in management, but are two of the five partners. The other three are Bill Muirhead, David Kershaw and Jeremy Sinclair (all former Saatchi & Saatchi directors). At the moment the CEO is Moray McLennan.

From the beginning, Maurice and Charles Saatchi built their new agency on their old success factors: simplicity, creativity and charisma. They also devised a global communications strategy for their company, as they did before in the 1980s. M&C Saatchi also realised that no one company is the best at everything, but that an integrated approach is the best way for a successful campaign. For this purpose they have built relationships with 64 independent companies to handle the different fields like Public Relations, New Media, Event Management and so on. This is called the 'M&C Saatchi village' (with the motto: integration by disintegration), where M&C Saatchi guides its clients through the partnership-network for the best possible result. The company also has an alliance with Publicis for the markets in which they are not located. M&C Saatchi claims to be 100% Saatchi, i.e. they have built all their agencies themselves, not by acquisitions (Maurice and Charles apparently learnt their lesson).

As M&C Saatchi is not publicly traded, no information about the operational performance and profitability of M&C Saatchi is available through public channels. What is known is the size of the billings, £195 million, and the notion by industry experts that M&C Saatchi is quite successful. According to these industry experts, the 'new' Saatchi is beating the 'old' Saatchi and establishing itself definitively as the 'real' Saatchi agency. "Also people in the ad community think that M&C Saatchi has the mantle because it is doing the sort of things which made Saatchi famous. Using power at high levels to get in and see clients. Everyone was envious of that in the Eighties, and they still are." (Martin Jones, managing director of the Advertising Agency Register, in *The Independent*, October 27, 1998)

EXHIBIT 4
World Advertising Expenditures, Year on Year Change (%), Current and Constant Prices
(Source: Advertising Age)

	1998 vs. 1997		1999 vs. 1998		2000 vs. 1999		2001 vs. 2000	
	current	constant	current	constant	current	constant	current	constant
North America	5.4	4.5	3.9	2.4	4.2	2.5	4.5	2.6
Europe	6.0	4.6	3.8	2.2	4.9	2.2	5.0	2.3
Asia/Pacific	-3.0	-5.5	4.1	1.8	6.2	2.8	6.8	3.3
Latin America	7.7	-	6.1	-	8.0	-	9.8	-
Africa/M. East/ROW	8.2	-	6.4	-	9.9	-	11.3	-
Total	**3.9**	**1.9**	**4.2**	**2.2**	**5.3**	**2.5**	**5.8**	**2.7**

References

Abrahams, B., Cordiant distances itself from Saatchis, *Marketing*, November 9, 1995.
Advertising Age (www.adage.com).
Green, H., One name, two agencies, *The Independent*, October 27, 1998.
M&C Saatchi homepage (www.mcsaatchi.com).
O'Sullivan, T. Cordiant three-way split adds fuel to take-over speculation, *Marketing Week*, April 24, 1997.
Saatchi & Saatchi homepage (www.saatchi-saatchi.com).
The Economist, Cordiant v Saatchi: Bittersweet, December 23, 1995.

TEACHING NOTE 20 A&B: CAP GEMINI SOGETI

Case by Tom Elfring, Ron Meyer & Herve Amoussou

Teaching note by Ron Meyer

Case Synopsis

In the 1980s and 1990s Cap Gemini Sogeti (CGS) has moved from being a very focused firm to being a large corporation with a complete offering of IT services. At the same time Cap Gemini's presence outside of France has increased substantially. The forces driving the company's internationalization and its swift move into a full-service offering corporation have been both external and internal. Externally, an important factor was that clients of the original professional services group (IT consulting, customized software, and education and training) increasingly started asking for related services such as management consultancy, facilities management, and systems integration. Furthermore, CGS wanted to remain one of the top players in the rapidly concentrating IT market. Acquisitions and alliances offered a quick way of building up market share. The international expansion by acquisitions and alliances has also been partly knowledge driven, as the targeted local firms have been able to fill in the gaps in CGS's skill portfolio.

Case A ends at the 1992 company-wide conference, the Prague Rencontre, where decisions need to be made on how to integrate the new acquisitions and allies into a cohesive international organization. The company believes that it should not remain a decentralized federation, but that it should increase its cross-border coordination and cooperation, and become an integrated network – a transnational organization. However, it is not clear how the organization should be structured, which processes would need to be standardized across borders, and how a true transnational mentality could be created.

Case B describes the steps that CGS takes towards becoming a transnational organization between 1992 and 1995. In this change process the first step is to reorganize CGS into a dual organization, in which each of the regions also receives the responsibility for coordinating worldwide efforts within a certain industry sector. The second step is to standardize services and working methods across all country units. The third step is to emphasise the human resource management and communication aspects needed to create a transnational culture. The case ends in January 1995, as the company looks back upon the completed reorganization with mixed feelings. The company is somewhere on its way from being a decentralized federation to becoming a transnational organization, but it is unclear whether the steps taken will be sufficient to complete this transformation. Furthermore, it is unclear whether the German ally, Debis, will be willing to stay in the group. A further issue is the integration between CGS and Gemini Consulting, which has barely been explored yet. Pressure was on CEO Kampf to come up with some answers, as the financial results were still far from satisfactory – closer to the nightmare that Kampf feared, than to his dream.

Teaching Objectives

When used in conjunction with chapter 10, this case can be employed to meet the following teaching objectives:

- *Understanding the nature of globalization pressures*. Cap Gemini has experienced a variety of demands that pressure the company to organize its activities across national borders. These globalization pressures are partially due to increased international similarity (allowing for scale advantages through international standardization and cross-border learning), but also due to increased international integration (requiring international coordination of activities). The case can be used to discuss these various drivers of globalization (link to introduction, 10.1 Levitt, 10.2 Douglas & Wind, and 10.3 Prahalad & Doz).

- *Understanding the nature of localization demands.* The Cap Gemini Sogeti case also makes clear that strong pressures for local responsiveness can remain. Specific local demands and close local relationships can be clearly witnessed in the CGS case (link to introduction, 10.2 Douglas & Wind, and 10.3 Prahalad & Doz).

- *Distinguishing micro, meso and macro level globalization.* This case allows for a discussion on the difference between the globalization of economies (macro level), the globalization of businesses (meso level), and the globalization of companies (micro level). CGS operates in different economies and businesses, and it can be discussed how this affects the extent of globalization the company itself should pursue (link to introduction).

- *Understanding the paradox of globalization and localization.* CGS is in the difficult situation in which both the pressures for globalization and localization are strong, although this varies between industry segments. It seems that CGS must reconcile the conflicting demands, but it is not directly clear how this can be achieved (link to introduction, 10.3 Prahalad & Doz, and Bartlett & Ghoshal).

- *Discussion of the global convergence and international diversity perspectives.* In designing a new organization, CGS will need to formulate its vision of whether globalization will further increase or whether international differences will remain significant (link to introduction, 10.1 Levitt, and 10.2 Douglas & Wind).

- *Determining the existence of national diamonds.* CGS is very dependent on leading edge customers for building up its industry specific IT know-how. In line with Porter, CGS believes that certain clusters of advanced customers exist in specific countries. The question is however whether this is true for all industries (link to 10.4 Porter).

- *Examining organizational options to fit with international operations.* CGS's strategy of international coverage through the acquisition of a number of national IT companies raises the question of how these companies must be integrated to achieve the optimal amount of local responsiveness, efficiency, learning and innovation (link to 10.5 Bartlett & Ghoshal).

Teaching Guideline

As can be seen in the chapter coverage table, this case covers a wide variety of strategic issues and it is therefore an appropriate case for use towards the end of a course. What I find particularly appealing about this case, is that it can be used to surface and discuss a number of student biases I have found to be common. First, many students believe, without too much questioning, that globalization is an inevitable fact of life. Especially in something so obviously 'non-cultural' as information technology, there seems to be little doubt that localization is for the has-beens. The CGS case helps to create a more balanced perspective, as in this industry there have been no moves yet towards global organizations.

Second, in my experience many students strongly believe that growth and internationalization by means of acquisition and alliance are the logical and preferred paths of development. This case helps to draw attention to the problems of cross-border 'growth by assembly', thus shedding light on the advantages of less-spectacular organic growth.

Third, most students tend to believe that in a multinational corporation coordination tasks and taking initiatives should be done by headquarters. Usually they implicitly assume that all coordination responsibility and capability development takes place at the center. "Especially in a French company," some smart student will often say, "Paris is the center of the world, where all decisions are made and all developments take place". This, however, is not the case in the transnational solution as was finally developed by CGS after the Prague Rencontre. In their organizational structure, international diversity is exploited - CGS tries to benefit from the particular strengths of each of the different countries. This has led to a network type of structure, without a dominating head office.

Finally, most students have a preference for broad, sweeping strategies, implicitly regarding such 'boring details' as organizational design to be matters that can be addressed at a later stage. This case, however, shows that the complexities of creating a workable transnational organization largely limit what is strategically possible and preferable. Students are forced to deal with these hands-on 'implementation issues' such as organizational design, corporate culture and human resource policy, otherwise they will be unable to judge the suitability and feasibility of the various strategic options.

The case has been structured chronologically into two sections. Section A covers all acquisitions and alliances up until the Prague Rencontre in 1992, where the transnational organization needs to be devised. Section B describes the transnational solution that the company came up with and explains how it was implemented up until 1995. In this teaching note it will be assumed that professors are using cases A and B sequentially (in two separate sessions is best). However, if time does not allow for two separate sessions, there are two alternatives:

- *Only case A.* Case A can be used as a stand-alone case to discuss most of the main issues involved in organizing international companies. Case B can be used to illustrate 'what happened after the case'.

- *Case A and B simultaneously.* Both cases can be prepared for simultaneous discussion, but knowledge of case B will pre-empt discussion on most of the case A questions. Therefore most attention will shift to the case B questions.

Suggested Questions

Case A

1. What are the pressures for global coordination and integration and the pressures for local responsiveness in the information technology services industry? Are these pressures equally strong in all industry sectors in which CGS is active?

2. Does CGS's strategy to internationalize fit with these external developments?

3. What type of international strategy do you think CGS should pursue in future? Should the company have a more global, locally responsive, or multi-focal approach?

4. What are the advantages and disadvantages of CGS's expansion through acquisition?

5. How can the existing organizations be integrated and "welded" more cohesively together? What should the organizational structure look like and how much cross border coordination should be undertaken? How can worldwide learning and innovation be achieved?

Case B

6. What are the major advantages and disadvantages of the 'transnational solution' as pursued by CGS?

7. How can the new organizational structure be made to work? What type of organizational systems and culture must be established to further the integration processes?

8. Would you advise further geographic expansion? If so, to which regions, and by which mode (acquisition, alliance or organic)? How should a new country be integrated into the firm?

9. Should Gemini Consulting be more strongly integrated into the company, and if so, how could this be achieved?

10. What should be CGS's next step? Would you advise further business expansion?

Case Analysis

1.   What are the pressures for global coordination and integration and the pressures for local responsiveness in the information technology services industry? Are these pressures equally strong in all industry sectors in which CGS is active?

Pressures for global coordination and integration. The need for strategic coordination is largely due to the following factors:

- *Client demand.* Clients increasingly demand IT systems that are compatible across borders. As client companies increasingly work on a global/European scale, they require services that can support their cross-border activities. They often prefer to work with only one (IT) service-provider, sometimes because it is necessary (systems must be linked together) but also because it is easier (they already know each other). Especially in the field of IT, companies are plagued by border-crossing nightmares and therefore opt to work with one organization.

- *Cross-selling opportunities.* A related factor pushing for strategic coordination across borders is the possibility of international cross selling. Of course, the very reason for CGS to expand to four businesses was to offer a full range of services and to achieve cross selling. This cross-selling, however, often takes place across borders (see the example in the case of Mobil Oil, where a consultancy contract in the US led to an IT contract in Europe).

- *Cross-border learning.* A further reason for strategic coordination is to be able to innovate more quickly and more efficiently. As new solutions to particular IT problems are found in one of the local units, CGS can try to transfer this knowledge to other parts of the organization as quickly as possible. In this way the organization avoids reinventing the wheel in each national market and the scarce 'good ideas' are optimally leveraged. Especially in the fast-paced IT market, where knowledge is the key competitive advantage, but where a knowledge lead also deteriorates quickly, cross-border learning is essential.

- *Competitive pressure.* Finally, an important reason for cross-border coordination is that key competitors are doing the same. If CGS doesn't benefit from cross-border coordination it will fall behind its main competitors.

It is important to note that while there seem to be significant advantages in strategic coordination, there are few pressures for operational integration. In the readings it is mentioned that increased competition is often followed by efforts to reach economies of scale and by the relocation of activities to increase, for example, plant size. These policies are difficult to realize in service industries, such as the IT business, due to the often non-standardized delivery of the services in close contact with the client. Therefore the opportunities for achieving economies of scale in IT service delivery remain slim. One possibility might be the research and development function at CGS. This activity is not necessarily in direct contact with customers, benefits from economies of scale and consequently it could be organized in one central location.

Pressures for local responsiveness. To the casual observer it might seem that something so universal as information technology should not require much local responsiveness. The IT business should be Levitt's showcase example of "The Republic of Technology" leading to global standardization. However, the opposite is the truth. IT hardware might be the same everywhere, but services such as facilities management and consulting are highly sensitive to local peculiarities. These are some of the most obvious differences:

- *Localized customers.* Large segments of the market are dominated by locally oriented organizations. Obviously, government, health and education organizations have a strongly local profile, but in most countries sectors such as retailing, professional services, tourism, banking, insurance, building and utilities are also largely local. Even in more internationally oriented industries such as consumer goods, industrial goods, and transportation, there are still significant numbers of local players.

- *Different levels of development.* Not all countries are moving at the same pace when it comes to the implementation of information technology.

- *Different buyer-supplier relationships.* Companies from different countries have strongly differing ideas about the ideal buyer-supplier relationship (see chapter 7), although these cultural preferences are often not made explicit. For instance, CGS has encountered that in the market for facilities management client companies in the UK want to have strong control, while in the Scandinavian countries joint ventures with equal shares are most common, and in the Netherlands partnerships with minority shares are the preferred mode.

- *Different organizational models.* The layers of hierarchy and level of control also differ across countries, resulting in different demands placed on IT systems.

- *Different service expectations.* In different countries there are widely differing expectations about the service level that should be offered.

- *Different cost and price levels.* Employee wage levels differ significantly from country to country, and as wages are the largest proportion of cost, cost levels are also quite uneven. Prices and margins also differ considerably.

- *Local relationships.* Having IT consultants come in closely resembles having dental surgery – nobody enjoys the process, but its best to go through the ordeal with someone you trust. Therefore, many contracts are acquired on the basis of good personal relationships at the local level. Of course, to work well with the local organization, knowledge of the local language is not an unnecessary luxury.

- *Localized competitors.* In most of the markets in which CGS must compete, they must be able to respond to the specific moves of important local competitors.

Clearly, it is impossible to generalize about the globalization and localization pressures, as these differ from industry sector to industry sector, and even from client to client. It should be clear, however, that globalization pressures are only dominant among international clients in globally oriented businesses such as manufacturing, telecommunications and transport.

2. Does CGS's strategy to internationalize fit with these external developments?

The answer to this question depends on whether students think that the globalization pressures will increase, while the localization pressures will recede, as expected by proponents of the global convergence perspective. If students agree, then CGS's early move to internationalize might have been prophetic, allowing it to establish itself early on as the prime international IT service provider. This would put CGS in the best spot to gain globalizing customers, project a leading edge image, and reap cross-border learning opportunities.

However, taking the international diversity perspective students could also argue that CGS could have remained a strong local competitor in France, with a much higher profitability. By focussing on the French market, CGS could have benefited from superior local knowledge compared to its major competitors such as IBM, Andersen and EDS. To satisfy the needs of its international customers it could have formed partnerships with other foreign independents, even forming occasional consortia to take on large international projects. This point assumes, however, that local knowledge would remain important as the basis of a competitive advantage.

3. What type of international strategy do you think CGS should pursue in future? Should the company have a more global, locally responsive, or multi-focal approach?

The answer to this question will depend strongly on the analysis performed in the previous questions. Two additional issues should be brought forward for discussion:

- *Standard solution for all sectors or differentiated approach.* Some industry sectors will have a more global profile than others. The question is whether CGS should pursue the same international strategy for all sectors, or whether they could have a global strategy for one and a local strategy for another.

- *Withdrawal from countries or sectors.* An alternative could be for CGS to withdraw from sectors requiring too much globalization or to withdraw from countries or sectors requiring too much localization.

I usually close this open-ended debate by stating what CGS has chosen: a standard solution for all sectors in all countries. CGS decided to remain largely locally responsive, while attempting to reap some international benefits, through cross-border selling and cross-border learning. In the terminology of Prahalad & Doz this is a multi-focal strategy with an area emphasis.

4. What are the advantages and disadvantages of CGS's expansion through acquisition?

The company has grown largely by acquisition and alliance, as opposed to expansion through internal growth. Growth by means of acquisition has a number of advantages and disadvantages, and it should be debated whether the advantages have actually outweighed the disadvantages in the case of CGS. In a nutshell the main advantages are (link to chapter 5 and 6):

- *Local expertise.* The accumulated knowledge about the local environment and their needs is a valuable resource that can be acquired.

- *Existing customer base.* Especially if there are switching costs or customers are slow to try new service providers, buying a customer base is a quick way of getting a foothold in the market.

- *Name recognition.* Especially in mature markets, building up name recognition and a quality image can be a slow and costly affair. Buying a respected name can be a useful shortcut.

- *Speed.* All of the previous points make entry through acquisition a relatively fast way for getting into a new market.

- *Not enlarging capacity.* A green-field operation usually means that more capacity is added to the industry, while an acquisition is capacity neutral.

The main disadvantages that can be debated are the following:

- *Divergent organizational systems.* Achieving cross-border coordination may be very difficult due to the very different organizational structures, decision-making procedures and policies common to each of the organizations.

- *Divergent corporate cultures.* An even more difficult part of the acquiree's historical baggage is often its corporate culture, which may prove hard to fit into the existing corporate culture of the acquirer.

- *Absence of network of informal relationships.* Cross-border communication, coordination and learning often also hinge on the existence of multiple informal contacts, but in the case of a takeover these must slowly be developed.

- *Overlapping or incompatible product ranges.* The acquired company's product range might overlap, requiring costly pruning, or might be incompatible with the products of the acquirer.

- *Mobility of main assets.* In professional services, if one buys a company, one is largely buying people. However, after a company is acquired key people can easily quit, leaving the acquirer with an empty shell.

5. *How can the existing organizations be integrated and "welded" more cohesively together? What should the organizational structure look like and how much cross border coordination should be undertaken? How can worldwide learning and innovation be achieved?*

Stated differently, this question asks how CGS's strategy can be implemented. From the analyses in the previous questions, two important organizational design criteria can be drawn. First, CGS will be looking for a multi-focal structure to fit with its multi-focal strategy of being strongly locally responsive, while striving for an intermediate level of strategic coordination. Second, CGS will be looking for a way to bridge the existing gaps between the constituent organizations to form a more cohesive company, while taking the disadvantages of growth by acquisition into account.

The discussion will have to touch on these major points (the discussion will be most efficient if this order is followed):

- *Primary structure.* CGS's primary structure (excluding Gemini consulting) needs to be multi-focal, probably with a geographic emphasis. In practice this means that CGS should have a matrix-like structure, with geographic units (by country or by region, depending on the similarity of local customers and competitors) as the main building blocks, and functional and business coordination between these units. It could be discussed whether an exception should be made for fundamental R&D, which would probably benefit from not being organized geographically, but functionally - in other words, all fundamental R&D for all countries and all businesses put together in one unit. In countries where CGS units coexist with acquired or ally companies (e.g. in the Benelux there is a CGS organization and an ally, Volmac), the two should be integrated.

- *Operating structure.* Within each geographic unit a further split could be made by function, product, customer group or geography. As the company wants to offer each customer the full range of IT services, a split by product would seem unwise. A further geographic split into local cells would only be useful if there are large differences between various regions of a country. For IT services, however, the differences between regions within a country are far less important than the differences between the needs of customers from various industry sectors. Building up expertise in IT applications per sector is a key success factor and therefore a split within each country unit into sector-oriented sub-units (e.g. utilities, banking, transportation) would seem the most obvious choice.

- *Cross-border coordination.* Three types of cross-border coordination would seem to be essential to be able to capture the cross-border synergies suggested in CGS's strategy:

  - *Project coordination.* If cross-border customers require a project to be carried out in a number of countries, CGS units in these countries need to coordinate their activities. This coordination will be determined on a project by project basis.
  - *Functional coordination.* Functional experts need to exchange their skills to be able to develop faster. This type of cross-border learning can be in the field of operations (e.g. Hoskyns people teaching others about their facilities management skills) and marketing.
  - *Sector coordination.* Most projects and the transfer of function skills will take place within the same sector (the utilities unit of Cap Programator will coordinate with the utilities unit of CGS in France). In other words, joint activities, learning and innovation will primarily take place on a sector by sector basis, making international coordination mechanisms between the

same sector-oriented units the primary focus of cross-border cooperation.

It should be discussed how the cross-border coordination should be organized. There are a number of possibilities: coordination could be spontaneous (self-organization, see 9.2 Stacey); it could be formalized through regular meetings between equals; it could be managed by a special coordination officer stationed at headquarters; or one geographic unit could be appointed lead country. In the case of a lead country, each country could be the leader in a different sector, depending on local expertise. For instance, given the strong financial services cluster in England and the larger chance that IT innovations for financial services will develop faster in such a dynamic cluster (link to 10.4 Porter), CGS's UK unit would probably take the lead in this sector. In this way CGS could tap into the world class clusters in each of its geographic markets and transfer its learning in each of these state-of-the-art markets to other countries. However, as with any type of matrix organization, there seems to be a threat of bureaucracy, and it must be resolved how to avoid excessive coordination costs. (This analysis largely coincides with the actual situation at CGS as described in case B).

6. *What are the major advantages and disadvantages of the 'transnational solution' as pursued by CGS?*

Most of the major advantages of the chosen structure have been outlined in the answer to question 5:

- Retention of local responsiveness

- Ability to undertake cross-border projects for international clients

- Potential for sector-based cross-border learning

- New structure can be implemented through evolutionary change

What needs to be emphasized, however, is that the 'solution' that CGS has devised is not really transnational, as described by Bartlett & Ghoshal (reading 10.5). The new CGS organization is somewhere between a *decentralized federation* and the *integrated network* proposed by Bartlett & Ghoshal. As in a decentralized federation, local autonomy has remained significant and there are only loose and simple control mechanisms. Despite CGS's attempts to standardize the service offering portfolio and working methods, it is doubtful whether the intended cross-border synergies will actually materialize. The major weaknesses are the following:

- *Non-structural approach to international projects.* As international projects are not the bread and butter of the organization, but are carried out on an occasional basis, CGS will find it difficult to develop the competencies necessary to successfully run such complex activities. Furthermore, as each geographic region has its own priorities, some SBA's might be less interested or committed to some international projects, sending their best people to local customers. This will place CGS at a disadvantage if competitors do establish dedicated international business units.

- *Few mechanisms to share customers.* In the new CGS organization customer accounts are still managed locally. However, the local managers have no incentive to attempt cross-selling CGS services in other geographic regions. On the contrary, they might be afraid to send their customers to other CGS units just in case something goes wrong and this adversely affects the relationship.

- *Few mechanisms to share knowledge.* While it is often remarked that 'knowledge flows', it doesn't, especially not across organizational and cultural barriers. Transferring knowledge across units is hard work and it needs to be organized in some way. More difficult still, many people understand that knowledge is power and are less than enthusiastic to give their knowledge away. The new CGS organization does cluster sector experts into common cross-border divisions, but there are few mechanisms in place to actually ensure that knowledge is shared between country units.

7. *How can the new organizational structure be made to work? What type of organizational systems and culture must be established to further the integration processes?*

Integration stimuli can already be inherent in the structure of the organization. As argued by Bartlett & Ghoshal, creating an organizational structure based on the principle of interdependence can in itself force regional units to coordinate. In the case of CGS, establishing a dual geography-sector structure with lead countries makes the geographic regions partially dependent on one another.

In this question, however, I want students to move beyond the 'anatomy' of the organization, to consider the physiology (systems) and psychology (culture) needed to be an effective international organization (Bartlett & Ghoshal, 1989, see further readings). Some organizational systems that would help to alleviate the weaknesses identified in the previous question could be:

- *Knowledge systems.* CGS could use its own IT know how to create a system for exchanging knowledge. In fact, CGS did try this, at first by getting all project managers to write reports that could be put into the information system for later retrieval. However, this system did not work well, as managers were not motivated to write reports, while the essential knowledge could not be easily articulated. Later, CGS changed its policy by requiring project managers only to state the essential details of their projects on the system, so that other managers could find out later who had previous experience.

- *Human resource management systems.* If people know that their careers will be within one geographic unit, and that international experience is not essential to advancement, there will be little motivation to work on complex international projects. Therefore, CGS must start hiring more people with an international orientation and must make international experience an essential criterion for career advancement. CGS could go even one step further by managing the careers of a number of high potentials at the group level, instead of at the country level.

- *Global account management system.* For some clients it will be highly beneficial if all contacts and knowledge are coordinated on a global scale. CGS could appoint global account managers or teams to ensure this coordination.

To encourage a transnational culture, CGS could take the following measures:

- *Stronger communication of the company mission.* Top management must outline, communicate and try to embed a common organizational mission. Especially if this mission encompasses both rational (strategic logic) and emotional (values) elements, a joint sense of mission can evolve (see 11.5 Campbell & Yeung). It is especially important for CGS to make sure that the mission does not sound hollow. If the mission is to become transnational, top management must take the lead, by moving to other geographic regions and leading international projects.

- *Joint education and socialization.* If managers from all of CGS's regional offices are sent to joint programs, they will start to share ideas, views and knowledge at the rational level, while at the same time they will undergo a joint process of socialization, calibrating their values, expectations and beliefs. This will not only help to understand one another and to grow towards one another, but also simply to get to know one another. In other words, joint programs offer the opportunity of building up informal networks.

- *Joint projects and taskforces.* In the same way, simply working together in itself can help to integrate the company. Especially if incentives (financial and career) are linked to cross-border coordination, joint work can be a beneficial integration factor.

8. *Would you advise further geographic expansion? If so, to which regions, and by which mode (acquisition, alliance or organic)? How should a new country be integrated into the firm?*

Much can be said for consolidation and not 'over-eating'. Resources, both in terms of money and people, are in relatively short supply. The financial position of the company is weak and there are plenty of integration problems without even further expansion.

On the other hand, the competitive logic that has led them to internationalize to approximately 10 countries would argue for further internationalization. Logical expansion would be to markets where CGS's many international customers also require IT-services and to markets where state-of-the-art IT services are being developed (countries with strong sector clusters). In order of significance this would mean Canada, Central Europe, Japan and Southeast Asia. CGS might also prefer to penetrate more deeply into a number of existing markets, where the company only has a relatively modest market share (e.g. the US, Spain, Switzerland, and Austria). Furthermore, CGS must worry about the prospect of its German ally, Debis, pulling out of the group, leaving an enormous hole in the middle of the CGS map.

As for foreign market entry mode, acquisitions are currently not financially viable. So, CGS must either start with a green-field operation, which might be appropriate in a relatively undeveloped market, or it must find a local ally with the potential of gradually merging into the group.

9. *Should Gemini Consulting be more strongly integrated into the company, and if so, how could this be achieved?*

CGS's multi-business strategy raises a number of questions, which can be tackled by referring back to chapter 6. The main questions are:

- *Existence of synergies?* The main justification for having four businesses 'under one roof' is the existence of cross-selling opportunities. This seems a clear argument for the three IT businesses, but are there really cross-selling opportunities between IT services and consulting? One incidence (Mobil Oil) is not convincing enough and it clearly does not justify more than a casual alliance. Yet, some of CGS's major competitors, such as Andersen, actually combine consulting and IT services (the former usually leading to the latter).

- *Organizational fit?* CGS and Gemini Consulting have significantly different profiles. CGS is much larger and has a broader geographic coverage. CGS is also organized by sector and has a technologically oriented culture. It is clear that the two do not fit like a glove and therefore can not be easily integrated.

10. What should be CGS's next step? Would you advise further business expansion?

Given the current financial and integration difficulties, further business expansion does not seem obvious. CGS also has enormous growth opportunities geographically, so these seem to most students to be the most obvious priorities.

However, I often use this question to challenge students to look beyond the immediate operational issues, towards the future of the IT industry. How might the industry be changing and how might CGS be at the leading edge of developments? I also ask them to think of the company today (which is not very different from the situation described in the case). Might the boom in the IT business be over, now that the Y2K and Euro projects are being wound down? What might the industry look like after 2002? Anticipating these changes might require action now, despite the current difficulties and preoccupations.

Other Teaching Issues

In the case analysis there have already been quite a few links made to other chapters. In addition, this case can be used to illustrate the following issues:

- *Internationalization as a planned or incremental process.* This case allows for a discussion on the extent to which a process of internationalization can be planned. CGS definitely had prior intentions, but a large part of their strategy seems to be emergent. Opportunities for takeovers and alliances, and the ensuing strategic possibilities and difficulties could hardly have been foreseen and set in a strategic plan. However, once the main acquisitions and alliances had taken place, the Genesis project could be launched in a relatively deliberate fashion (link to chapter 3).

- *Strategy making in an international professional organization.* It is interesting to discuss the use of company-wide conferences ("rencontres") as a means of focussing organizational attention and legitimizing strategic choices. Obviously, Serge Kampf realizes that keeping together a rag-tag group of professionals, who can leave at any moment, requires building up a common mission, culture and sense of community. His approach borrows a number of incrementalist strategy making features, such as building commitment, overcoming resistance to change, focusing organizational attention, building political support and gaining widespread acceptance (link to chapter 3).

- *Advantages and disadvantages of evolutionary change.* The integration process at CGS has been a continuous process, without whole-scale restructuring activities. Both the advantages and disadvantages are illustrated in the case (link to chapter 4).

- *Competing on capabilities.* This case can be used to illustrate the importance of continual capability development as the basis of competitive advantage. In the IT services business the company can only differentiate itself on the basis of its capabilities, while these capabilities have a very short life cycle (link to chapter 5).

- *Managing partnerships.* CGS has staged takeovers, but has also created partnerships with foreign IT companies. It can be discussed what the relative benefits of both options are (link to chapter 7).

- *Interaction with the industry context.* Is CGS adapting to the pressures in the IT services market, or is it attempting to change the rules of the game? Of course the question can also be asked whether any firm is in a position to change the rules of the game (link to chapter 8).

- *Control vs. chaos in an international professional organization.* The question can be discussed to what extent Serge Kampf can and should try to control the organization. Furthermore, it can be debated whether a company with a strong French heritage can transform itself into a transnational organization (link to chapter 9).

What Happened after the Case?

Since the end of case B in 1995, Cap Gemini has lost part of its name (Sogeti was dropped) but has picked up quite a bit of extra business. Operating revenue has grown from 2259 million Euro in 1996 to 3955 million Euro in 1998. The company ranks as one of the word leaders in information technology and management consulting. Some of the major events since 1995 are summarized below:

- *Transnational organization.* Cap Gemini has slowly progressed towards further cross-border coordination, although the SBA's are still dominant within the organizational structure. Careers are still largely national, while international projects are mostly carried out on a project by

project basis. The biggest move has been towards the creation of more Global Market Units (GMUs) that operate on a global scale, while also integrating IT services and management consulting (see Exhibit 1). For example, the GMU Utilities was formed in 1998, because of an increased number of privatizations in this sector in both Europe and the United States, combined with the growing globalization of the industry.

EXHIBIT 1

The group's organizational structure as of January 1 1999

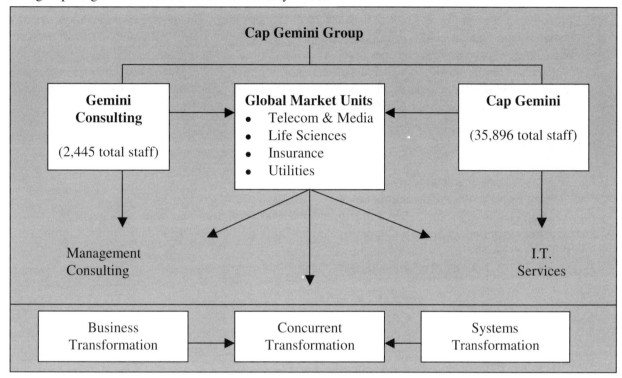

- *Organizational integration.* In a move to make the international transfer of personnel easier, the Cap Gemini group attempted to acquire the outstanding shares of Cap Gemini NV of the Netherlands. Almost all of these shares, traded on the Amsterdam stock exchange, were eventually obtained during 1999, although one of the original owners of the Volmac organization, who holds more than 5% of the shares, did not take the offer to sell. The Dutch unit therefore retains a separate listing on the Amsterdam exchange and is still not fully integrated into the corporate structure.

- *Organizational convergence.* Since 1995 Cap Gemini and Gemini Consulting have been moving more towards convergence, although they remain organizationally and physically separated. By 1999 approximately 25% of Gemini's business was carried out in projects together with Cap Gemini.

- *Growth.* The group has made a drive towards growth through internal growth as well as numerous acquisitions the last few years, e.g. the acquisition and subsequent integration of the Bossard Group into Gemini Consulting in 1997/1998. More recently Cap Gemini acquired Beechwood Data Systems, a telecom operations support systems integrator, to enlarge their offering of capabilities on the telecom market and to establish themselves among U.S. carriers.

- *Repositioning.* Cap Gemini has been very successful with to its Y2K and Euro-currency offerings. But as these issues pass, the company will be hard-pressed to meet the danger of new entrants into the various sector-markets, which could result in the commoditization of service-offerings and increasing competition on price. Cap Gemini believes that the programs that will bring high growth in the future will be won on the basis of quality relationships, not just delivery capability. Therefore Cap Gemini has changed it's strategy to concentrate on attracting bigger, higher-profile clients that will bring the kinds of challenging assignments that require Cap Gemini's size and particular level of expertise. The leaders of Cap Gemini UK that were forming this strategy described this strategy as "swimming for the deeper water", where only those with the richest skill and experience base can succeed. Because of the need for talented people, especially with this strategy, Cap Gemini also has to fiercely compete for new talent and has to retain good people.

- *European Company of the Year.* In June 1999 the European Business Press Federation (EBP) declared Cap Gemini as the 'European Company of the Year'. The EBP counts 47 top European business newspapers and magazines in 23 countries. Over 5 500 companies were rated. Initially the Dutch Cap Gemini subsidiary was judged for financial performance. Since European presence is one of the most important criteria and the Cap Gemini Group meets the financial performance, the award was accepted on behalf of the Cap Gemini Group by Geoff Unwin, Vice Chairman.

References

Business Week, Star Search at Cap Gemini, July 27 1998, page 22.
Cap Gemini website, www.capgemini.com
Europe, Cap Gemini: European Firm Profiting from Millennium Solution, May 1998, page 18.
Strategy & Leadership, Gaining a competitive edge: Building business from knowledge, March/April 1999, page 36-37.
Telephony, Integration revisited, June 28 1999, page 34.

TEACHING NOTE 21: BURROUGHS WELLCOME AND AZT

Case by Ram Subramanian

Teaching note by Bob de Wit and Ron Meyer

Case Synopsis

Burroughs Wellcome is a US pharmaceutical company owned by the UK-based firm Wellcome PLC. It was the first company to introduce an anti-AIDS drug, AZT, to the market in March 1987. The initial price of the drug was set at $10,000 for a year supply. This case describes the ethical controversies surrounding the company's introduction of the drug.

Two issues prompted AIDS patients to stage widespread protests against the company and for the House Subcommittee on Health and the Environment to conduct a hearing on the company's activities. First, Burroughs Wellcome decided to use placebo trials to test the drug, knowing that the group receiving the placebo would probably die much more quickly. Secondly, the drug was priced as one of the most expensive in history, although most insurance schemes did not cover its costs.

The case focuses on the issue of whether the company acted ethically or not. More fundamentally, however, the question is to what extent pharmaceutical companies have a responsibility towards patients. Are patients just customers or the very *raison d'être* of pharmaceutical companies?

Teaching Objectives

If employed in conjunction with chapter 11, this case can be used to meet the following teaching objectives:

- *Understanding the paradox of profitability and responsibility.* The case describes how Burroughs Wellcome must secure its own profitability under uncertain circumstances, while there is a strong (external) demand for the company to take on the responsibility of saving as many AIDS patients as possible. This allows for a discussion on the general tension between profitability and responsibility (link to introduction).

- *Understanding the impact of an organization's mission on policy choices.* The choice of trail method and pricing policy are not objective, stand-alone ethical decisions, which are unaffected by the company's mission. On the contrary, the case can be used to illustrate how important decisions are based on top management's conception of the organization's purpose and the values dominant with the company (link to introduction and 11.5 Campbell & Yeung).

- *Understanding the broader governance system.* The policy choice of Burroughs Wellcome was not disallowed by its own Board of Directors, but two other forces did attempt to enforce what they perceived to be the company's responsibility. Both the regulatory framework (government) as well as societal pressure (activists and the media) were brought to bear on Burroughs Wellcome's top management (link to 11.4 Demb & Neubauer).

- *Discussion on the shareholder value perspective.* Burroughs Wellcome behaved in accordance with the shareholder value perspective. This case therefore allows for a discussion of the main aspects of this perspective (link to introduction and 11.1 Rappaport).

- *Discussion on the stakeholder values perspective.* Most of the protesters believed that Burroughs Wellcome was misusing its patent monopoly and was not displaying any notion of corporate responsibility. This case therefore allows for a discussion on how a stakeholder values perspective might lead to different corporate behavior (link to introduction and 11.2 Freeman & Reed).

Teaching Guideline

The case of Burroughs Wellcome's introduction of AZT has become a classic example of the clash between the simple business logic of profit maximization and widespread public demands for responsible corporate behavior. It is a useful case for teaching purposes as it clearly illustrates the tension between profitability and responsibility, and because there is no 'right' answer. Whether the actions of Burroughs Wellcome are viewed as ethical or not depends strongly on one's views of what a business organization's purpose should be.

The case questions have been structured in such a way that students are required to look at both sides of the case. An alternative approach is to use the case as the basis of a role playing exercise, whereby half of the class is asked to act as Burroughs Wellcome executives and the other half as ACT-UP activists. Another possibility is to simulate the House Subcommittee hearing, whereby one group defends the position of Burroughs Wellcome, a second group defends the position of the activists, while the rest of the class acts as committee members.

Case Questions

1. What should the strategy of Burroughs Wellcome have been if it had strictly followed the shareholder value perspective?

2. What could the strategy of Burroughs Wellcome have been if it had adopted the stakeholder values perspective?

3. What would you have done if you were the manager in charge of bringing AZT to the market?

Case Analysis

1. What should the strategy of Burroughs Wellcome have been if it had strictly followed the shareholder value perspective?

If the company had strictly followed the shareholder value perspective, it should have tried to maximize the value of Burroughs Wellcome's shares by reaping the highest possible benefit from the AZT drug. Its pricing policy should have been designed to maximize profitability over the drug's probable life span (possibly until the expiry of its patent in 2005, but more likely until a more potent drug was discovered, which could be at any moment). The company would, of course, have to keep the demands of key stakeholders in mind when determining its strategy, but only compromise if stakeholders (such as the government and the AIDS activists) had enough power to thwart the company's plans. In other words, the company should have engaged in active stakeholder management (which is different than managing to the benefit of all stakeholders).

Ethically, Burroughs Wellcome could argue that it was merely pursuing its organizational purpose as an economic entity. If society (or the government representing it) believed that the plight of AIDS patients required special attention, it could make money available to purchase these drugs. They could argue that it should not be left up to private companies to decide which causes deserve to be subsidized. And if society believed that the company was reaping windfall profits, it could use legal means to change the patent period or could introduce new tax measures.

In practice, the strategy followed by Burroughs Wellcome seems to be largely in line with the shareholder value perspective. However, the company is careful not to speak of profit maximization. Publicly it argues that its costs are high and that its profits are average. It also points to the need to recover its R&D costs quickly, before other drugs come on to the market. Yet, the company does not disclose financial figures that may back up its claim to 'good corporate citizenship'.

2.   What could the strategy of Burroughs Wellcome have been if it had adopted the stakeholder values perspective?

If the company had adopted the stakeholder values perspective, it would have identified patients worldwide as one of the major reasons why the company exists. In the most extreme situation it could have formulated the 'maximization of health' as its organizational objective, instead of the 'maximization of profit'. In such a case the company would try to supply as many patients as possible, as quickly as possible, within the confines of what is financially feasible.

Ethically, Burroughs Wellcome would then argue that while it needs profits to survive as a company, it believes it has the responsibility not to let people die as an unintended consequence. It would argue that pharmaceutical companies, much like doctors, should be committed to heal the ill, not to use others' misfortune as a means of excessive personal enrichment.

3.   What would you have done if you were the manager in charge of bringing AZT to the market?

In the answer to this question we try to encourage students to formulate a number of options that balance the demands for profitability and responsibility. We first ask students whether the entire affair actually adversely affected any AIDS patients, or whether they primarily felt misused as corporate money-spinners. As the latter is largely the case, it could be argued that better stakeholder management might have solved many of the problems. Actually, in most cases the pharmaceutical industry and patient organizations work closely together to ensure that the government and medical insurance organizations are willing to pay the bills.

Some options that could have been explored by Burroughs Wellcome are:

- *Advisory board.* Burroughs Wellcome could have actively solicited the opinions of AIDS patients by instituting an advisory board.

- *Joint lobbying.* Burroughs Wellcome could have used the support of AIDS patients to get more government support and quicker inclusion in health care coverage.

- *Establishing a support fund.* Burroughs Wellcome could have channeled some of the Wellcome PLC charity money into setting up a fund to subsidize AZT for poor AIDS patients. Wealthy individuals could also be asked to join in.

- *Open reporting.* Burroughs Wellcome could have given more insight into its finances and could have indicated how profits would be used for further AIDS research.

All of these options do not really require Burroughs Wellcome to transform itself as a company. If it were really serious about 'maximizing health' as its mission, it would probably have to go much further in changing its core values and market positioning (see The Body Shop case in this book as an example).

Other Teaching Issues

The case also raises a number of issues that are relevant to other chapters in the book. These other teaching issues are:

- *Managing external relationships.* Burroughs Wellcome seems to consider its 'buyers' as a group with which it wishes to maintain an arm's length relationship. Whether intended or not, the company's policies and behavior are viewed as selfish and arrogant. This not only indicates that the company's communication policy is poor, but that the relationship with patients and the media was not cooperative to begin with. It can be debated whether this is the best approach to managing the company's external relationships (link to chapter 7).

- *Behavior emerges from history?* Was the policy of Burroughs Wellcome a deliberate choice by the company to deal with the totally new situation of an AIDS crisis and the discovery of a breakthrough drug? Or were the company executives merely following the 'standard operating procedures', which they had learned during their years of working on less spectacular drugs for arcane diseases (link to chapter 9)?

What Happened after the Case?

The case runs until 1990. This section describes the major developments in the AZT dispute, the different anti-AIDS drugs that emerged and the corporate responsibility at Burroughs Wellcome after 1990. Visit our website (www.itbp.com) for the most up-to-date information and valuable further links.

The AZT protests and new drug developments

- *Sales and profit.* A study in 1993 by the Harvard School of Medicine concluded that through August 1993, Burroughs Wellcome reaped almost $600 million in profits on total AZT sales of $1.4 billion, a profit margin of 43%. According to the study, cumulative profits on worldwide AZT sales were expected to increase to $1.3 billion by August 1996.

- *Price drops.* After 1994, however, the price of AZT was lowered. The main reason was that studies revealed that AZT was not the wonder drug hoped for, as HIV could become resistant to it. This crushed the hopes for a quick solution of the AIDS problem. It also changed the mentality of the activists, who came to realize that the pharmaceutical companies needed to be stimulated to keep on searching for new anti-AIDS drugs. The activists also accepted the necessity of thorough testing, even if it meant that the approval of new drugs would be slower (unlike in 1990 when speed was the most important criterion).

- *Court battles.* In 1991 and 1992 Burroughs Wellcome filed lawsuits against Barr and Novopharm Ltd., when these companies began taking steps to produce a generic version of the HIV and AIDS treatment patented by Burroughs Wellcome. The two companies argued that the National Institutes of Health should also be named as patent holder, due to the fact that much of the development and testing had been carried out and paid for by public institutions. In their view, the six Burroughs Wellcome patents were thus invalid. In a court ruling and an appeal in 1994 the judges ruled in favor of Burroughs Wellcome, validating the patent until 2005. In 1995, Barr got FDA approval for its AZT equivalent after 2005.

- *New anti-AIDS products.* The lucrative profit margins have since drawn many new players into the anti-AIDS market. Below are the 16 FDA approved anti-AIDS drugs or 'cocktails' as of the beginning of 1999 and their manufacturers.

- *New customer groups.* In 1994 a study revealed that giving AZT to pregnant women infected with HIV for several months prior to birth could reduce transmission of the virus to infants by two-thirds. In March 1998, researchers in Thailand found that a shorter treatment—just three weeks of AZT pills given to women daily—halved transmission rates. This opened up a whole new market for the producers of anti-AIDS drugs. Only weeks after this last discovery, Glaxo Wellcome announced that it would give a 75% discount for pregnant women in poor countries, making the treatment more available for an estimated 3 million HIV-infected mothers.

- *Prices of AZT continued to drop.* As of the beginning of 1999, the price of an AZT treatment is about $1,000 a year. The newer products, such as Glaxo Wellcome's Ziagen (approved in

December 1998), are about $3,000 a year for wholesalers (about $3,800 at retailers), making better treatments possible at a much lower cost than in 1990.

EXHIBIT 1
Anti-AIDS Drugs as of January 1st 1999

Brand name (generic name)	MANUFACTURER
Retrovir (zidovudine, AZT)	Glaxo Wellcome
Epivir (lamivudine, 3TC)	Glaxo Wellcome
Hivid (zalcitabine, ddC)	Hoffmann-La Roche
Combivir (3TC + AZT)	Glaxo Wellcome
Videx (didanosine, ddI)	Bristol-Myers-Squibb
Zerit (stavudine, d4T)	Bristol-Myers-Squibb
Ziagen (abacavir)	Glaxo Wellcome
Rescriptor (delaverdine)	Pharmacia & Upjohn
Viarmune (nevirapine)	Boeringer Ingelheim
Sustiva (efavirenz, DMP-266)	DuPont-Merck
Crixivan (indinavir)	Merck
Invirase (saquinavar (hard gel))	Hoffmann-La Roche
Fortovase (saquinavar (soft gel))	Hoffmann-La Roche
Norvir (ritonavir)	Abbot Laboratories
Viracept (nelfinavir)	Agouron
Agenerase (amprenavir)	Glaxo Wellcome

Glaxo Wellcome

▪ *Merger with Glaxo.* In 1995, Burroughs Wellcome Plc. integrated with Glaxo Plc. to form Glaxo Wellcome Plc., the world's largest pharmaceutical company, with global sales in 1998 totaling $13.25 billion (at $1.66 exchange rate), with nearly $2 billion spent on R&D. After tax earnings in the same year amounted to $3.0 billion. The trading margin was 33.6% of total sales.

▪ *The sales future of Glaxo Wellcome's anti-AIDS drugs.* According to analysts at Dresdner Kleinwort Benson flat growth for the anti-HIV market overall is forecasted, as Western infection rates level off. Forecasted are sales of £280 million a year for Ziagen by 2002, compared with £390 million for Epivir and £640 million for Combivir, a tablet which combines Epivir and Retrovir. Analysts at Greig Middleton, however, forecast that Glaxo Wellcome's two new products (together with Agenerase, which received FDA approval in April 1999) are predicted to help the company retain leadership in a fast-growing AIDS and HIV market. They expect Glaxo Wellcome to maintain its market share of around 40 percent in the anti-HIV market that is forecasted to grow to £6.3 billion a year by 2004 from £1.7 billion a year in 1997.

EXHIBIT 2
Sales and Profit Figures Glaxo Wellcome 1996-1998 (Source: Annual Reports)

Year	Net Sales (US$ billion)	Trading margin (%)	After tax profits (US$ billion)
1998	13.25	33.6	3.03
1997	13.45	35.4	3.34
1996	12.09	37.5	2.75

EXHIBIT 3

Financial Summary Glaxo Wellcome 1995-1998 (Source: Annual Reports)

	1998 (£ billion)	1997 (£ billion)	1996 (£ billion)	1995 (£ billion)
Sales	7.98	7.98	8.34	7.64
Trading profit	2.68	2.82	3.13	2.58
Trading margin	33.6 %	35.4	37.5 %	33.8 %
Pre-tax profit	2.67	2.69	2.96	2.51
Earnings	1.84	1.85	2.0	1.79
Earnings per share	51.1p	52.0p	56.7p	50.3p
Dividends per share	36.0p	35.0p	34.0p	30.0p

References

- Annual Reports Glaxo Wellcome 1995, 1996, 1997 and 1998 (www.glaxowellcome.com).

- BioCognizance list of anti-HIV drugs (www.biocognizance.com/hiv)

- *Chemical Marketing Reporter*, 'Burroughs-Wellcome hit over high AIDS drug profits', June 28, 1993.

- *Chemical Marketing Reporter*, 'US court upholds five AZT patents', November 28, 1994.

- Henahan, S., Resistance fighters, *Drug Topics*, August 21, 1995.

TEACHING NOTE 22: THE BODY SHOP INTERNATIONAL

Case by Andrew Campbell

Teaching note by Bob de Wit and Ron Meyer

Case Synopsis

The Body Shop originates, produces, and sells naturally based skin and hair products and related items through its own shops and through franchised outlets. It opened its first shop in Brighton in 1976 and, despite a recession in retailing, the company has grown with great speed. In 1990 it had a turnover of £84.5m, with 457 shops, 139 in Britain and 318 in 37 other countries. A further 25 UK outlets and 180 overseas stores were due to open in the following year. The Body Shop has over 300 products specially made for its shops.

     The Body Shop is an unusual company and an unusual workplace. CEO Anita Roddick, who started the first Body Shop with a bank loan of £4000, promotes an ethical code of behavior for the global citizen. She aims to change the world for the better. The Body Shop has a very strong corporate philosophy, with a strong commitment to the animal rights, environmental care and community enhancement. The case focuses on The Body Shop's sense of mission and its usefulness for future growth.

Teaching Objectives

If used in conjunction with chapter 11, this case can be employed to meet the following teaching objectives:

- *Understanding the paradox of profitability and responsibility.* Anita Roddick is driven by a strong sense of responsibility, but also clearly realizes that profitability is an important organizational end. But while she experiences the tension between profitability and responsibility, she attempts to reconcile the two demands in The Body Shop formula. Therefore, this case allows for a discussion on the tension between profitability and responsibility (link to introduction).

- *Discussion of the shareholder value and stakeholder values perspectives.* The case describes The Body Shop's corporate philosophy, which strongly emphasizes corporate responsibility to a wide variety of stakeholder values. This allows for a discussion on how the stakeholder values perspective differs from the better-known shareholder value perspective (link to introduction, 11.1 Rappaport and 11.2 Freeman & Reed).

- *Illustrating the distinction between primary and secondary stakeholders.* The Body Shop employs a broad definition of stakeholders, not only including the direct participants in the economic value creation process (primary stakeholders). As global citizens, Body Shop employees believe that they have a responsibility to the world at large (secondary stakeholders) (link to introduction).

- *Clarifying the distinction between vision and mission.* The case allows for a discussion of the Body Shop's mission, while it will also become clear that the company may actually be in need of a vision for the future (link to introduction and 11.5 Campbell & Yeung).

- *Clarifying the distinction between mission and a sense of mission.* While most students have seen mission statements before, this case allows for a discussion on the sense of mission that can be achieved when missions are actually internalized (link to 11.5 Campbell & Yeung).

- *Debating the importance of a sense of mission.* Campbell & Yeung emphasize the importance of a sense of mission for achieving organizational results. Proponents of the stakeholder value perspective may see a mission statement merely as a way for getting the agent to acknowledge the interests of the principle (for which wages are paid in return). This case therefore allows for a discussion on the importance of a sense of mission for motivating employees (link to all readings).

Teaching Guideline

This case can be used as an example of a company that has successfully tried to resolve the paradox of profitability and responsibility. From the very beginning, Anita Roddick has tried to combine her sense of responsibility to the world at large with her desire to make a good living and to build up a viable company. Most students have difficulty envisioning such a synthesis, and therefore this case often proves to be a good way of sparking their imagination.

Besides illustrating the paradox of profitability and responsibility, this case also gets students to think about their own values and about the type of company they would like to work for. It is for this reason that discussions sometimes also become emotional. Students will often feel that the values that they hold are 'true' and therefore that some companies and missions are inherently superior to others. Some students will view The Body Shop as an excellent model for other companies to follow and would be happy to work for them. However, others might feel uneasy with so much 'unbusiness-like' ideological do-gooding, and would strongly prefer a sharper distinction between business activities and charitable works.

The interesting aspect of the Body Shop case is that it always creates controversy. The Body Shop is often in the press, sometimes because of its community projects, sometimes because of allegations of hypocrisy, and sometimes because of disgruntled shareholders. We usually encourage polarization by starting off the discussion with the question whether students think that Anita Roddick is genuinely concerned with the world, or just a very convincing salesperson. In other words, is the Body Shop's organizational purpose really to contribute to the broader community and the environment, or is it just a smart marketing ploy? This question usually separates the hard-nosed 'realists', who believe that the business of business is to make money and therefore that Roddick is just being cunning, from those who believe she is an honest 'bleeding heart'. We then start with the first formal question below.

Suggested Questions

1. What is The Body Shop's mission?

2. Does The Body Shop have a sense of mission?

3. How does The Body Shop attempt to resolve the paradox of profitability and responsibility?

4. How should the corporate governance of The Body Shop be structured to ensure that the corporate mission is pursued?

5. In what direction do you think The Body Shop should develop in future? Which threats and opportunities do you see?

Case Analysis

1. What is The Body Shop's mission?

This question can be addressed by using the Ashridge mission model outlined by Campbell & Yeung in reading 11.5:

- *Purpose*. In the case the slogan 'profit with principles' is used, but this still suggests that the main reason for being in business is profitability. However, throughout the case it is clear that Anita Roddick believes that The Body Shop can make a large contribution to the world as a whole and has the responsibility to do so. The Body Shop strives to meet the interests of all of its primary stakeholders, including customers, suppliers, franchisees, employees and shareholders, but even more importantly The Body Shop is committed to helping those who cannot help themselves. These secondary stakeholders include the environment, animals, poor parts of local communities and disadvantaged people in developing economies. In their 1998 Annual Report the company states succinctly that it is its purpose *"to dedicate our business to the pursuit of social and environmental change"*.

- *Strategy*. Here Campbell & Yeung refer to the underlying commercial logic of the organization. The Body Shop has positioned itself as a retailer of toiletries and cosmetics, distinguishing itself through specially manufactured products that employ natural ingredients and are environmentally friendly. A constant stream of new products are introduced exclusively for The Body Shop, while economies of scale are realized through a global chain of franchise outlets. This strategic positioning clearly fits with the above organizational mission.

- *Values*. The Body Shop Philosophy is built on a number of ideals, which the company has summarized as follows in their 1998 Annual Report:
  - "To creatively balance the financial and human needs of our stakeholders: employees, customers, franchisees, suppliers and shareholders."
  - "To courageously ensure that our business is ecologically sustainable: meeting the needs of the present without compromising the future."
  - "To meaningfully contribute to local, national and international communities in which we trade, by adopting a code of conduct which ensures care, honesty, fairness and respect."
  - "To passionately campaign for protection of the environment, human and civil rights, and against animal testing in the cosmetics and toiletries industry."
  - "To tirelessly work to narrow the gap between principle and practice, whilst making fun, passion and care part of our daily lives."

- *Behavior standards*. The above elements are translated into "an ethical code of behavior for the global citizen", which includes the following key features:
  - Vegetable rather than animal ingredients
  - No animal testing
  - Refill service for all products
  - Only biodegradable products
  - Waste is recycled
  - Use of natural, close-to-source ingredients
  - Minimal packaging
  - Information instead of advertising
  - Free training for employees

2. Does The Body Shop have a sense of mission?

Campbell & Yeung argue that a sense of mission is the emotional commitment felt by people to the company's mission. It occurs when there is a match between the values of the individual and the values of the company. Although it can not be said with certainty for all employees, it seems obvious that Anita Roddick and most of the employees see their personal values strongly reflected in the mission of the company, and therefore have a clear sense of mission.

3.   How does The Body Shop attempt to resolve the paradox of profitability and responsibility?

The Body Shop's approach is to try to make responsible behavior profitable. This approach works in two directions:

- *By appealing to consumers' sense of responsibility*. The Body Shop doesn't only sell toiletries and cosmetics – it 'sells' responsible behavior. It's products might be a little bit more expensive, but the consumer is willing to pay extra to a firm which it trusts to make a real contribution to community and the environment. The Body Shop is not quietly ethical, but wears its ethical behavior as a seal of quality, which demands a premium price.

- *By appealing to employees' sense of responsibility*. The Body Shop is able to attract highly motivated people to their company and to get them to work hard to make the company a success. This passion is not due to their dedication to the shareholders ("I can't wait to go out and create some shareholder value today!"), but due to their dedication to the company's mission. In Roddick's terms, "how do you ennoble the spirit when selling moisture cream"? By appealing to deeper held values of the employee.

However, this resolution of the paradox of profitability and responsibility is a constant issue, as the company must always ask itself how much profit is enough and how far the company should go in spending time and money on the public good. Especially with a large part of the shares in the hands of others than the Roddicks, the pressure to push up profitability can be expected to remain strong.

4.   How should the corporate governance of The Body Shop be structured to ensure that the corporate mission is pursued?

In other words, who should manage Anita Roddick? The case does not give any information on this issue, but students can think about the ideal corporate governance structure nonetheless. Given the company's balanced mission, it would seem obvious to make sure that a Board of Directors was chosen that shared this balanced perspective. This could be done in two ways:

- *Independents*. By seeking independent individuals, who also accept the need to reconcile the demands of profitability and responsibility.

- *Representatives*. By seeking the balanced representation of the company's various stakeholder groups (e.g. environmental activist, community worker, pension fund manager, employee representative).

At this point it is often useful to ask students to think of well-known companies that have been built up by an entrepreneur founder, are taken to the stock market and then end up with corporate governance difficulties. Among the cases in this book, Virgin and Saatchi & Saatchi have encountered such difficulties. Apple Computers is also a prominent example where the strong-willed entrepreneur came into conflict with his Board of Directors. In the case of Saatchi and Apple, the founders were eventually forced to leave (both starting new companies to prove they were right), while Richard Branson was able to buy out the publicly held shares of Virgin.

   We then ask students why they think such conflicts arise. After some discussion it becomes clear that many entrepreneurs who are 'self-made' and used to making decisions themselves on the basis of business instinct, have difficulty being checked and controlled by outsiders. Especially when a crisis arises and the Board of Directors feels it must intervene, captains who have built their own ships have difficulty accepting such meddling.

   We then ask whether they think this threat exists at The Body Shop. It can be argued that the difficult act of balancing profitability and responsibility makes the chance of conflict quite a bit larger. As long as growth continues, Roddick will probably be given full reign, but if major difficulties arise, and profitability or responsibility need to be sacrificed, then the paradox will be back in full force, and Roddick's decisions might be challenged. It is a matter of debate whether under such circumstances the board should be made strong enough to actually 'impeach' Roddick, or whether a predominately 'advisory' board would be more effective.

5. *In what direction do you think The Body Shop should develop in future? Which threats and opportunities do you see?*

Here a variety of issues can be brought forward. Some of the most important points are:

- *Retaining a sense of mission.* How can The Body Shop guard against the loss of its energy and ideals as it slips into middle age? Getting customers and employees enthusiastic is one thing, keeping them enthusiastic is quite another.

- *Retaining a competitive advantage.* For a while Roddick could see the industry march in one direction and could then move in the opposite direction. Now the industry is watching The Body Shop and tries to follow its moves. So, how can The Body Shop remain different with so many imitators?

- *Retaining growth momentum.* It is easier to keep shareholders satisfied if there is growth. So, how can The Body Shop keep up its growth once it has shops in most countries in the world?

- *Life after Roddick.* How must the company deal with the eventual retirement of Anita Roddick? Does it need another charismatic leader or is the organization strong enough to carry on without one?

Other Teaching Issues

The case also raises a number of issues that are relevant to other chapters in the book. These other teaching issues are:

- *Multi-business strategy.* As a part of The Body Shops future growth it can be discussed whether diversification would be a wise option (link to chapter 6).

- *The Body Shop as the strategic center of a web of partners.* Currently, The Body Shop runs only a few of its shops itself and hardly produces any goods on its own. Yet, The Body Shop system is much larger, with partner companies making goods especially for The Body Shop outlets and a large number of franchisees running the shops. It can be discussed whether this focus on the core activities is only due to a shortage of resources or is also a matter of choice. Should The Body Shop eventually strive towards forward or backward integration (link to chapter 7).

- *Breaking the industry rules.* Anita Roddick has made it her policy to constantly break the industry rules. But as a result The Body Shop is now the new rule maker. The question is whether there are any old rules left to break, or whether The Body Shop would now have to start breaking some of its own (link to chapter 8).

- *Mission as a means for facilitating self-organization.* Roddick empowers her employees and trusts that the initiatives that they come up with will fit with the company strategy. This trust is based on her belief that employees who embrace the company mission will make the right decisions (link to chapter 9).

- *Global appeal of values?* The Body Shop's values are very distinct, and one might expect them not to appeal to the same extent to people in all cultures. Still, the company is following a global strategy. It can be discussed whether this is a wise strategy. It can also be debated whether the company's poor performance in the US is due to a values mismatch, a lack of local adaptation or to the intense competitiveness of the US-market (link to chapter 10).

What Happened After the Case?

The case runs until 1990. This section describes the major developments at The Body Shop and in the company's ideals after 1990, and also whether The Body Shop is still capable of balancing profitability and responsibility. Visit our website (www.itbp.com) for the most up-to-date information and valuable further links.

The Body Shop's ideals

The reason for being for The Body Shop (according to their 1998 annual report) is: *"To dedicate our business to the pursuit of social and environmental change."*

- "To creatively balance the financial and human needs of our stakeholders: employees, customers, franchisees, suppliers and shareholders."

- "To courageously ensure that our business is ecologically sustainable: meeting the needs of the present without compromising the future."

- "To meaningfully contribute to local, national and international communities in which we trade, by adopting a code of conduct which ensures care, honesty, fairness and respect."

- "To passionately campaign for protection of the environment, human and civil rights, and against animal testing in the cosmetics and toiletries industry."

- "To tirelessly work to narrow the gap between principle and practice, whilst making fun, passion and care part of our daily lives."

The Body Shop clearly still seeks a synthesis between responsibility and profit. Note that shareholders are the last to be named as stakeholders. In this respect The Body Shop is (still) one of the few well-known companies in the world that actively strives to put this synthesis in practice, incorporating it in their management control and audit systems (see below).

The Body Shop, still very much personified by Anita Roddick, is also very active in a variety of environmental and social issues. These activities included supporting the Ogoni tribe in Nigeria against their government and trying to enforce a boycott of Shell (who had major activities in the Ogoni region) in 1994. Also, the clean up of nurseries in Romania to prevent HIV infection and work on 'cultural survival' in the Amazon basin (by producing botanical products that ensure the long-term viability of both the forests and the tribes people that live there).

Social and ethical auditing

The Body Shop's approach to social auditing is to use it as a practical tool for increased social accountability and transparency, as well as a strategic management tool with significant potential to facilitate continuous improvement in corporate social performance and stakeholder relationships.

There are three types of performance measurement in The Body Shop's approach to social auditing. They are:

1. *Performance against standards (performance indicators).* These should reflect nationally and internationally available information on best practices for activities and policies that describe the organization's social performance. Measures may be both quantitative and qualitative. Standards are agreed with relevant departments, which then have the responsibility for collecting relevant information. Data are submitted by the departments and validated by the audit and verification processes. Where appropriate, departments are encouraged to set internal benchmarks/ targets relating to individual standards, and to collate information on external benchmarks.

2. *Stakeholder perception of performance against core values.* These core values are essentially defined by the organization itself. Each stakeholder group is consulted to establish their perception of how closely the organization's performance matches its stated aspirations.

3. *Stakeholder perception of performance against specific needs of stakeholders.* These needs are particular to individual stakeholder groups. They are identified as salient through consultation with stakeholders in focus groups and measured in anonymous and confidential surveys of opinion.

Below is a figure that describes an overview of the ethical policies at The Body Shop. It was prepared by Maria Sillanpää, Ethical Audit Team manager of The Body Shop. The Ethical Audit department has six areas of professional expertise: Animal Protection, Environmental Protection, Social Issues, Health and Safety at Work, Information Management, and Training.

EXHIBIT 1
Overview of The Body Shop's Ethical Policies (Source: Maria Sillanpää, 1998)

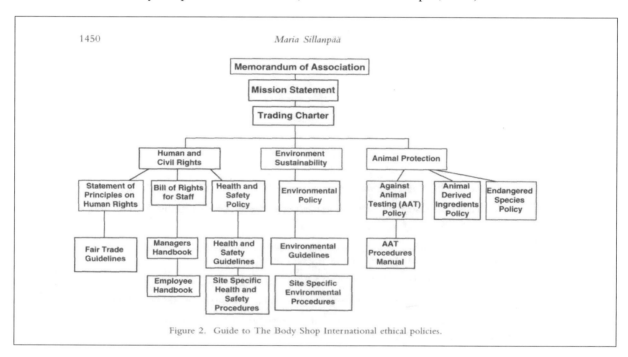

Figure 2. Guide to The Body Shop International ethical policies.

Given below is the structure of the Ethical Audit Department, showing how professional groups take responsibility for ethical issues of relevance to principal stakeholders. Each grouping also works through relevant departments.

The Body Shop argues that the emergent practice of social auditing is consistent with the key principles and best practice in environmental and total quality management as well as the philosophy of learning organizations and employee empowerment. The key premise of their view is based on the argument that a systems-based approach to stakeholder inclusion as reflected in the practice of social auditing will become an increasingly important component of corporate strategy in years to come.

In 1995 The Body Shop published the Values Report 1995, in which they presented three separate statements on the company's social, environmental and animal protection-related performance respectively. In an attempt to develop the company's reporting towards greater integration, the 1997 report comprised of a single document, structured throughout in a stakeholder-driven way, each stakeholder section reporting on those aspects of environmental, animal protection and social performance most salient to a particular stakeholder group.

In December 1998, The Body Shop linked up with the accountancy KPMG to offer advice to companies on social, ethical and environmental reporting. The operation is called Sustainability Advisory Services.

EXHIBIT 2
Structure of the Ethical Audit Department (Source: Maria Sillanpää, 1998)

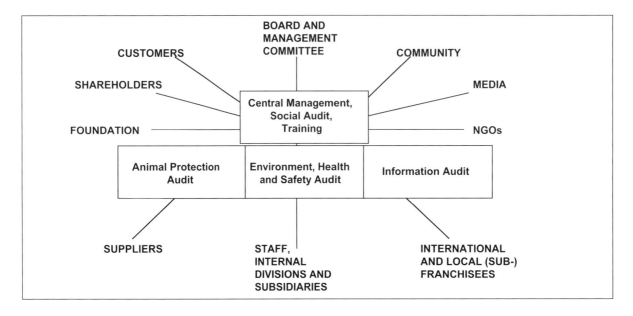

Further business developments

Since the end of the case, The Body Shop has witnessed some major upheaval. The most important developments are:

- *Slow down in growth and profitability.* By 1995 The Body Shop's business was losing its momentum due to intensified competition from a host of imitators such as Bath & Body Works and Boots, and due to an increasing amount of time spent by executives launching environmental projects rather than revamping the company's aging product line. In 1995, The Body Shop had a profit growth of just 13%, which was quite low compared to the growth rates in the previous years. The US operation was even losing money, due to the non-advertising philosophy of the company and its break-neck rate of expansion. In a short period of time, a number of senior executives were fired, suggesting that The Body Shop had lost its grip on the situation in the United States.

- *Bad publicity and criticism.* Since 1992 The Body Shop has been subject to bad publicity, with journalists and other critics accusing the company of making false claims about its stand against animal testing (the Roddicks sued for libel and won more than $400,000 in damages). In 1994 an American journalist, Jon Entine, broadened the charge of hypocrisy to include Body Shop's environmental standards, charitable contributions and efforts to buy materials from the Third World. Though Anita Roddick dismissed the allegations as 'recycled rubbish' and an independent research group later concluded that Entine's charges were 'broadly unfair', she was devastated by the negative press. This also negatively affected the already slowing business.

- *Private company?* In 1995, Anita Roddick and her husband, Gordon, the co-founder and chairman, were actively exploring ways to take the company private and turn it over to a nonprofit foundation that could use profits to finance good works rather than to pay dividends.

The plans were shelved shortly after when it became clear that the cost of financing the share buy-back would sap The Body Shop's aggressive global expansion plans.

- *Company makeover.* In an attempt to regain momentum, The Body Shop decided to launch a major makeover in 1996. Anita and Gordon Roddick stepped down from running day-to-day operations and installed board member Stuart Rose as managing director, who promptly began restructuring the company by changing the top management team, installing tighter inventory and control systems, and streamlining processes. Since then, the Asian market has produced explosive growth, and untapped areas like South Korea and the Philippines are coming on stream. In mature markets like Britain, the company launched new marketing strategies to revitalize sales. The company begun a program of direct mail and in-home sales. In the US, it started taking out ads in print and on radio for the first time ever. The Body Shop also revamped its product line and store design while trying to maintain its green ideals.

EXHIBIT 3

Key figures per region, 1998 (Source: Annual Report The Body Shop International 1998)

	UK	USA	Europe	Asia	Americas ex-USA	Austral-asia
Stores	263	290	527	308	130	76
Turnover (£ million)	116.2	78.0	42.0	37.5	12.8	6.6
Retail sales (in %)	27	16	25	18	8	6
Customer transactions (in %)	37	12	24	13	9	5
Operating profit (£ million)	11.2	-1.7	8.0	15.4	3.4	1.8
Retail sales growth (in %)*	+2	-2	+8	+5	+10	+2
Comparable store sales growth (in %)**	0	-3	+4	-14	+9	-4

* Retail sales are sales to consumers through all shops (franchised and company owned)
** Sales by all stores which have been trading for more than one year

- *Another restructuring.* Due to continuing trouble in the US market, the company was still not doing well financially in 1998. Its shares fell from a peak of 370 pence in 1992 to 123 1/2 pence on May 13th 1998. Investors were also unhappy with Anita Roddick's continuing influence on the company and pressed for new restructuring measures. On May 12th 1998 Anita Roddick announced that she would cede the post of chief executive to Patrick Gournay, a professional manager from Danone, a French food conglomerate. Roddick herself, with her husband, became co-chairmen. The American stores would also be farmed out to a non-executive director with retailing experience, who would be given an option to buy control of the American operation if it became profitable. The objectives of this second restructuring were to create a new operational and management structure, to optimize the franchise system and to regionalize and outsource manufacturing. Although not completely satisfied, investors hoped that this time Anita Roddick really would stay away from daily operations and that the move would result in a higher profitability. Investors were also suggesting that The Body Shop should turn itself from a retailer into a supplier. Analysts at B.T. Alex Brown commented that The Body Shop is about products: "They shouldn't have anything to do with running shops." The Body Shop partly ignored these views and as it is expanding, it is sticking to its more profitable franchising strategy, the approach that made the company successful in the first place. All but 12 of its 841 shops outside the U.S. and Britain are franchises. In December 1998, the company announced that it bought its German franchise operator Cosmo Trading for £7 million with plans to double the size of the operation in the next few years. In January 1999, the Body Shop announced that the company will withdraw from manufacturing, including the sale of its Littlehampton factory (where the headquarters is situated).

As of January 1999, The Body Shop sells its products in 47 countries through 1594 stores of which 209 are owned and operated by the company itself, while the others are franchises. Above are some figures for 1998, given per region. As can be seen in this exhibit, the Asian operations are the most profitable and the US operation is still losing money. For the whole company, some 3-year financials are given below. Judging from the figures, the two restructurings and the new focus of The Body Shop seem to be working in financial terms. The company also seems to have succeeded in maintaining its focus on social responsibility. Despite the formal 'removal' of the founder Anita Roddick, the company has become balanced again, successfully combining profits with social responsibility without leaning to the one or the other side too severely. Yet, the danger of emphasizing one to the detriment of the other exists.

EXHIBIT 4
Three year financials (£ million except per share data)
(Sources: Financial Times company profile and Annual Report 1998 The Body Shop International)

	1998	1997	1996
Total revenue	293.1	270.8	256.5
Pre-tax profit	38.0	31.7	32.7
Net income	22.8	17.6	18.6
Total assets	204.7	202.3	191.1
Total liabilities	74.4	72.2	68.5
Profit margin %	12.97	11.71	12.75
Return on equity %	17.53	14.36	16.82
Debt/Equity %	17.50	16.83	19.66
Turnover/Assets	1.43	1.34	1.34
Earnings per share	11.8	11.4	9.8
Dividend per share	5.6	4.7	3.4

References

Financial Times, "Company profile The Body Shop International".

Sillanpää, Maria, The Body Shop values report - Towards integrated stakeholder auditing, *Journal of Business Ethics*, October 1998.

The Body Shop International, *Annual Report 1998*.

The Economist, "Business: Capitalism and cocoa butter", May 16, 1998.

Wallace, Charles P., Can the Body Shop shape up?, *Fortune*, April 15, 1996.

Teaching Transparencies

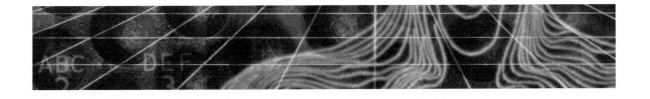

INTRODUCTION
Dimensions of Strategy

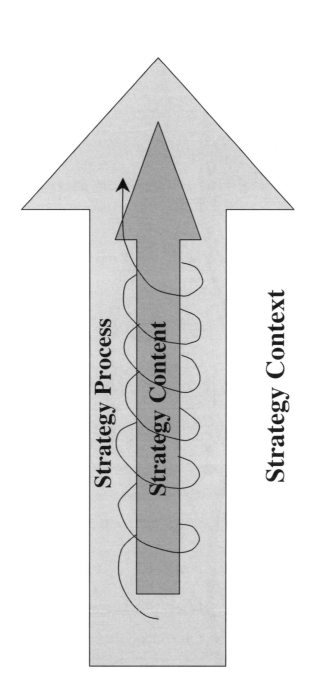

Strategy Process

Strategy Content

Strategy Context

De Wit & Meyer, *Strategy - Process, Content, Context: An International Perspective*, Chapter 1

LEVELS OF STRATEGY

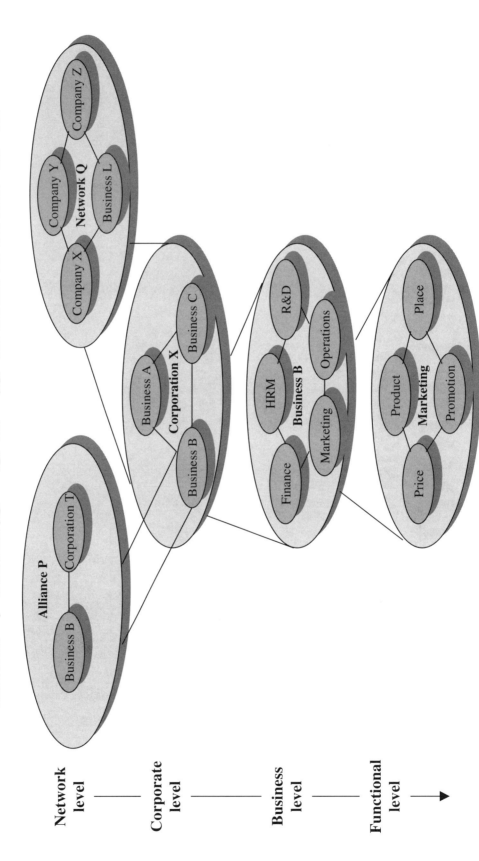

Network level

Corporate level

Business level

Functional level

De Wit & Meyer, *Strategy - Process, Content, Context: An International Perspective*, Chapter 1

INTRODUCTION
The 10 Strategy Tensions

De Wit & Meyer, *Strategy - Process, Content, Context: An International Perspective*, Chapter 1

STRATEGIC THINKING
The Paradox of Logic and Creativity

	RATIONAL THINKING	GENERATIVE THINKING
Emphasis on	Logic over creativity	Creativity over logic
Cognitive style	Analytical	Intuitive
Reasoning follows	Formal, fixed rules	Informal, variable rules
Nature of reasoning	Computational	Imaginative
Direction of reasoning	Vertical	Lateral
Value placed on	Consistency and rigor	Unorthodoxy and vision
Decisions based on	Calculation	Judgement
Analogy	Strategy as science	Strategy as art

De Wit & Meyer, *Strategy - Process, Content, Context: An International Perspective*, Chapter 2

STRATEGIC THINKING
Elements of Strategic Thought Process

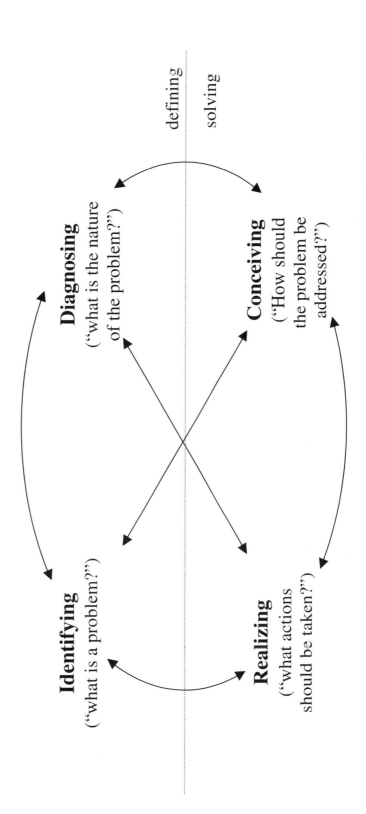

Diagnosing
("what is the nature
of the problem?")

Conceiving
("How should
the problem be
addressed?")

defining

solving

Identifying
("what is a problem?")

Realizing
("what actions
should be taken?")

De Wit & Meyer, *Strategy - Process, Content, Context: An International Perspective*, Chapter 2

STRATEGY FORMATION
Forms of strategy

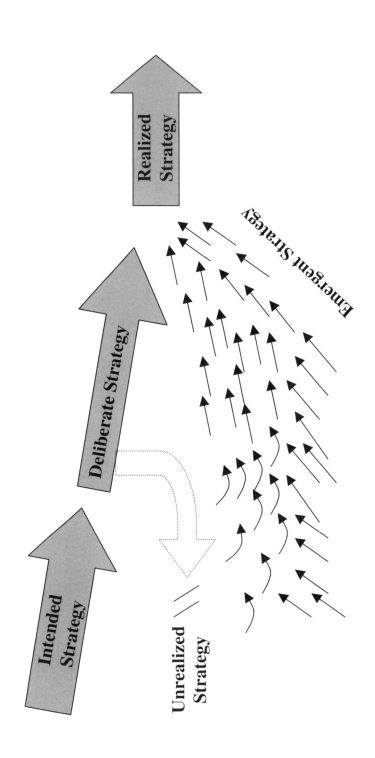

Intended Strategy

Deliberate Strategy

Realized Strategy

Unrealized Strategy

Emergent Strategy

De Wit & Meyer, *Strategy - Process, Content, Context: An International Perspective*, Chapter 3

STRATEGY FORMATION
Paradox of Deliberateness and Emergentness

	PLANNING PERSPECTIVE	INCREMENTALISM
Emphasis on	Deliberateness over emergentness	Emergentness over deliberateness
Nature of strategy	Intentionally designed	Gradually shaped
Strategy formation	Figuring out	Finding out
Formation steps	First think, then act	Thinking and acting intertwined
Formation process	Formal & comprehensive	Unstructured & fragmented
View of future	Forecast and anticipate	Unknown and unpredictable
Decision-making focus	Allocation/coordination	Experimentation
Implementation focus	Programming	Learning

De Wit & Meyer, *Strategy - Process, Content, Context: An International Perspective*, Chapter 3

STRATEGIC CHANGE
The Paradox of Revolution and Evolution

	DISCONTINUOUS CHANGE	CONTINUOUS CHANGE
Emphasis on	Revolution over evolution	Evolution over revolution
Strategic change as	Disruptive innovation/turnaround	Uninterrupted improvement
Change process	Creative destruction	Organic adaptation
Change magnitude	Radical, comprehensive, dramatic	Moderate, piecemeal, undramatic
Pace of change	Abrupt, unsteady, intermittent	Gradual, steady, constant
Change requires	Sudden break with status quo	Permanent learning and flexibility
Environmental jolts	Trigger shock therapy	Require continuous adjustment
Change pattern	Punctuated equilibrium	Gradual development

De Wit & Meyer, *Strategy - Process, Content, Context: An International Perspective*, Chapter 4

STRATEGIC CHANGE
The Magnitude of Change

Scope of Change

	Broad	**Narrow**
High	Revolutionary Change	Focussed Radical Change
Low	Comprehensive Moderate Change	Evolutionary Change

Amplitude of Change

De Wit & Meyer, *Strategy - Process, Content, Context: An International Perspective*, Chapter 4

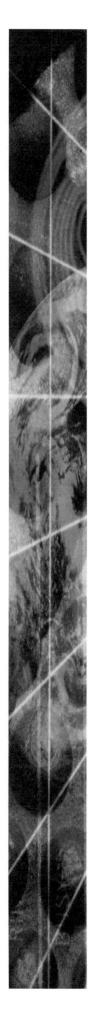

STRATEGIC CHANGE
Levels and Spheres of Organizational Change

	Changes in Organization (State)	Changes in Strategy (Direction)
More Conceptual (Thought)	Culture	Vision
	Structure	Positions
	Systems	Programs
More Concrete (Action)	People	Facilities

De Wit & Meyer, *Strategy - Process, Content, Context: An International Perspective*, Chapter 4

BUSINESS LEVEL STRATEGY
The Paradox of Markets and Resources

	OUTSIDE-IN PERSPECTIVE	INSIDE-OUT PERSPECTIVE
Emphasis on	Markets over resources	Resources over markets
Orientation	Market-driven	Resource-driven
Starting point	Industry structure	Company strengths
Fit through	Adaptation to environment	Adaptation of environment
Strategic focus	Attaining strong position	Developing resource base
Tactical move	Acquiring needed resources	Industry entry & positioning

De Wit & Meyer, *Strategy - Process, Content, Context: An International Perspective*, Chapter 5

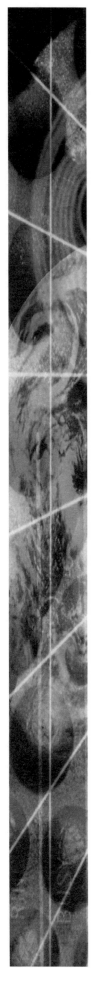

BUSINESS LEVEL STRATEGY
Industries, Markets and Businesses

Markets

	London-Paris Transport	London-Jamaica Transport	London-Benidorm Transport
Airlines		Charter Business	
Railways			
Shipping			

Industries

De Wit & Meyer, *Strategy - Process, Content, Context: An International Perspective*, Chapter 5

BUSINESS LEVEL STRATEGY
Types of Firm Resources

Firm Resources

Intangible Resources

Tangible Resources
- Land
- Buildings
- Materials
- Money

Relational Resources
- Relationships ('contracts')
- Reputation ('brands')

Competencies
- Knowledge ('patents')
- Capabilities ('program')
- Attitude

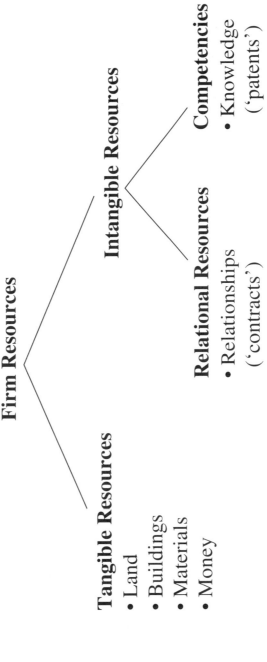

De Wit & Meyer, *Strategy - Process, Content, Context: An International Perspective*, Chapter 5

CORPORATE LEVEL STRATEGY
The Paradox of Responsiveness and Synergy

	PORTFOLIO PERSPECTIVE	CORE COMPETENCE
Emphasis on	Responsiveness over synergy	Synergy over responsiveness
Firm composition	Potentially unrelated	Shared competence-base
Synergy through	Cash flow optimization	Joint competence building
Task of head office	Allocate capital to SBUs	Competence management
Central control style	Setting financial objectives	Joint strategy development
Position of SBUs	Highly autonomous	Highly integrated
Coordination	Low, incidental	High, structural
Acquisitions	Simple to accommodate	Difficult to integrate

De Wit & Meyer, Strategy - Process, Content, Context: An International Perspective, Chapter 6

CORPORATE LEVEL STRATEGY
Directions of Diversification

Supplier
Businesses

(Backward
Vertical
Integration)

Current
Business

Other
Businesses

(Horizontal
Integration)

Buyer
Businesses

(Forward
Vertical
Integration)

De Wit & Meyer, Strategy - Process, Content, Context: An International Perspective, Chapter 6

CORPORATE LEVEL STRATEGY
Corporate Coordination Mechanisms

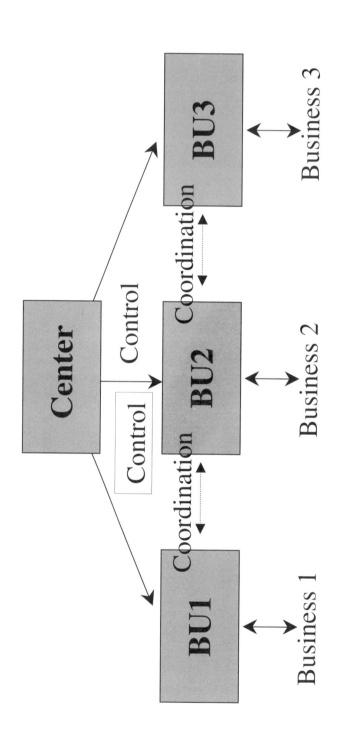

De Wit & Meyer, *Strategy - Process, Content, Context: An International Perspective*, Chapter 6

NETWORK LEVEL STRATEGY
The Paradox of Competition and Cooperation

	DISCRETE ORGANIZATION	EMBEDDED ORGANIZATION
Emphasis on	Competition over cooperation	Cooperation over competition
Environment	Discrete/atomistic	Embedded/networked
Firm boundaries	Distinct	Fuzzy
Preferred position	Independence	Interdependence
Interaction outcome	Mainly zero-sum (win/lose)	Often positive-sum (win/win)
Use of collaboration	Temporary arrangement	Durable partnership
Collaboration basis	Power and calculation	Trust and reciprocity
Collaboration form	Limited, contract-based	Broad, relationship-based

De Wit & Meyer, *Strategy - Process, Content, Context: An International Perspective*, Chapter 7

NETWORK LEVEL STRATEGY
The Firm and Its Relationships

Sociocultural
Forces

Economic
Forces

Suppliers

Vertical Upstream Relations

Competitors

Direct Horizontal

The Firm

Vertical Downstream Relations

Buyers

Entrants
Substitutes
Outsiders

Indirect Horizontal

Political/Legal
Forces

Technological
Forces

De Wit & Meyer, *Strategy - Process, Content, Context: An International Perspective*, Chapter 7

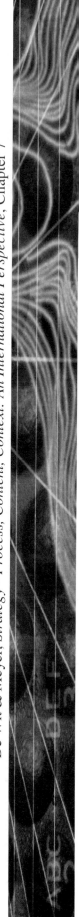

NETWORK LEVEL STRATEGY
Types of Cooperative Arrangements

Extent of Interorganizational Dependence

Negligible

→ Low

→ Moderate

→ High

Technical training/start-up assistance agreements

Production/assembly/buyback agreements

Patent licensing

Franchising

Know-how licensing

Management/marketing service agreement

Nonequity cooperative agreements in

- Exploration
- Research partnership
- Development/coproduction

Equity Joint Venture

De Wit & Meyer, *Strategy - Process, Content, Context: An International Perspective*, Chapter 7

THE INDUSTRY CONTEXT
The Paradox of Compliance and Choice

	INDUSTRY EVOLUTION	INDUSTRY CREATION
Emphasis on	Compliance over choice	Choice over compliance
Industry changes	Uncontrollable evolution	Controllable creation
Change dynamics	Environment selects fit firms	Firm creates fitting environment
Success due to	Fitness to industry demands	Change of industry demands
Industry malleability	Low, slow	High, fast
Strategy	Play by the rules (adapt)	Change the rules (innovate)
Firm profitability	Industry-dependent	Firm-dependent

De Wit & Meyer, *Strategy - Process, Content, Context: An International Perspective*, Chapter 8

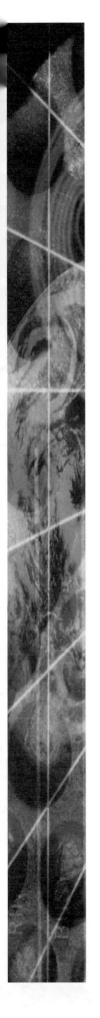

THE ORGANIZATIONAL CONTEXT
The Paradox of Control and Chaos

	ORGANIZATIONAL LEADERSHIP	ORGANIZATIONAL DYNAMICS
Emphasis on	Control over chaos	Chaos over control
Organization changes	Controllable creation processes	Uncontrollable evolution processes
Change process	Leader commands behavior	Behavior emerges from history
Change determinants	Leader's vision and skill	Politics, culture and learning
Form of change	Top-down, mechanistic	Interactive, fermentation
Malleability	High, fast	Low, slow
Adaptation direction	Organization follows strategy	Strategy follows organization
Point of view	Voluntaristic	Deterministic

De Wit & Meyer, *Strategy - Process, Content, Context: An International Perspective*, Chapter 9

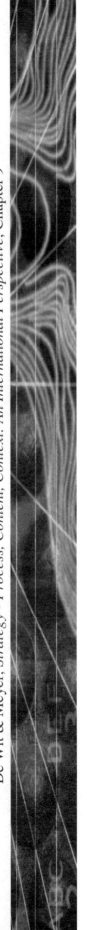

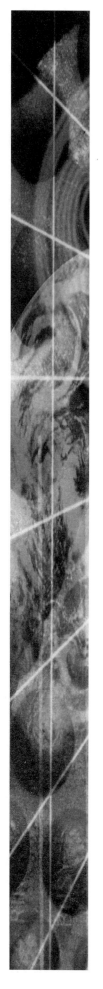

THE INTERNATIONAL CONTEXT
The Paradox of Globalization and Localization

	GLOBAL CONVERGENCE	INTERNATIONAL DIVERSITY
Emphasis on	Globalization over localization	Localization over globalization
International variety	Growing similarity	Remaining diversity
International linkages	Growing integration	Remaining fragmentation
Major drivers	Technology, communication	Cultural and institutional inertia
Diversity	Costly, to be avoided	Reality, to be exploited
Strategic focus	Global-scale efficiency	Local responsiveness
Preference	Standardize/centralize unless	Adapt/decentralize unless
Innovation process	Center-for-global	Locally-leveraged
Organizations	Global	Transnational

De Wit & Meyer, *Strategy - Process, Content, Context: An International Perspective*, Chapter 10

ORGANIZATIONAL PURPOSE
Paradox of Profitability and Responsibility

	SHAREHOLDER VALUE	STAKEHOLDER VALUES
Emphasis on	Profitability over responsibility	Responsibility over profitability
Organizations are	Instruments	Joint-ventures
Purpose	To serve owners	To serve all parties involved
Measure of success	Share price & dividend	Stakeholder satisfaction
Major challenge	Principle-agent problem	Balancing interests
Governance by	Independent outside directors	Stakeholder representation
Social responsibility	Up to individuals	Up to individuals and organizations
Society served by	Pursuing self-interest	Pursuing joint-interests

De Wit & Meyer, *Strategy - Process, Content, Context: An International Perspective*, Chapter 11